Preface

What business doesn't want quality in its own publications and at a feasible price? What publisher doesn't want to produce a professional-looking product and still be competitive? Desktop publishing satisfies both, and with the release of Xerox Ventura Publisher 2.0, you'll have more control over the publication and production process than ever before.

Since Ventura was first released, it has rapidly earned a reputation as the most sophisticated page layout program available for personal computers. With Ventura 2.0, it is now possible to compose an entire publication electronically, including not only the usual text and graphics elements, but also the use of photographs and spot color in the form of digital halftones and color overlays. The ability to transmit complete digital pages to the printer offers virtually every business office in the country unprecedented speed and flexibility in producing its printed materials. Although this technology has been available for years in expensive high-end systems, Ventura is now at the leading edge of the new generation of desktop publishing tools that are redefining the future of electronic publishing.

Indeed, Ventura offers exciting possibilities for both neophytes and seasoned publishers. However, it takes time to learn how to use this publishing program proficiently. Those experienced in electronic publishing are often used to embedding codes in manuscripts using a word processor, but not in formatting a document interactively with a page layout program and a mouse. Others approach Ventura strictly in terms of a specific application, such as a newsletter or manual, and only learn how to use the features required to create that type of document. Yet because of Ventura's abundant options, there are often many ways to accomplish a publishing task, and some methods offer more advantages than others.

This book will provide you with a solid foundation on how Ventura works, and will serve as a guide for producing numerous types of publications. It is intended to complement Ventura's documentation by offering additional explanations and examples of the many program features. If you are still considering whether or not Ventura is the solution for your desktop publishing needs, or if you are about to cross that technological Rubicon and begin using a personal computer for the first time, this book is also for you.

In Part I, "Introducing Ventura Publisher," the emphasis is on what you should know before you begin using Ventura. Veteran desktop publishers can skim this section, but novices and those who need to set up a desktop publishing system will find several important guidelines. Part II, "Getting Started," covers Ventura's graphic interface and thoroughly examines each of the program's four functions, or modes of operation. Key concepts such as style sheets and automatic pagination are also explained.

Part III, "Taking Command," explains, step by step, how to use Ventura's menu options, dialog boxes, and related features. It also includes a host of tips and techniques on managing style sheets and working with text and graphics files. To make this part of the book easy to use as a reference, the actual menus are printed in the margins to help you quickly locate information about specific options. Part IV, "The Professional Extension," offers a guided tour of the add-on program that turns Ventura into an industrial-strength publishing tool. Included are special sections on using the automatic table function, sophisticated equation editor, and other expanded features.

The typographical and naming conventions used in this book follow those in Ventura's documentation. Function and menu names appear in capital letters, filenames in all caps, and text codes in brackets. When mentioning specific paragraph tags and dialog box options, the terms are enclosed in quotation marks; when discussing the program's more generic features, such as the side-bar, assignment list, and item selectors, they are printed in lower case.

Finally, to take full advantage of Ventura Publisher 2.0, and the Professional Extension, in particular, invest in the fastest computer system you can afford (including expanded memory), and continue to save your chapter files and archive your work as often as possible.

Richard Jantz
Berkeley, California

Ventura Publisher ® 2.0

Mastering Desktop Publishing

Richard Jantz

WILEY

John Wiley & Sons, Inc.
New York • Chichester • Brisbane • Toronto • Singapore

This book is dedicated to my parents, Frederick and Wanda Jantz.

Publisher: Stephen Kippur
Editor: Therese A. Zak
Managing Editor: Frank Grazioli

Library of Congress Cataloging-in-Publication Data

Jantz, Richard J., 1947–
   Ventura Publisher 2.0

   Bibliography: p.
   1. Desktop publishing. 2. Ventura publisher (Computer program) I. Title.
   Z286.D47J35 1989   686.2'2   89-5501
   ISBN 0-471-50302-9

Reproduced by John Wiley & Sons, Inc. from camera-ready art supplied by the author and Tulpa Productions, P.O. Box 10185, Berkeley, CA 94709, using Ventura Publisher: Professional Extension.

Printed in the United States of America

89 90 10 9 8 7 6 5 4 3 2 1

Acknowledgments

*A*mong the many talented people who contributed to the production of this book, no one deserves more credit than Jo Magaraci for her valuable assistance in editing the manuscript, proofreading the camera-ready pages, and providing unconditional support throughout the entire project.

I'm grateful to several magazine editors who inspired or encouraged me as a computer journalist. These include Eric Knorr, Karl Koessel, Rich Landry, Robert Luhn, and William Rodarmor of *PC World*, James Felici, Susan Gubernat, Bob Weibel, Christine Whyte, and Jake Widman of *Publish!*, and Adrian Mello of *Macworld*. Special thanks to author Ted Nace, of Peachpit Press, and publications pro Bruce Anderson, who gave me my first job as a magazine editor.

The cooperation of the Ventura Software staff — John Meyer, Don Heiskell, Lee Lorenzen, John Grant, and Michele Polliard — was invaluable in producing this book. As busy as they were, working on the Xerox Ventura Publisher family of software products, someone always took time to answer my latest questions. Many people at Xerox Corporation were also helpful, including Lori Bertley, Art Coles, Randi Doecker, Carolyn Grossman, Jan James, and Beatrice Morgan. For supplying copies of Ventura Publisher and the Professional Extension, my thanks to Brenda Beck and her Ventura public relations colleagues at Hill and Knowlton.

Finally, my deepest appreciation goes to publisher Stephen Kippur and others at John Wiley & Sons for their innovative attitude toward using desktop publishing technology to produce this book. I'm particularly indebted to managing editor Frank Grazioli, for commandeering the editorial review and production process, and to acquisitions editor Teri Zak and managing editor Ruth Greif, for their professional guidance and unlimited enthusiasm since the beginning of this project. Thanks also to Nana Clark, Laura Lewin, Corinne McCormick, and copy editor Sheck Cho for a job well done.

Production Note

On the software side, Microsoft Word and WordStar were used to write the manuscript for this book. Publisher's Paintbrush was used to produce the Ventura screen shots and to scan and edit many of the bit-mapped images; PC GrayScan, Scanit, and Scanning Gallery were used to produce the gray-scale TIFF images. Adobe Illustrator, GEM Artline, Corel Draw, and VersaCAD were used to produce object-oriented graphics. Ventura Publisher: Professional Extension was used to produce all of the camera-ready master pages.

On the hardware side, a 20-MHz 386-based computer (Dell System 310), with 4MB of RAM and a 90MB hard disk, was the primary computer used to produce this book. However, several other systems were also used to run Ventura in various configurations during the research phase of the project, including an IBM PS/2 Model 70, with 6MB of RAM and a 120MB hard disk, as well as PC-AT and PC-XT compatibles. The displays used included an IBM 8514/A, NEC MultiSync, PC's Limited VGA Monochrome, and Wyse WY-700. Scanned images were created with AST TurboScan, Dest PC Scan 2020, Hewlett-Packard ScanJet, Howtek ScanMaster, and Microtek MSF-300G scanners.

All of the camera-ready master pages were printed on Hammermill Laser Plus paper stock, using PostScript fonts (primarily Times, Helvetica, and Helvetica Narrow) available on an Apple Laser-Writer Plus. Each of the high-resolution digital halftones in this book was output on an Allied Linotype Linotronic 300 and imaged twice: first as a paper positive for proofing purposes, and second as a film negative for preparing the printing plate.

If you are involved in producing a formidable publication, such as this book, and would like to learn more about the pros and cons in using Ventura with various laser printers, typesetters, scanners, digital halftones, color overlays, and so forth, or would like to share your own experiences in working with Ventura, the author can be reached at Tulpa Productions, P.O. Box 10185, Berkeley, CA 94709.

Contents

Trademarks

The companies listed below hold trademarks on the following product names (printed in italic) which are mentioned in this book. The use of any additional trademarks is for reference purposes only.

3Com Corp. *3-Plus, 3-Plus Share*
3M *Post-It Note Pads*
Adobe Systems, Inc. *Adobe Type Library, Illustrator, PostScript*
Apple Computer Inc. *Apple, Apple Laserwriter, Apple LaserWriter Plus, Apple LaserWriter IINTX, Apple Lisa, MacDraw, Macintosh, MacPaint*
Ashton-Tate *dBASE , FullPaint, MultiMate*
AST Research *AST TurboLaser, AST TurboScan*
Autodesk, Inc. *AutoCAD*
Birmey Graphics *Birmeysetter*
Bitstream, Inc. *Fontware*
Borland, International *SideKick, SuperKey*
Canon USA *LBP-8II*
Compugraphic Corp. *Compugraphic CG 400-PS*
Conographic Corp. *Conofonts, ConoVision*
Corel Systems Corp. *Corel Draw*
Cornerstone *Cornerstone Dual Page Display System*
Cricket Software *Cricket Draw*
Dell Computers *Dell System 310, PC's Limited VGA Monochrome*
Dest Corp. *PC Scan 2020*
Digital Research, Inc. *GEM, GEM Artline, GEM Desktop, GEM Draw Plus, GEM Graph, GEM Paint, GEM Presentation Team, GEM Scan*
DP-Tek *LaserPort Grayscale*
Epson America, Inc. *Epson*
General Parametrics, Inc. *VideoShow*
Graphic Software Systems, Inc. *Computer Graphics Metafile*
Hammermill Papers *Hammermill Laser Plus*
Hercules Computer Technology *Hercules Graphics Card*
Hewlett-Packard Corp. *Hewlett-Packard (HP), HP Graphics Language, HP LaserJet, HP LaserJet Fonts, HP LaserJet Plus, HP LaserJet Series II, HP Printer Control Language HP ScanJet, HP Scanning Gallery*
Howtek, Inc. *Scanit, ScanMaster*
Innovative Data Design *MacDraft*
Intel *Visual Edge*
International Business Machines Corp. *Document Content Architecture, IBM, IBM 8514/A, IBM Color Graphics Adapter, IBM DisplayWrite, IBM Enhanced Graphics Adapter, IBM Personal Computer, IBM Personal System/2, IBM PS/2 Model 70, IBM PC, IBM PC-AT, IBM PC-XT, IBM PCNet, IBM Video Graphics Arrary*

International Microcomputer Software, Inc. *DP Graphics*
International Typeface Corp. *ITC Zapf Dingbats*
Lifetree Software, Inc. *Volkswriter*
Linotype Corp. *Helvetica, Helvetica Narrow, Linotronic 300, Linotype, Times*
Lotus Development Corporation *Freelance Plus, Lotus, 1-2-3, Symphony*
McIntosh Laboratories, Inc. *Macintosh*
Media Cybernetics Inc. *HALO DPE*
Mentor Graphics Corp. *Mentor Graphics*
Micro Display Systems, Inc. *The Genius*
Micrografx *Designer*
MicroPro International *MicroPro, WordStar, WordStar 2000*
Microsoft Corp. *Microsoft, Microsoft Chart, Microsoft Excel, Microsoft Word, Microsoft Windows, MS, MS-DOS, Windows Executive*
Microtek Lab, Inc. *GLZ, MSF-300G, PC GrayScan*
Moniterm Corp. *Viking 1, Viking 1 Portrait, Viking 2400*
NEC Home Electronics *NEC MultiSync, NEC MultiSync Plus*
NEC Information Systems *SilentWriter LC 890*
Novell *Novell Netware*
Pantone, Inc. *Pantone Matching System*
QMS, Inc. *QMS ColorScript 100*
Samna Corp. *Samna Word*
SoftCraft, Inc. *LaserFonts, Publisher's Font Solution Pak, SoftCraft Font Editor*
Symsoft Corp. *Hotshot Grab*
Tall Tree Systems *JLaser*
Varityper *VT600*
Ventura Software *Ventura Publisher, Ventura Publisher: Professional Extension, Ventura Publisher: Network Server*
VersaCAD Corp. *VersaCAD*
VS Software *FontGen, VS Fontpaks, VS Fonts*
Weaver Graphics *LJ Fonts*
Word Perfect Software *WordPerfect*
Wyse Technology *WYSE, WY-700*
Xerox Corp. *Interpress, Xerox, Xerox 4020 Color Ink Jet Printer, Xerox 6068 Full Page Display, Xerox Star, Xerox Writer III*
XyQuest, Inc. *XyWrite III*
ZSoft Corp. *PC Paintbrush, PC Paintbrush Plus, Publisher's Paintbrush, Publisher's Type Foundry*

Part I

Introducing Ventura Publisher

Chapter 1

The Publishing Renaissance

*W*hen Johann Gutenberg pulled the first printed page off his crude printing press in 1455, it coincided with a revitalized interest in philosophy, the arts, and the sciences. Today, as countless businesses and individuals pull typeset-quality pages from personal computer systems, another renaissance is taking place. More than ever people are learning how to design and print their own publications.

Ads. Annual reports. Books. Brochures. Business reports. Catalogs. Flyers. Forms. Journals. Legal documents. Magazines. Manuals. Newsletters. Newspapers. Pamphlets. Proposals. Sales materials. Scientific and technical documents. From A to Z, today's electronic Gutenbergs — publishers and printers rolled into one — want to do it all, and with the right equipment, you can.

At the forefront of this phenomenon known as "desktop-publishing" stands the *Xerox Ventura Publisher* family of software products for the IBM Personal Computer (IBM PC) and compatibles. Armed with this powerful resource, virtually anyone can produce their own library of professional-looking publications. *Ventura Publisher 2.0,* the base product, provides all the essential tools you need to create both short and lengthy documents, from one-page newsletters to 100-page manuals. For advanced applications, *Ventura Publisher: Professional Extension* is an add-on software program that allows you to produce larger documents, control more typesetting features, automatically generate complex tables, incorporate scientific and mathematical equations, and more.

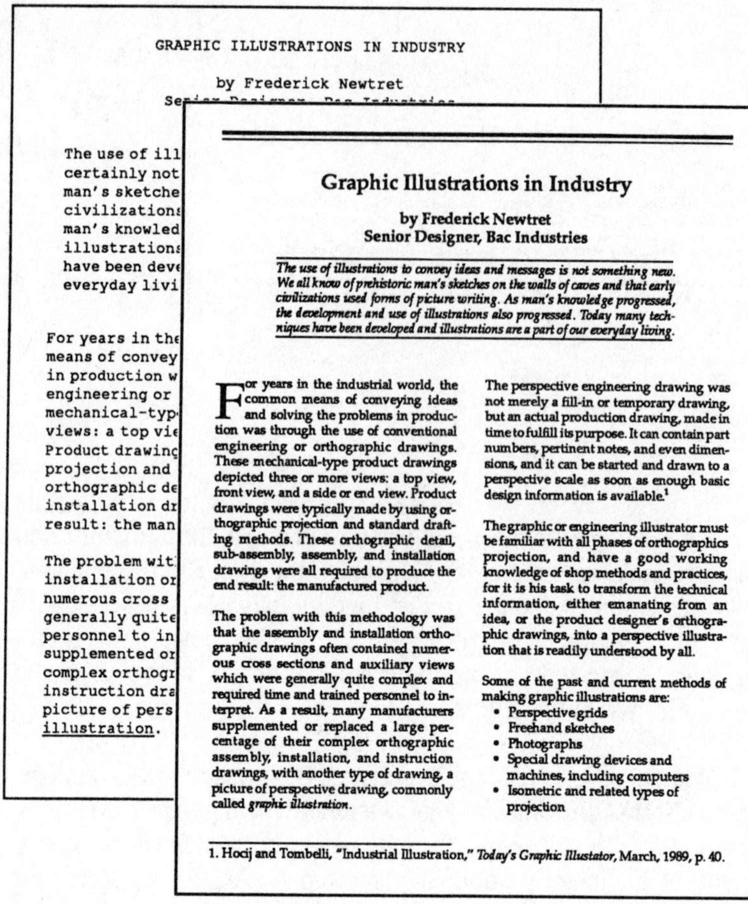

GRAPHIC ILLUSTRATIONS IN INDUSTRY

by Frederick Newtret
Se---- D------, --- Ind------

The use of ill
certainly not
man's sketche
civilizations
man's knowled
illustrations
have been deve
everyday livi

For years in the
means of convey
in production w
engineering or
mechanical-typ
views: a top vie
Product drawing
projection and
orthographic de
installation dr
result: the man

The problem wit
installation or
numerous cross
generally quite
personnel to in
supplemented or
complex orthogr
instruction dra
picture of pers
illustration.

Using Ventura Publisher, ordinary text files from a standard word processor can be easily formatted and turned into typeset-quality documents.

Graphic Illustrations in Industry

by Frederick Newtret
Senior Designer, Bac Industries

The use of illustrations to convey ideas and messages is not something new. We all know of prehistoric man's sketches on the walls of caves and that early civilizations used forms of picture writing. As man's knowledge progressed, the development and use of illustrations also progressed. Today many techniques have been developed and illustrations are a part of our everyday living.

For years in the industrial world, the common means of conveying ideas and solving the problems in production was through the use of conventional engineering or orthographic drawings. These mechanical-type product drawings depicted three or more views: a top view, front view, and a side or end view. Product drawings were typically made by using orthographic projection and standard drafting methods. These orthographic detail, sub-assembly, assembly, and installation drawings were all required to produce the end result: the manufactured product.

The problem with this methodology was that the assembly and installation orthographic drawings often contained numerous cross sections and auxiliary views which were generally quite complex and required time and trained personnel to interpret. As a result, many manufacturers supplemented or replaced a large percentage of their complex orthographic assembly, installation, and instruction drawings, with another type of drawing, a picture of perspective drawing, commonly called *graphic illustration*.

The perspective engineering drawing was not merely a fill-in or temporary drawing, but an actual production drawing, made in time to fulfill its purpose. It can contain part numbers, pertinent notes, and even dimensions, and it can be started and drawn to a perspective scale as soon as enough basic design information is available.[1]

The graphic or engineering illustrator must be familiar with all phases of orthographics projection, and have a good working knowledge of shop methods and practices, for it is his task to transform the technical information, either emanating from an idea, or the product designer's orthographic drawings, into a perspective illustration that is readily understood by all.

Some of the past and current methods of making graphic illustrations are:
• Perspective grids
• Freehand sketches
• Photographs
• Special drawing devices and machines, including computers
• Isometric and related types of projection

1. Hocij and Tombelli, "Industrial Illustration," *Today's Graphic Illustator*, March, 1989, p. 40.

For businesses where writers, editors, graphic designers, and others all participate in the publishing process using several computers, *Ventura Publisher: Network Server* is another add-on program that can be used on local area networks, in which multiple computer workstations and printers are connected together.

With Ventura Publisher (Ventura) installed in your office, you can apply it in numerous ways on a daily basis. You can easily transform the prosaic text of a word processor, database, or spreadsheet program into a dynamic business communication. To enhance the visual impact of a publication, you can incorporate pictures and illustrations from a variety of graphics software programs and image scanning devices. Instead of the traditional method of pasting up type galleys and artwork on a mechanical layout, Ventura turns the

The perspective engineering drawing was not merely a fill-in or temporary drawing, but an actual production drawing, made in time to fulfill its purpose. It can contain part numbers, ~~pertinent notes, and even dimensions, and it~~ can be started enough basic

The Perspective Grid

One of the greatest reasons why industry continues to use graphic illustrations is because this type of drawing can be read with such ease and rapidity. Since this type of drawing is easier to interpret, a definite savings in time is effected. Today's busy executives do not necessarily have the time to spend studying a complicated orthographic layout. The pictorial perspective presents the situation in a form that is clear and highly perceptive, thus enabling those in charge to make more rapid decisions.

For years, the most popular method for graphic illustration has employed the use of a perspective grid. It makes accuracy and uniformity possible in the work, and permits several illustrators to work on a single drawing. By using a common grid, each drawing can be a separate part or section of an assembly, which can be later combined accurately into one major illustration.

Based on a mechanically accurate method of perspective, the grid has predetermined vanishing points. It consists of a series of multiple cubes stacked together. Any point can be located or plotted horizontally, vertically, at the front or rear according to a definite dimension. A series of these points form a line when connected and, when enough lines have been added, suitable shading can be applied to add depth to the drawing. This method is the opposite of the manner in which an orthographic drawing is made, where a single point is laid out in three separate views.

There are many types of grids for the varied usages of these picture perspectives, and

be familiar with
have a good
ices, for it is
tion, either
ner's
llustration that

ic illustration
It makes
k, and permits
wing. By using a
part or section
accurately into

e method of
g points. It

where a single
is laid out in
separate views.

are many types of
for the varied
s of these picture
ectives, and each

hic drawing is

Figure 1: Parallel planes from the center of vision as illustrated in an old drawing.

2

Pictures and drawings from graphics programs and image scanners can be added to any Ventura document.

computer screen of your desktop publishing system into an electronic drawing table. This highly visual environment enables you to interactively place text and graphics in a document and see what each page will look like on the computer screen before you print it.

You can enlarge each on-screen page of your document to see the various text and graphics elements in greater detail or reduce it to get a bird's-eye view. As you zoom in on a page, you can see actual typographic characteristics, including type size and spacing, boldface, italic, and other text attributes, accurately depicted on the screen. Business graphics, logos, scanned photographs, and other images are also clearly represented. Most important, if you aren't satisfied with the arrangement of text and graphics on a page, you can easily make changes and immediately view the results.

Once you've finished laying out a document, you can print copies on a standard office laser printer, using Ventura's versatile output features, including collated and duplex printing. Or you can use the laser-printed pages as camera-ready masters that can be photocopied or used for offset printing. If you prefer the sharper quality of a commercially produced publication, a Ventura document can be printed on higher-resolution typesetting equipment, such as the Allied Linotronic series of PostScript typesetters. You can also print a document in color with a color ink jet or color PostScript printer, or output color overlays that can be used by a commercial printer to add spot color to your publication.

Federal Government Directory   Page 1

Office	Phone	Address	City	State	Zip
The White House	(202)456-1414	1600 Pennsylvania Ave. N.W.	Washington	DC	20500
Department of State	(202)632-4910	2201 C St. N.W.	Washington	DC	20520
Department of Treasury	(202)566-2533	15th St. & Pennsylvania Ave.	Washington	DC	20220
Department of Justice	(202)633-2001	10th St. & Constitution N.W.	Washington	DC	20530
Department o					20240
Department o					20250
Department o					20230
Department o					20210
Department o					20590
Department o					20410
Council of E					20506
Office of Ma					20500
Office of Po					20500
Regulatory I					20037
Bureau of th					20233
Bureau of Ec					20230
Economic Dev					20230
Social Secur					20530
Antitrust Di					20530
Community Re					20815
Internal Rev					20224
IRS Business					20224

Federal Government Directory

The White House
(202)456-1414
1600 Pennsylvania Ave. N.W.
Washington, DC   20500

Department of Commerce
(202)377-2112
14th & E Streets S.W.
Washington, DC   20230

Department of State
(202)632-4910
2201 C St. N.W.
Washington, DC   20520

Department of Labor
(202)523-8271
200 Constitution Ave. N.W.
Washington, DC   20210

Department of Treasury
(202)566-2533
15th St. & Pennsylvania Ave. N.W.
Washington, DC   20220

Department of Transportation
(202)426-1111
400 Seventh St. S.W.
Washington, DC   20590

Department of Justice
(202)633-2001
Tenth St. & Constitution Ave. N.W.
Washington, DC   20530

Antitrust Division
(202)633-2481
Tenth St. & Constitution Ave. N.W.
Washington, DC   20530

Department of Interior
(202)343-7351
C & 19th Streets N.W.
Washington, DC   20240

Economic Development Admin.
(202)377-5113
Commerce Building
Washington, DC   20230

Department of Agriculture
(202)447-3631
14th St. & Independence Ave. S.W.
Washington, DC   20250

Bureau of Economic Analysis
(202)523-0793
1401 K St. N.W.
Washington, DC   20230

Bureau of the Census
Data User Services Div.
(301)568-1200
Silver Hill & Suitland Rds.
Suitland, MD   20233

Regulatory Information
Service Center
(202)653-7246
2100 M St. N.W.
Washington, DC   20037

1

You can use Ventura to format and publish any database list or report that can be generated in the American Standard Code for Information Interchange (ASCII) text file format.

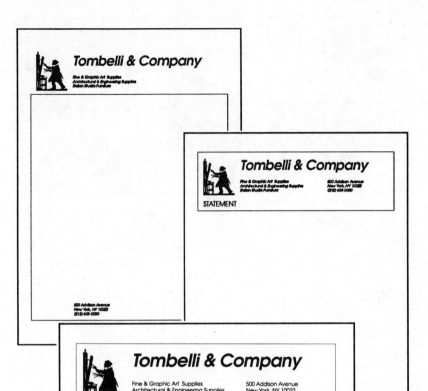

Tombelli & Company

Fine & Graphic Art Supplies
Architectural & Engineering Supplies
Italian Studio Furniture

500 Addison Avenue
New York, NY 10022
(212) 605-0050

INVOICE

Sold to:					
Billing Address:					
Order Date:		Ordered by:		P.O. No.	

Quantity	Stock No.	Description	Unit	Amount

A finance charge of 1.5% per month is charged on past due accounts, which is an annual percentage rate of 18%.

Subtotal	
Sales tax	

Customer Signature

Total	
Deposit	

X _____
This signature acknowledges this order as correct

Balance Due	

Business forms provide an excellent example of how useful Ventura's built-in drawing function can be. Except for the scanned logo image, all the type and graphics shown here were created with Ventura.

Single-sheet documents, such as advertisements, business mail, circulars, and bulletins, can be printed on a variety of page sizes using either a horizontal- or vertical-page orientation.

APE ART

A rare exhibit of lithographs by naturalist Renaldo Estevez

Last year a crate containing over fifty lithographs by Renaldo Estevez was discovered in the basement of the Pongo Museum Center for Nonhuman Primates at Bac Island, North Borneo. According to museum records, Estevez sent the prints in 1916 to the personal attention of Josef Janowicz, the Center's field anthropologist, but Janowicz was on a trip at the time and died of typhoid before returning to Bac Island. The unopened crate was subsequently placed in storage for Janowicz's heirs who failed to claim it. Seventy years later, the crate has finally been opened and the contents revealed.

These well-preserved lithographs represent many years of Estevez's work as a field researcher in the early 1900s studying apes and monkeys in their natural habitats throughout the world. Although his name is well-known in the natural science world, Estevez has only recently been recognized for his artistic efforts. His realistic renderings of animals provide a glimpse of a wild kingdom that is vanishing all too rapidly from the face of the earth.

This rare collection of art is being presented by the Pongidae Foundation as part of a special month-long exhibit called "The Art of Bac Island," which will be on display at the Metro Art Museum from June 6 through July 6, 1987. Adults $5, children $1. All proceeds will go to the World Center for Preservation of Endangered Species, Washington, D.C.

A few of the specialized printed forms you can create include awards and certificates, labels, calendars, wine cards, placemats, and menus.

Captain Ahab's
House Specialties

Blackened Louisana Redfish – on fried green tomatoes with creole sauce

Shellfish Stew – clams, mussels, scallops, and crab with mushrooms in a light tomatoe sauce

Rainbow Trout – stuffed with wild rice and bay shrimp, napped with brown butter sauce

Sea Scallops Saute – in puff pastry with shallot butter and caviar

Seafood Lasagna – shrimp, scallops, and crab layered in fresh spinach pasta and cheese

With Ventura, you no longer need to turn to someone else or use high-end publishing equipment to produce professional-looking publications. Even those with limited experience in producing print media often find that desktop publishing makes the traditional services provided by professionals more accessible and affordable for the average person or business. As desktop publishing systems become more prominent on the business landscape, the difference in equipment and functions associated with desktop publishers and with professional publishers will become even harder to distinguish.

FIELD REPORT

THE
Taming
OF
THE Boa

BY SALVATORE C. MELLINI

As a child growing up in southern Louisiana, I hated all snakes with a passion. However, my discomfort in seeing them slither across a neighborhood field never stopped me from seeking out their caged habitats whenever I went to the zoo. I was especially curious—and not just a little bit anxious—about the manner in which snakes devoured their meals.

If anyone had told me back then that I would someday learn how to handle an adult boa constrictor — *Constrictor constrictor*, a notorious member of the largest snake family in the world — I would have imagined the beast coiling itself around me and pulverizing each of my bones with chiropractic precision before swallowing me within minutes. It's also doubtful that I would have ever stepped foot in a zoo again.

Yet it wasn't until I began studying biology in college that I finally heard a herpetologist explain that much of what I thought I knew about snake behavior was, in fact, nothing more than a lot of fanciful lore gathered over the centuries. Since then, I have come to regard the 2,600 species of

snakes known to exist in the world today with much more appreciation and respect.

Beauty and the Boidae
Of the four principal snake families — the Boidae, the Colubridae, the Elapidae, and the Viperidae — the

Boidae family contains the largest and the most primitive of all snakes. Included in the Boidae family are the pythons of the Old World tropics, along with the New World anacondas and boas — many of which possess the most beautiful and naturally harmonious skin patterns of all snakes.

But while other snake families include members which use elaborate techniques of injecting poisonous venom, the members of the Boidae family are strictly constrictors: they overpower their prey by skillfully wrapping their bodies around it and squeezing.

Like all snakes, the feeding technique of the boa is one of its most distinctive features, as it involves several unique structural modifications of the head and jaws. In addition to reductions in the facial skeleton — which free the boa's jaws from its brain case — the brain itself is enclosed in bone as a guard against contact with any oversized food.

Salvatore C. Mellini is a professor of biology at Cummins University.

ZOO LIFE 18

You can place scanned photographs in Ventura documents and obtain digital halftones, such as the Tagged Image File Format (TIFF) gray-scale image used in this sample document, which was output as a film negative on an Allied Linotronic typesetter at a resolution of 1,270 dots per inch.

With the ability to produce such a broad spectrum of publications available to anyone using a desktop publishing system, it's no surprise that there's a synchronous surge of interest in the aesthetics of effective print communication. Many users find that working with Ventura causes them to take a closer look at the barrage of print media that passes through their daily lives, trying to identify the formulas for success. Although Ventura won't teach you what makes one document better than another, it will provide you with excellent tools for producing top-quality publications. Once you begin using the program, your appreciation of print media may never be the same. Like thousands of other desktop publishers, you may find yourself pleasantly revivified by the power of the printed word.

One of the singlemost popular applications for Ventura is to produce all kinds of newsletters.

The Micro Advisor

Volume 3, Number 4   For Microcomputer Consultants   Winter 1987

What Price Really?

The Savvy Buyer's Guide to Computer Shopping by Mail

Question: What do Alpine cow horns, accordians, stereos, microwave ovens, tropical fish, diamond jewelry, monogrammed matchbooks, relaxation tanks, and microcomputer products have in common? Answer: All of them can be purchased by mail.

➡ IN THIS ISSUE

Industry Update:
New Graphics Computers
Introduced   2
Interview:
Roth Powers of Powers,
Cox & Associates   4
Taxes without Tears?

How New Tax Laws Are
Affecting Consultants
Desktop Publishing
Goes Hollywood   6

Today you can buy just about anything by mail. From African violets to Zeiss binoculars, from Yves St. Laurent outfits to Elvis Presley wallpaper — you name it and, chances are, there's a mail-order dealer who will happily send it to you.

The mail-order universe is so vast, in fact, that it has become a $100-billion-a-year industry, expanding at 14 to 18 percent annually.

One of the fastest-growing areas in mail order is the microcomputer marketplace. Many of the magazines and newspapers that cater to computer users are full of mail-order ads for virtually everything a novice or veteran could want: microcomputers, monitors, disk drives, printers, modems, disks, disk storage boxes, and an endless proliferation of software packages.

The Mail-Order Sizzle

The main advantage of buying any computer products through the mail is lower prices. Because most mail-order dealers pay less over-head than retailers and buy big quantities of computer merchandise at reduced prices, they can offer customers larger inventories at sizable discounts.

Depending on whether it is hardware or software, a mail-order dealers often sell products at 20 to 50 percent off the manufacturer's list price. When you figure that most average computer buyers spend $6,000 during their first two years of involvement, the mail-order option could mean signficant savings.

Mail-order dealers offer the additional advantage of saving you some time and effort, since shopping by mail or phone is generally easier than traveling store to store. And, if you don't live near a computer store, or if your local retailer doesn't stock the items you want, mail-order computer shopping may actually be your only choice.

Savings, selection, and convenience. For these and other reasons, many shoppers consider mail-order transactions an attractive alternative to the retail marketplace.

But what about the disadvantages of buying computer products by mail? What will you get in terms of support and service? What risks do you face with mail-order dealers and, if anything does go wrong, what can you do about it?

Frugal or Foolish?

Although it's true that computer shoppers can save money initially by using mail order, just how provident is it in the long run? The final answer depends less on the product itself, and a lot more on the person using it. The real key to success in mail-order buying, most all authorities will agree, is to know your own level of computer expertise and to properly research a product *before* you buy it.

Many users find that mail order is a very economical way to obtain add-on hardware and software packages. Business people, for example, who need additional copies of a
(Continued on page 3)

Chapter 2

A Desktop Publishing System

*V*entura Publisher is a software program that enables you to perform an array of publishing tasks. Like the professional electronic publishing systems that predated it, Ventura combines sophisticated type composition with page layout features, making it possible to compose text and graphics interactively on the computer screen and view pages before you print them. By streamlining the process of creating document pages manually, computer-aided publishing allows you to eliminate several time-consuming steps and to reduce labor, materials, and typesetting charges.

But unlike high-end publishing systems that often require a sizable investment in dedicated computer workstations, Ventura operates on a standard IBM PC or IBM compatible. For small businesses as well as large corporations, the implications are profound. The continuous tasks of document creation, page formatting, typesetting, and output can all be performed on smaller, more cost-effective equipment. Better still, many businesses that already have PCs in the office can use the same equipment as part of a desktop publishing system.

The phrase *desktop publishing system* refers to both PC hardware and software components. This chapter explains those components in general and suggests which are vital and which are not. First, the

11

"System Hardware" section tells you what equipment you need to use Ventura. It also looks at some of the optional equipment available for setting up a full-powered desktop publishing system. The "System Software" section provides an overview of Ventura's prominent role as a publishing tool and includes information on using word processing, graphics, and printer software with Ventura.

System Hardware

Because PCs are now available in more configurations than ever, the hardware most appropriate for a desktop publishing system is best determined by the type of work required, ranging from the stringent demands of corporate and professional publishing efforts to the more moderate needs of small businesses and individuals.

If your work involves basic word processing and database filing in addition to desktop publishing, an inexpensive IBM PC-XT or compatible, with an older-generation Intel 8088 or 8086 processor, may be all you need. Spreadsheet and accounting tasks may require the speed of an IBM PC-AT or compatible, with a faster Intel 80286 processor. Sophisticated graphics and scientific applications often demand a 386-based system, such as a high-end IBM Personal System/2 (PS/2), with a maximum speed Intel 80386 processor.

But don't think that you're hamstrung without the best technology available. Although a high-performance system provides more computing power for data-intensive applications, it's by no means a necessity. You can still produce plenty of publications with Ventura even with an ordinary PC-XT as your publishing platform, which is one of the reasons for the program's popularity.

The Computer
At the very least, you need a PC-XT or compatible, with 640K RAM (kilobytes of random access memory) and between 1.5 and 3.5MB (megabytes) of available hard disk space in order to set up and run Ventura. The exact amount of disk space you need depends on which printers and fonts you install with the program, but you should still have another 2 to 3MB of disk space free after installation for storing your documents. If you expect to use a lot of graphics in your documents, or plan to use your computer system for other applications, a 30MB (or larger) hard disk is a wise investment.

To complete a basic system, you need a graphics adapter and display (monochrome or color), a mouse (which you use along with the keyboard), and an output device ranging from a dot-matrix to a black-and-white or color laser printer. If you must, you can operate Ventura using the keyboard instead of a mouse, but it's much more awkward and time-consuming to work without one of these relatively inexpensive input devices made by various manufacturers.

A more robust publishing system might include a 286-based computer running at a clock speed of 10 MHz (megahertz) or faster; at least 1.5MB RAM; a 40MB hard disk; and high-resolution graphics. For a full-blown system, you need a 386 computer running at 20 MHz (or faster); at least 2.5MB RAM; a 70MB (or larger) hard disk; and full-page, high-resolution graphics. Other options include a tape backup unit to preserve copies of important files and documents, and a scanner to convert artwork or text into computerized files that you can incorporate into Ventura documents.

Memory Considerations

To use Ventura proficiently, you should understand the different types of memory used by the various systems on which you can run the program. All IBM PCs (including PC-XT, PC-AT, PS/2, and 386 machines) and compatibles contain *conventional* memory, which is limited to a maximum of 640K RAM. This base memory space is where most software programs, including Ventura, reside when you run them. Because Ventura is a large program, it requires as much conventional memory as possible. Therefore, when running Ventura you should avoid installing any RAM-resident utilities or drivers that take up conventional memory and reduce the space available.

After you load Ventura, between 100K and 150K of conventional (640K) memory remains free for creating documents. When your document contains more data than the program can place in the remaining memory, it stores the extra part on the computer's hard disk, up to a maximum of about 500K of text on a monochrome system (color systems leave even less memory available). If you try to go beyond that limit, the program issues an error message that explains there isn't enough memory left to load additional text. However, Ventura can manage larger documents if your computer contains more memory beyond the conventional memory. This extra memory, called *extended* and *expanded* memory, is supported by all

IBM PCs and compatibles except the older PC-XTs. While only a few applications currently use extended memory, many other programs, including Ventura and the Professional Extension, provide support for expanded memory, based on the Lotus-Intel-Microsoft (LIM) Expanded Memory Specification, also called EMS memory.

If your computer has extended memory, you can convert it to EMS memory by using a LIM/EMS-compatible driver (version 3.0 or later), provided with the computer or purchased separately. No other special procedures are required; Ventura will automatically make use of all EMS memory available. If your computer has at least 128K of EMS memory free, Ventura will place up to 108K of its program code in EMS memory, thereby leaving an extra 108K of conventional memory for creating documents. The Professional Extension goes a major step further and can store documents in EMS memory, as well as program code, which enables you to create much larger publications than with the base product.

Two other ways to improve Ventura's performance on a system with extended or EMS memory are to use some of that memory to create a disk cache or a RAM disk. A disk-caching program, available from several software companies, allows an application to access frequently used data faster by keeping it in the computer's memory, rather than constantly reading it from, and writing it to, the hard disk. A RAM disk, available to Ventura users with a computer that contains at least 1.3MB RAM, enables you to configure any extended or EMS memory to emulate a disk drive, which is capable of running the program much faster.

Graphics Adapters and Displays

Computer screen images are composed of small picture elements called *pixels,* and screen resolution is commonly expressed as the number of vertical pixels times horizontal pixels. Ventura supports several graphics systems (adapters and displays) of varying resolution, including the Hercules Graphics Card, IBM Color Graphics Adapter (CGA), IBM Enhanced Graphics Adapter (EGA), IBM Video Graphics Array (VGA), and compatibles.

Most Ventura users find that a CGA system's low resolution (640 by 200 pixels) is unsuitable for long work sessions, which makes it the least desirable graphics system to use. An EGA (640 by 350 pixels), VGA (640 by 480 pixels), or extended VGA (800 by 600 pixels) system provides better resolution and gives you the choice of using a monochrome or color display. If you work with scanned images, you'll need a VGA adapter with an analog display (standard in PS/2 systems) to see up to 16 shades of gray in a gray-scale image, which is like looking at an actual photograph on the screen. Although you can still use gray-scale images without an analog display, it's harder to judge how they will look until they are printed.

If you run Ventura in color, you can view 16 colors on an EGA or VGA color display, and the program's "loose lines" feature also operates in color (i.e., loose lines are highlighted in red rather than gray). On a VGA system, you can change the screen colors (or grays) by using the program's Define Colors feature and see the resulting colors on screen. Without a VGA system, you can still change the colors but you won't be able to see the results on screen. Because running Ventura in color slows down the program's speed, color operation is only recommended if you intend to use a color printer, such as the QMS ColorScript 100 laser printer or Xerox 4020 Color Ink Jet printer, or to print spot color overlays for color publications.

Ventura also includes drivers for higher-resolution systems, which are capable of depicting a larger amount of readable information on screen at one time. This more sophisticated and costly hardware includes the MDS Genius Full Page Display (720 by 1,000 pixels), Wyse WY-700 (1,280 by 800 pixels), and Xerox 6068 Full Page Display (720 by 992 pixels). You can also use other high-resolution systems, such as the Cornerstone Dual Page Display System (1,600 by 1,280 pixels), Moniterm Viking 10 (1,024 by 768 pixels), and NEC MultiSync Plus (960 by 720 pixels), which all supply their own software drivers for running Ventura. Each of these graphics systems allows you to view and read the contents of a full page while remaining in Ventura's reduced page view. This saves you time and effort because you don't have to change the page view as frequently as you must with the standard graphics modes, or use the scroll bars as often to move from one side of the page to the other.

Printers

A laser printer is a high-resolution output device that makes a dot-matrix or letter-quality printer look like a toy. With the ability to print 300 dots of xerographic toner per inch, a laser printer can produce pages that look commercially typeset, and it can produce multiple copies much faster than traditional printers. The most powerful laser printers contain a built-in software program called a *page description language* (PDL). When used with a PDL laser printer, Ventura tells the machine how to construct a complete page image as a series of procedures and parameters, rather than telling it the location of every single dot. After the printer receives the information, it processes it and prints the entire page all at once.

Ventura supports two primary PDLs: Adobe Systems' PostScript, generally accepted as the *de facto* standard, and Xerox's Interpress. One of the most powerful features of PDL printers is the support of resident fonts in outline form that can be scaled to any size, just like graphics. PDL printers are also device independent, that is, you can output a document on any printer based on the same PDL. For example, you can use Ventura's PostScript device driver to print the same document on an Apple LaserWriter IINTX laser printer at 300 dots per inch (dpi), a Compugraphic laser printer at 400 dpi, a Varityper laser printer at 600 dpi, an Allied Linotronic phototype-setter at 1,270 and 2,540 dpi, and a Birmy Graphics BirmySetter phototypesetter at 3,000 dpi.

A secondary PDL supported by Ventura is the Hewlett-Packard (HP) Printer Control Language (PCL), used by the HP LaserJet Plus, LaserJet Series II, and compatibles. Although these printers are highly regarded as speedy, cost-effective workhorses, they use bit-mapped rather than outline fonts and lack the broad range of resident typefaces, type sizes, and graphics capabilities provided by PostScript PDL printers. However, you can usually access more fonts and print larger graphics with a PCL printer by increasing the printer's memory with a RAM expansion adapter. You can also increase the printing speed or resolution of many PCL printers by installing a printer enhancement adapter, available from such companies as Conographic, DP-Tek, Intel, LaserMaster, and Talltree.

With Ventura, you can also use a dot-matrix printer, including Epson, NEC, and Toshiba models, instead of a laser printer. How-ever, the program's real power is short-circuited on dot-matrix printers since they lack the professional quality offered by laser printers and phototypesetters. Unless you're on a limited budget, plan to use a dot-matrix printer for rough proofs only.

Scanners

In a desktop publishing system, a scanner is an input device that serves as a bridge to the world of artwork and photographs. With a scanner, you can turn logos, drawings, and other hard copy illustrations into digitized images, made up of tiny black-and-white dots, which can be placed into Ventura documents along with text and output on a laser printer or phototypesetter. With the proper software, many scanners can also be used as optical character recognition (OCR) devices, which let you convert typewritten hard copy into a text file that can be edited with your word processing program.

A scanner system includes a scanning unit, interface adapter (which you install inside the PC), cables, and software that controls the scanning process. Aside from installing and configuring a scanner system to work with your computer, most scanners are fairly easy to use. With sheetfed models (which operate like facsimile machines), an internal set of rollers pulls a letter-size (or smaller) page through the machine and a stationary sensing element, called a charge-coupled device (CCD), converts the image on the page into digital information. With flatbed models (which work like photocopy machines), the page is placed on a glass platen and remains still while the CCD moves back and forth below it. Flatbed scanners are bigger and heavier than most sheetfed scanners, however, they can be used for scanning images from bound volumes and oversize originals. Although handheld scanning systems and video image capture devices are also available, flatbed and sheetfed scanners generally provide the best image quality (300 dpi or more).

Scanner systems provide different modes of operation for scanning two types of images: black-and-white line art, such as pen and ink drawings, and continuous-tone pictures (containing shades of color or gray), such as photographs. With line-art images, virtually any scanner can produce excellent results; with continuous-tone images, you will get the best results if you use a gray-scale scanner, a more sophisticated device that converts continuous tone into true shades of gray rather than just black-and-white dots. The current generation of gray-scale scanners for desktop publishing can produce 16, 64, or 256 shades of gray. Exactly how many shades of gray a scanner can record is a function built into the hardware and controlled by the software that drives the scanner. Both gray-scale and black-and-white scanned images can be used in Ventura documents.

System Software

Software is the unique set of instructions that directs computers to perform specified tasks, as opposed to the hardware devices that execute them. All computer programs are considered software, and all computers include a software operating system to control the basic functions of the computer. For the IBM PC and compatibles, this system is called DOS (Disk Operating System) and it is provided on magnetic floppy disks. When you purchase a computer, the software operating system is supplied as part of the package.

In addition to DOS, some programs use an alternative operating system that places a "shell" over DOS to create a graphics-based user interface. Ventura is an example of a program that uses this type of environment — which, in this case, is called Graphic Environment Management (GEM) Desktop by Digital Research. Another well-known example of a graphics-based user interface is Microsoft Windows by Microsoft Corporation. Because the software necessary to create Ventura's graphics-based interface is included as part of the program, no additional software is required to run Ventura.

About Ventura Publisher

Desktop publishing programs like Ventura are also referred to as *page makeup* software. All page makeup programs provide you with similar electronic printing functions, including the abilities to:

- Compose and typeset text in various sizes and styles
- Create or input graphics and illustrations
- Design pages merging text and graphics
- Output the results to a page printer or typesetter

In addition to these fundamental abilities, Ventura offers two other outstanding attributes. The first is its ability to automatically format and paginate an imported text file. Because of this feature, referred to as *automatic pagination*, many users characterize Ventura as a document processor, or document-oriented program. Simply stated, when you import or "load" a text file from a word processor and place it on the first blank page of a Ventura document, the program automatically places the text on as many additional pages as required to paginate the entire file. And as you add or edit the various text and graphics elements (e.g., increase the point size for all body text, or enlarge the size of a picture), the program will continue to automatically reformat all pages.

Due to its automatic pagination, Ventura is adept as an assembly-line page processor, composing and producing structured documents or any publication with a consistent style, such as books, manuals, reports, and catalogs. At the same time, the program's emphasis on documentwide formatting doesn't preclude its usefulness for producing less conforming documents, where the design changes from page to page, as with brochures, newsletters, and magazines.

Ventura's second important distinction as a page makeup program is that it uses powerful master guides called *style sheets* to manage its documentwide formatting tasks. In short, a style sheet is a Ventura file that tells the program how to automatically format an entire document according to page layout and typographic specifications you've already defined. As you import a word-processed text file, Ventura uses whatever style sheet you designate as its master guide for composing all of the text in your document.

Whenever you make a change to a style sheet, Ventura automatically reformats the entire document and changes all affected paragraphs or pages. This feature makes it possible for you to try various "what if" scenarios with widely divergent style sheets and quickly see your document reconfigured in any number of ways. For example, you can easily see how a document looks using different type styles, margin settings, or page sizes by merely instructing the program to use another style sheet and let it reformat the entire document according to a different set of specifications.

Best of all, although you can have a skilled graphic designer create your company's style sheets, you don't have to be a trained designer to use them. With style sheets, anyone can format pages quickly and obtain a consistent look throughout a document. Style sheets also make it easy to customize a document by applying different formats for different audiences or by incorporating the same information in different publications. For instance, an article on company growth published in a house organ can be instantly transformed into a news release, business proposal, or annual report. Because the program includes a default style sheet and several samples, it isn't necessary for you to create your own style sheets from scratch.

With Ventura serving as the foundation for your desktop publishing software, there are several other applications that you can include as members of your publishing software family. In addition to word processing, spreadsheet, and database software, many users supplement their publishing libraries with one or more graphics software packages, including electronic clip art collections. With extra printer software, such as font library disks and a font editor, you can expand the selection of fonts available for use with most laser printers. The remainder of this chapter presents an overview of these additional software publishing tools.

Word Processing Software
Ventura contains a built-in text editor, however, it's usually more efficient to prepare most of your text files with a word processing program, and then import those files into Ventura. With a word processor, you can use rapid cursor commands, block copy operations, search and search-and-replace functions, and other features that greatly reduce the amount of time it takes to produce the final text. You can also take advantage of a spelling checker, thesaurus, keyboard macro program, and other word processing aids.

With Ventura, you can import text files from virtually any word processing program and place them in a document. The program will specifically incorporate the file formats of the following word processors: Microsoft Word, MultiMate, WordStar, WordPerfect, Xerox Writer, XyWrite, and any program that creates IBM Document Content Architecture (DCA) files, such as DisplayWrite, Samna Word, Volkswriter, and WordStar 2000. Text created in different file formats can also be mixed within the same document. You can even use Ventura to convert a text file from one word processing format to another.

Ventura translates many of the character attributes you assign to a word-processed file — boldface, underlining, and italic — but it doesn't use printing or formatting information, such as margins, indents, and centering. Instead, the program relies on whatever style sheet is active to determine those specifications. You can also import text from any word processor or program that generates ASCII files, including spreadsheets, databases, and utilities with text editors. (See the Index for discussions on specific programs.)

Using other programs to prepare text to place in Ventura documents makes it easy for a publishing group to split up the work and become more productive. It also makes it possible for several people to share the same desktop publishing system when Ventura is being used to produce output on the only laser printer in the office. While some workers use word processors, databases, and other programs to prepare text files, others can use Ventura to paginate and print them.

Graphics Software

To add graphics to your Ventura documents, you have two choices. For simple graphics, you can use the program's built-in drawing function to create a variety of rules and objects, including squares, rectangles, and ovals composed of different line weights and fill patterns. For more sophisticated graphics, you must go outside Ventura and use a graphics software program with a broader range of tools for creating artwork. Although Ventura offers compatibility with several different graphics file formats, the two basic types of graphics software are draw programs and paint programs. Each type offers different tools for creating graphics, and desktop publishers can profit by including both types of programs in their publishing software repertoire.

Draw programs produce "object-oriented" graphics, which means that everything you draw is treated as a distinct object, such as a circle or rectangle. After selecting the object with the cursor, you can move it, resize it, change its line weight, fill it with a pattern, and perform other operations, depending on the complexity of the program. Although you can produce object-oriented graphics with Ventura's built-in drawing mode, the selection of tools is modest. However, with the broad range of drawing capabilities offered by such programs as GEM Draw Plus and Windows Draw Plus, you can create polygons, arcs, and freehand sketches, and group individual elements together as a single object that can be copied, rotated, and flipped vertically or horizontally. Adobe Illustrator, Corel Draw, Designer, and GEM Artline add the ability to trace over a scanned image to their drawing toolboxes. With specialized computer-aided drawing (CAD) programs, such as AutoCAD and VersaCAD, you can generate complex architectural, mechanical, structural, and electronics illustrations.

Paint programs produce "bit-mapped" graphics, which means you control an entire image as a collection of dots, or pixels. Although you can create geometric objects with a paint program, you cannot select and manipulate individual objects as easily as you can with a draw program. Once an object is added to an image, it becomes part of the overall collection of dots. Tools like pencils, erasers, airbrushes, and paintbrushes enable you to manipulate an image in a variety of ways, including the ability to zoom in and turn each individual pixel on or off. With paint programs such as Halo DPE, PC Paintbrush Plus, and Publisher's Paintbrush, you can flip, rotate, reverse, shrink, and enlarge an image or part of an image.

If you use a scanner to convert line-art illustrations into digitized images, the images can also be loaded into a paint program and edited as bit-mapped graphics. You can even use some paint programs to operate the scanner itself, which makes it easier to edit scanned images before incorporating them into a Ventura document. There are also dedicated scanning programs, such as GEM Scan and ScanDo, that specialize in providing tools for editing scanned images. However, if you're using gray-scale scanned images (which are different than bit-mapped scanned images), you'll need to use a program that supports gray-scale image editing.

The popularity of desktop publishing has also led to the emergence of electronic clip art software, featuring either object-oriented or bit-mapped graphics. With a clip art library, you can use the artwork as it is, or modify it and then paste it into your document. For the business user, clip art libraries typically offer symbols of commerce, communication, transportation, and industry. Maps of assorted cities, states, and countries are particularly handy for sales and marketing documents, and images of people at work or at home are also very useful. Since these packages vary in quality, however, it's best to see a printed version of an entire library beforehand so you know it matches the style and tone of your publication.

In addition to importing pictures from draw and paint programs, scanners, and clip art libraries, you can also incorporate files from several business graphics programs into Ventura documents. For example, the program will directly import pie charts, bar graphs, and line graphs in the native file formats of GEM Graph, 1-2-3, Symphony, Freelance Plus, and others. In some cases, you can improve a business graphics file before bringing it into Ventura by first transferring it into another graphics program to enhance it. For instance, you can load a 1-2-3 graphics file directly into Publisher's

Paintbrush and use that program's versatile tools to jazz up an otherwise routine chart or graph.

Printer Software

With Ventura, the word *font* refers to a typeface (e.g., Helvetica or Times Roman) in a specific size, style, and orientation (portrait or landscape). Style refers to light, normal, bold, heavy, light italic, normal italic, bold italic, and heavy italic. Although the fonts supplied with Ventura can be used to produce bushels of publications, there comes a time when many desktop publishers yearn for a larger selection of type. To expand the number of fonts you can use with Ventura, you can purchase additional fonts designed for your printer from a variety of font vendors, or you can use a font editing program to create your own custom-made fonts if you desire.

If you have a PCL printer (e.g., the HP LaserJet Series II) or a dot-matrix printer, you can use the Bitstream Fontware Installation Kit, which is bundled with Ventura, to generate additional fonts for Swiss, Dutch, and Symbol typefaces at any point size. You can also buy more font packages for either PCL or PostScript printers from Adobe Systems, Hewlett-Packard, VS Software, Weaver Graphics, and many other font vendors. Not all font libraries offer designs of equal quality, but plenty of excellent font software is available.

In order for Ventura to use any additional fonts you purchase, it accesses the font width tables you install to provide information about each individual character in the new fonts. The program uses this information to determine the line breaks, letter spacing, kerning, and other aspects of type composition for all of the text in your document, and to display the correct font name and sizes in the font dialog boxes. If font width tables are not supplied by the font vendor, you must create these files by using Ventura's font conversion utilities, and then load them into the program using the width-table merging function, located in the Add/Remove Fonts menu option.

Depending on the type of printer, additional font files are stored on your PC's hard disk or within the printer's memory. Before you purchase new fonts, however, consult Ventura's documentation to find out if any font support limitations are involved in using the program's device drivers with your printer. For example, Ventura's HP LaserJet Plus driver can handle 220 fonts and any point size that the printer is capable of producing, but with the addition of more than 220 fonts, the printer will not print. Also, the drivers Ventura supplies for the AST, Cordata, and JLaser can all handle at least 500 fonts, but the AST and Cordata drivers cannot handle above 30 points, and the JLaser driver cannot manage above 48 points.

Because the resolution and aspect ratio of a computer screen and a laser printer are different, the fonts Ventura displays on the screen will not precisely match the fonts when they are printed. Although this may not be critical in some cases, there are times when you'll wish for a more accurate screen representation of the actual printer fonts (e.g., when using display-size type or kerning a headline). The solution is to install specially designed screen fonts that match your system's printer fonts. Fortunately, you can use the Bitstream Font-ware Installation Kit to create many matching screen fonts for both PCL and PostScript PDL printers. Other font vendors that offer matching screen and printer fonts, include Adobe Systems, Cono-graphics, Hewlett-Packard, SoftCraft, and VS Software.

In order to be most useful, screen fonts should also match the resolution of your system's graphics adapter and display. If you don't install screen fonts to match the fonts your printer uses, Ventura automatically substitutes generic screen fonts — serif, sans serif, symbol, and courier styles — that are supplied with the pro-gram. Exactly which generic screen fonts are used by the program depends on the display and printer installed with your system.

Finally, if your printer uses bit-mapped rather than outline fonts, you may also want to use a font editor or printing utility program. Font editors, such as FontGen, Publisher's Type Foundry, and SoftCraft, will let you build or modify bit-mapped fonts used with HP LaserJet, Cordata, Canon, NCR, and other laser printers. Some font editors, such as Publisher's Type Foundry, can also be used to create outline fonts for PostScript printers. Printer utility programs enable you to download fonts to your printer and provide print spooling. In most cases, you won't need a printer utility since Ventura automatically locates and downloads font files to the printer as necessary, but you can also turn off Ventura's automatic downloading routine and use a customized printer utility if you prefer.

Part II

Getting Started

Chapter 3

A Tour of the Program

*I*n the short history of PC desktop publishing, few products have enjoyed the "overnight" success that Ventura has earned in business offices throughout the country. But the seeds for this powerful IBM PC software program were actually planted back in the early 1970s, when Xerox Corporation founded the Palo Alto Research Center (PARC) to explore future office technology. Among the many innovations that PARC pioneered was a graphics-oriented interface that made it easier for people to communicate with computers.

Based on the notion that computers could be operated by using symbols and pictures as well as words, the PARC interface introduced a bit-mapped screen display that included icons (pictographic representations), drop-down menus, pop-up screens, windows, and a mouse as an alternative means of moving the screen cursor.

With the PARC interface, operating a computer was much more intuitive. As you moved the mouse on a flat surface, the cursor correspondingly moved on the screen. To activate a program function, you pointed the cursor at one of the screen icons and pushed a button on top of the mouse. Menu options and other commands were selected by using the same "point-and-click" technique.

In the early 1980s, the Xerox Star become the first commercial computer to apply the PARC interface. A few years later, the Apple Lisa appeared, which featured a modified version of the PARC interface. However, the cost of these machines was still too high for many businesses and individuals. It wasn't until Apple Computer launched the Macintosh, an affordable graphics-based computer, that the PARC interface finally gained widespread recognition.

As the Macintosh grew in popularity, so did the interest in adding a PARC interface to the IBM PC. But installing a graphics interface on a standard PC was much more difficult because it wasn't built into the hardware as it was in the Macintosh. The solution was to create it by means of the software itself, and two popular programs eventually emerged with the ability to replace the DOS system prompt with a full-screen graphics display. These programs were Digital Research's GEM (Graphics Environment Manager) Desktop and Microsoft Corporation's Windows.

While the GEM and Windows operating systems differ in several respects, they invite comparison because of their graphics orientation and shared linkage to the historic PARC interface. Both systems use a bit-mapped graphics interface replete with icons, pull-down or drop-down menus, scroll bars, dialog boxes, item selectors, and mouse and keyboard control. GEM and Windows also provide the same basic interface for other applications that run under their respective operating systems, in much the same way that all Macintosh programs share a constant interface. That makes it easier to use different applications since you only have to learn one interface, and there are several GEM-based and Windows-based word processing, draw, paint, and business graphics programs available.

One of the advantages of using GEM-based applications is that they run efficiently on older generation PC-XT computers as well as on PC-AT and 386-based machines. Windows applications, however, require an AT-class or better machine in order to run properly because Windows is a multitasking operating system that places heavier demands on the computer's processor. For instance, with Windows you can send output to a printer from one application while proceeding to work in another, and you can run multiple applications on screen at the same time, switching back and forth from one program to another.

Ventura Publisher is an application based on the GEM operating system, which means its user interface is similar (but not identical) to that of other GEM applications, such as Digital Research's GEM Artline and GEM Presentation Team. It also means Ventura can be put to immediate use in offices that are already equipped with PC-XTs or compatibles, which is good news for businesses that are not inclined to invest in hardware upgrades just for desktop publishing. Bear in mind, though, that Ventura works more proficiently on faster and more expensive PC-ATs and 386-based computers, as explained in Chapter 2.

Ventura can also be accessed from Microsoft Windows if you install and select the Program Information File (VP.PIF) provided on the Ventura Publisher Utilities disk, or simply select the VP.BAT file. Although Ventura does not operate as a Windows application when run in this manner — it still uses its GEM interface rather than a Windows interface — you will automatically return to the Windows operating system after exiting Ventura. This capability is provided as a convenience for those who use Windows regularly but would also like to access Ventura as quickly and easily as possible.

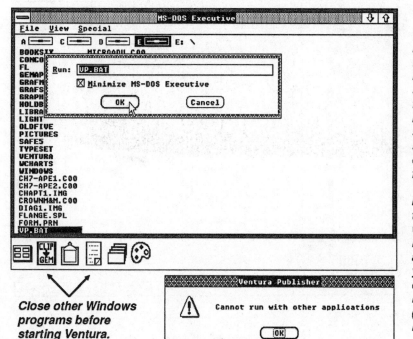

Close other Windows programs before starting Ventura.

With Windows, you can run Ventura from the MS-DOS Executive program by clicking the mouse cursor on the VP.PIF or VP.BAT file and selecting the File menu's Run command (as shown here). Or, as a shortcut, you can simply double click on the filename. In either case, Ventura will automatically begin to load and replace the Windows interface with its GEM interface. However, you will receive an error message when you try to start Ventura if other Windows programs have already been loaded (represented by the icons in the lower-left corner).

User Interface

Studies indicate that productivity often increases when computer users face a lively full-screen graphics display rather than one based solely on text characters. Yet as visually oriented as Ventura's interface is, it still takes getting used to, especially if you've never used a mouse-driven program before. If you're already adept at using a Macintosh, you'll find it easy to adapt to Ventura. But if you haven't worked with a Macintosh or used any other GEM or Windows program applications, plan on spending some time to adjust to this new type of working environment.

In this chapter, you'll learn about each distinct component of Ventura's user interface. As you read through the various sections, including "Mouse and Menu Operations," you may want to practice certain maneuvers at the same time. What you'll see on your screen will look similar to the screen shots shown here and throughout this book but may vary somewhat in size and shading depending on the type of graphics adapter and display you're using.

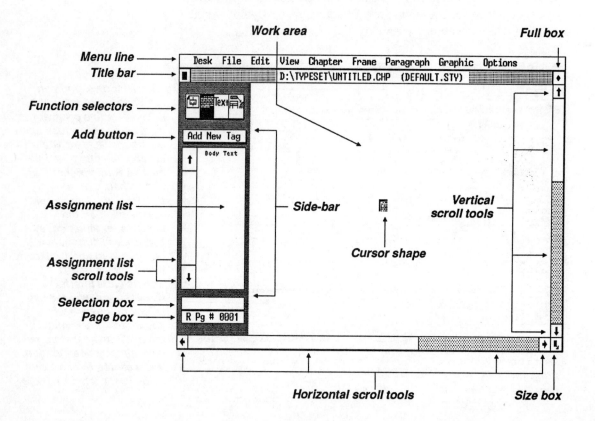

Main Screen

With Ventura, you perform all work on one main screen, which
essentially consists of a *menu line* and *title bar* on top, a box called
the *side-bar* on the left, and a large *work area* where you'll lay out
your documents. On the bottom and right side of the work area are
scroll tools (bars and arrows) that enable you to see other parts of a
page, depending on the page view you're using. All these components are described briefly in this section and examined in greater
detail later on in this and other chapters.

Ventura Publisher's User Interface		
Area	**What it contains**	**What it does**
Menu line	Menu names	Provides drop-down menus
Title bar	Chapter and style sheet	Identifies the active files
Side-bar	Function selectors, add button, assignment list, selection box, page box	Provides other functions
Function selectors	Function icons	Activates main functions
Add button	Command name	Adds a frame, tag, or text attribute
Assignment list	Filenames or commands	Displays files loaded in chapter, tag commands, or text commands
	Scroll tools	Moves different filenames or commands into the assignment list
Selection box	Filename, tag, or graphic tool	Identifies current selection
Page box	Page side and number	Identifies current page
Work area	Large blank area	Contains underlying page frame for document layout
Scroll tools	Bars (sliders) and arrows	Moves different areas of the page into the work area
Size box	Small black box and arrow	Makes the main screen area smaller and larger
Full box	Small black diamond	Makes the main screen return to original full size

```
┌─────────────────────────────────────────────────────────────────┐
│ Desk  File  Edit  View  Chapter  Frame  Paragraph  Graphic  Options │
└─────────────────────────────────────────────────────────────────┘
```

Menu Line

The menu line (shown above) contains nine drop-down menus, which are represented by the words Desk, File, Edit, View, Chapter, Frame, Paragraph, Graphic, and Options. By using these menus, you can invoke over 80 different program options. Some of these options provide immediate commands, such as quitting the program and exiting back to the DOS system prompt. Other options display *pop-up windows* — messages that overlay the main screen — to provide you with, or ask you for, additional information. All menu options that produce pop-up windows are indicated by the presence of ellipses (...) after the option name in the drop-down menu.

As you might expect with so many options, it takes time to learn which of these menus to use in order to perform various tasks. After using the program for awhile, however, you'll become acquainted with each menu's domain and find it easier to locate the exact option you want. There are also a number of keyboard shortcuts available that enable you to invoke different options by typing various key combinations. For instance, you can save your work at any time you're using Ventura by entering the Control-S command from the keyboard (holding down the Control key and typing the letter S) instead of using the File menu to invoke the same (Save) command.

```
┌─────────────────────────────────────────────────────────────────┐
│ ▌       C:\TYPESET\UNTITLED.CHP   (DEFAULT.STY)                    │
└─────────────────────────────────────────────────────────────────┘
```

Title Bar

Under the menu line is the title bar (shown above), which is used for displaying the location and name of the chapter file you're working on and the name of the style sheet file you're using. The location includes the disk drive and subdirectory (or subdirectories) where the chapter file is stored. All chapters use the same .CHP filename extension and all style sheets use the same .STY filename extension. When you start Ventura for the first time, the title bar will contain the chapter and style sheet file information displayed in the above example (which shows "C" as the hard drive designation). Thereafter, each time you start the program, the title bar will display an untitled chapter file and the style sheet file in use the last time you saved a chapter file.

When a page in the work area is displayed in the Normal View, as shown here, the scroll tools can be used to move other parts of the page into view. For example, using the four scroll arrows you can move the page up, down, left, or right in small increments.

Vertical scroll arrow

Horizontal slider

The Work Area and Scroll Tools

The large blank area that occupies most of the main screen is the work area. This is where you'll place the text and graphics elements in your documents, arranging everything just the way you want on simulated pages, and using Ventura's editing and graphic drawing tools to finalize each layout. When displaying your document in the work area, you have a choice of four different page views: (1) look at an entire page in Reduced View, (2) work on a page in Normal View, (3) see a page in Enlarged View, and (4) for double-sided documents, you can view a two-page spread in Facing Pages View.

When viewing a page in the Normal or Enlarged View, you can only see part of the page in the work area on a standard graphics system. (If you're using a high-resolution, full-page monitor, you'll be able to see an entire page in the Normal View.) In order to view and move to different areas of the page, you can use the scroll tools, which are located on the bottom and right side of the main screen. These tools, which you use with the mouse cursor, consist of scroll bars and scroll arrows. Inside each scroll bar is a white box, called a *slider,* and a shaded area that represents the amount of the page that isn't currently displayed in the work area. By using the scroll tools on the right side of the work area, you move the page vertically. With the scroll bar at the bottom of the work area, you can move it horizontally. In order to move the page by small increments, you use the scroll arrows.

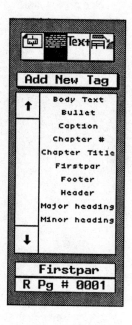

At the lower right corner of the screen where the horizontal and vertical scroll tools meet is a small icon called the *size box,* and at the upper right where the title bar and vertical scroll tool meet is a small icon called the *full box* (both shown on the left). These icons are technically part of the GEM interface but they have no pertinent use with Ventura. Nevertheless, with the size box you can reduce the size of any GEM application's main screen (except for the menu line) by selecting and dragging the box to a new location. (Incidentally, it's also possible to move the main screen by selecting and dragging a program's title bar.) If you later select the full box, the application's main screen automatically returns to its full size. Although you don't need to use these controls to operate Ventura, if you ever accidentally reduce or move the program's main screen, you can always return it to normal by simply selecting the full box.

Side-Bar

The *side-bar* (shown on the left) is the white and shaded area on the left part of the main screen that contains program options in addition to those found in the drop-down menus. In some cases, you can select the same program tool by using either the side-bar or a menu. But unlike the menus, which must first be selected before you can pick an option, you can keep the side-bar constantly on the screen. In cases where you would like more space for the work area, however, you can also remove the side-bar from the screen.

At the top of the side-bar are the *function selectors* (represented by icons), which are like buttons you press to enable Ventura's four operating modes: Frame Setting, Paragraph Tagging, Text Editing, and Graphic Drawing. The active function is easy to spot, because it's the only one that is highlighted (white icon in black box). A full explanation of what each function does and how to use it is provided in Chapter 4. (With the Professional Extension to Ventura, a fifth function called Table Edit is also available in the side-bar.)

Located directly below the function selectors in the side-bar are two more tools called the *add button* and *assignment list.* The contents of both these items depends on which function is enabled. As you change the active function from Frame Setting to Paragraph Tagging or to Text Editing, the contents of the add button and assignment list will also change. The assignment list can display up to 12 different selections at a time. When it contains more than 12, you can view

Function	Highlighted icon	Add button	Assignment list
Frame Setting		Add New Frame	Names of text and graphics files
Paragraph Tagging		Add New Tag	Names of style sheet tags
Text Editing		Set Font	Text attribute commands
Graphic Drawing		Add New Frame	Replaced by drawing tools

In Ventura's side-bar, the function selector that is highlighted (the white icon in the black box) is the active operating mode.

the additional selections by using the vertical scroll tools on the left side of the assignment list. These tools operate in the same way that the vertical scroll tools on the right side of the main screen are used to move the page contents within the work area. The scroll arrows move the list one item at a time, and the scroll bar moves the list by several items at a time.

When you change the active function to Graphic Drawing, the add button remains but the assignment list is replaced by six icons (shown on the right) that you can select, just like the function selectors, in order to draw a variety of lines, circles, square- and round-cornered boxes, and special boxes — called *box text* —that are designed to contain text, such as diagram words.

At the bottom of the side-bar are the *selection box* and *page box*, which provide you with additional information regarding currently selected items that appear in the work area. In the Paragraph Tagging mode, for example, if the active tag you're using is labeled "Firstpar" (for first paragraph), the selection box will contain that tag name (as shown on the right). With the Frame Setting mode, whenever you select a frame that already contains a file, the name of the file is identified in the selection box. If a selected frame does not contain a file, however, the box will read "EMPTY." The page box works in a similar fashion and identifies the side (right or left) and number of the page displayed in the work area. For example, the opening right page of a document is always shown as "R Pg # 0001" in the page box.

Mouse and Menu Operations

With Ventura, you perform program operations by using a mouse and a keyboard. A mouse is a hand-operated pointing device with buttons that you press to input various commands. As you move the mouse across your desk, a pointer, or mouse cursor, moves on the screen. Although some mice come with one or more buttons, all mouse-driven actions that can be performed with Ventura require only one button, which is always the left-most button on a multi-button mouse. Throughout this book, a number of terms are used to indicate various mouse operations, as described below.

Mouse Operations	
Term	**What it means**
Point	To move the mouse cursor on top of something on the screen
Click	To press and release a mouse button
Double click	To press and release a mouse button twice in fast succession
Drag	To hold down a mouse button and move the mouse until the cursor is where you want it, then release the mouse button
Release	To stop holding down a mouse button
Select	To point on a menu, scroll tool, or other object; or to pick text or graphics so they can be manipulated by your next action

Although a mouse will speed up your ability to move the cursor around the screen and perform various program functions, there are also many keyboard shortcuts available. Some shortcuts use the keyboard only, whereas others take advantage of mouse–keyboard combination commands. In order to use the mouse with the work area scroll tools, you can use a combination of point, click, and drag techniques. If you point and click on the scroll arrows or on the shaded part of the horizontal or vertical scroll bar, the page displayed will move in either small increments or big increments, respectively. You can also move the page with the slider by pointing the cursor on top of the white box and dragging it across the shaded part.

One of the main time-saving aspects of using a mouse is the double click shortcut for executing a command. For example, when selecting a file to load into Ventura, pointing the cursor on top of the filename and double clicking the mouse button is equivalent to selecting it and "OK" at the same time. Otherwise, you must select "OK" separately before the program will execute your command. It's also possible for you to adjust the double-click speed in order to make Ventura run a bit faster. The double-click speed setting is found in Options menu's Set Preferences selection. If you aren't using a mouse or the double-click shortcut, you can set the double-click speed preference to "Fast" in order to lessen the amount of time the program will wait before executing all selection operations.

Cursor Shapes

As you select each different function and perform various tasks, the cursor assumes different shapes (as shown on the right). These different shapes help you to see at a glance which function — Frame Setting, Paragraph Tagging, Text Editing, or Graphic Drawing — or specific function task is active. When the Graphic Drawing function is selected, for example, several additional cursor shapes are used to show which drawing tool is active. As you continue to spend time using the program, you'll become more familiar with each of the cursor shapes.

When working on a page layout and trying to position the cursor with precision, use the Options menu's Show Rulers command to display the program's horizontal and vertical rulers, and select the Enlarged View of the page to see the most detailed ruler increments. These on-screen rulers furnish valuable points of reference and include sliding indicators that move across the face of each ruler as you maneuver the cursor on the page, providing the precision required to accurately align the various elements in a layout.

Using Menus

The menu line that runs across the top of the main screen contains nine menus — Desk, File, Edit, View, Chapter, Frame, Paragraph, Graphic, and Options — and each menu contains its own list of additional program options and commands. To choose one of these menus, you simply touch the menu name with the cursor and the menu "drops down" like a window shade and remains on the main screen, displaying all the choices you can select from that menu. To choose an option after the menu drops down, move the cursor to the appropriate line, which becomes highlighted (white letters on a black bar), and click. Ventura then proceeds to carry out the selected command.

Cursor Shapes

Frame Setting	✚
Add new frame	FR
Resize frame	👉
Crop frame	✋
Move frame	✥
Paragraph Tagging	▦
Text Editing	I
Graphic Drawing	◤
Box text	Te
Line drawing	✎
Circle drawing	⊕
Rectangle drawing	⌐
Rounded rectangle drawing	⌐

To "pull down" a program menu, move the cursor on top of the menu name at the top of the screen, and a list of that menu's options is displayed. To select one of these menu options, move the cursor down on top of the option to highlight it, and then click the mouse button.

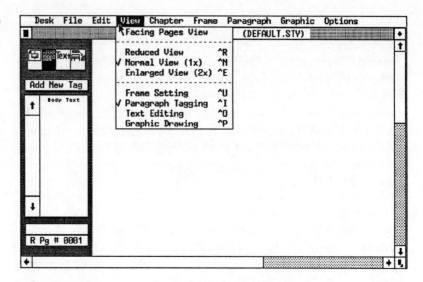

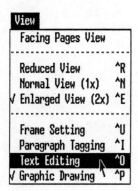

In some cases, menu options will appear in gray rather than black type, and you can't select them. A command is gray when it does not apply to the task you are performing or is not currently available. To the right of some options, the menus also list keyboard shortcuts, which entail using the Control key, represented by the caret (^) character, in tandem with a designated character key. If you select a menu but decide not to use its options or commands, you must first clear the menu from the screen by pointing the cursor on another part of the screen and clicking. Or, if you happen to choose the wrong menu, simply move the cursor to the menu name you do want to access and that menu will appear instead.

You can also adjust the way in which you access the menus by changing one of the default interface settings in the Options menu's Set Preferences selection. Instead of drop-down menus, you can pick the "Menu Type: Pull-Down" setting and from then on, each menu will appear only as long as you hold the mouse button after touching the menu name. As soon as you release the button, the menu list is automatically removed from the screen. To choose an option from a pull-down menu, you drag the cursor downward and highlight the option you want before releasing the button.

As mentioned earlier, Ventura often requires additional data from you before it can carry out a menu option. To obtain this information, the program displays a pop-up window — a message box that overlays the center of the main screen — and prompts you for it. For example, the program typically uses a pop-up window to ask if you want to "Save" or "Abandon" changes to the current chapter when you select the File menu's Quit option. The two main types of pop-up windows that Ventura uses are *dialog boxes* and *item selectors*. In brief, dialog boxes are used for choosing various program features, and item selectors are used for retrieving or saving the many types of files you use with Ventura. If you decide not to use a dialog box or item selector after it pops up, click on the "OK" or "Cancel" command inside the pop-up window, or press the Enter key, which is the equivalent of using the "OK" command.

Using Dialog Boxes

As shown below, dialog boxes list features on the left and choices or blank spaces on the right. When choices are provided, they take the form of *button controls*, which are rectangular boxes that contain text, such as "Left Page" and "Right Page," and additional pop-up menus. To select a button control, you simply click it on with the mouse cursor and the box remains highlighted to indicate your choice. The pop-up menus in a dialog box are located wherever you find the arrow (⬍) symbol. To select a pop-up menu, point the cursor on the arrow, click, and hold (as shown on the right). Move the cursor over the other selections and keep holding down the button until the selection you want is highlighted, then simply release the button. If a button control is gray rather than black, it is not currently available.

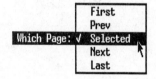

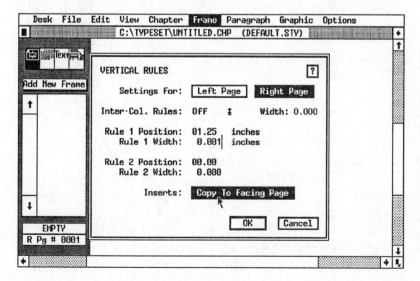

Dialog boxes are filled out by using the mouse and the keyboard. With the mouse, you often select an option by moving the cursor on top of a box, or "button control," and clicking. Like the buttons in a car radio, when you select a button control, the previous selection is disengaged. With the keyboard, you type in text or numeric values.

Ventura's dialog boxes also contain pop-up help menus that provide brief help screens associated with the various features found in the dialog box. Help menus are found in the boxed question mark in the upper-right corner of a dialog box.

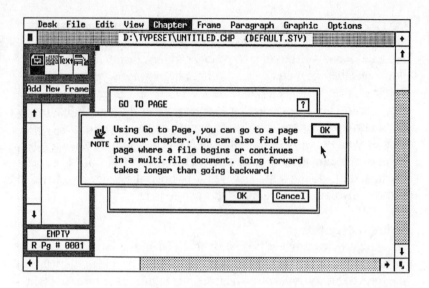

Help menus are another type of pop-up menu found in dialog boxes. In order to access a help menu, move the cursor on top of the boxed question mark at the upper-right corner, click, and hold. Ventura displays a list of topics related to the various features in the dialog box (as shown on the left). After you select the topic you need help with (by highlighting it and releasing the mouse button), the program displays a brief help message (as shown above). Most help messages are limited to a single pop-up screen, and as soon as you read the message and click "OK," the program returns to the original dialog box. One of the most useful help menus of all is in the Publisher Info dialog box, located in the Desk menu. This help menu provides nearly a dozen help screens that list all of the keyboard and mouse-keyboard commands you'll probably use most often in producing documents.

When a dialog box contains blank spaces or numeric values, you type in text or numbers by using the keyboard. The arrow keys and tab key are used to move the typing cursor (a thin vertical bar), which is always located on the first available blank space or numeric value. If a blank space or numeric value isn't currently available, it is displayed in gray rather than black type. To change the text or numeric value, you can use the Backspace, Delete, or Escape key to erase the contents, then type in the new information. If you only need to change a single value, you can use the mouse to move the cursor to the appropriate line and click.

In order to enter numeric values in a dialog box, Ventura allows you to use four different units of measurement: inches, picas and points, centimeters, or fractional points (which provide the greatest precision). At any time, you can change the measurement unit by pointing to it and clicking until the unit you want to use appears. As you change from one measurement unit to another, Ventura automatically adjusts all affected numeric values within the dialog box to reflect the active unit of measurement. For example, if you set the position of a vertical rule at 01.25 inches, pointing at the word "inches" and clicking changes the measurement to 03.18 centimeters. Clicking again changes it to 07,06 picas and points (the 7 refers to picas, the 06 to points). Clicking a third time changes it to 90.00 fractional points. Because the largest fractional points value that can be displayed is 99.99, or about 1.4 inches, the program uses tilde characters (~~.~~) if the fractional point value is out of range. Also, some dialog boxes display more than one unit of measurement to control different features within the same dialog box, and you can change one unit without affecting the others.

```
01.25   inches
03.18   centimeters
07,06   picas & points
90.00   fractional pts
```

A set of equivalent values using the four units of measurement supported by Ventura.

Using Item Selectors

Item selectors make it easy to retrieve or save a file by providing a fast and efficient way to move between the DOS directories where you keep the various files used for your Ventura documents. All item selectors include a directory line, selection line, and directory list, as well as an "OK" and "Cancel" execution command.

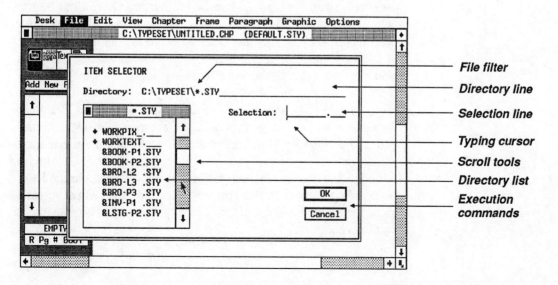

Backup button

Directory symbol

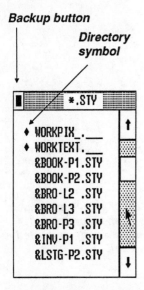

By clicking the mouse cursor on the backup button, you can access files from other disk drives.

The example on the preceding page shows the item selector Ventura uses whenever you pick the Load Different Style option in the File menu. In this case, the directory line shows "C:" as the active drive, "TYPESET" as the current directory, and ".STY" as the file extension (which is used for style sheets). The asterisk (*) preceding the file extension is a standard DOS wildcard character that can be used with any file extension for the purpose of filtering, or searching for and displaying, all files with the same extension. In Ventura, the asterisk and file extension are called a *file filter*.

The directory list shows the name of the active file extension and displays up to nine directories or filenames at a time. To help you tell the difference between a directory and a filename, all directories are preceded by a black diamond. The small black square in the upper-left corner of the directory box is the *backup button*. If you click on the backup button, the names displayed in the directory list change to the previous level in the directory structure, all the way to the root directory and your computer's disk drives.

On the right side of the directory list are vertical scroll tools to help display additional filenames. If you have more than nine files or directories, you can display the additional names by using the scroll tools the same way you use them with the assignment list in the side-bar. After locating the desired filename, you select it by placing the cursor on it and clicking; the filename is then highlighted and the name is automatically placed on the selection line. Click on the "OK" command to confirm it's the file you want to load and Ventura proceeds to load the file, then returns you to the main screen.

You can also use the keyboard to enter the name of a file on the selection line directly. Just use the typing cursor (which is on the selection line) the same way you use it in a dialog box. If you press the up arrow key on your keyboard, the cursor will move up to the end of the directory line and you can also change that information if you wish. For example, you can replace the default file filter with a filename extension of your own choice. Or, if you enter the DOS wildcard characters "*.*" on the selection or directory line, you can view the entire contents of any directory or floppy disk without exiting Ventura.

Chapter 4

Using the Program Functions

*P*roducing high-quality publications generally requires several skilled professionals — from editors and graphic designers to typesetters and printers — using specialized tools and equipment to perform their jobs. With Ventura, the task of constructing and printing a publication may involve the same skills, but when it comes to the tools required, most of what you need is included within the program itself.

Ventura's publication tools are grouped into four separate functions, or operating modes: Frame Setting, Paragraph Tagging, Text Editing, and Graphic Drawing. Each function offers its own set of features for performing a host of related publishing tasks. Ventura also uses a series of menus to organize the work tasks related to each function. Some menus are always available as you use the program, whereas other menus or specific menu options are linked to a certain function, as follows:

Function		Related Menu
Frame Setting	⇨	Frame menu
Paragraph Tagging	⇨	Paragraph menu
Text Editing	⇨	Edit menu
Graphic Drawing	⇨	Graphic menu

This chapter discusses these four functions and explores how to use them to design, lay out, and format a document. It also presents an overview of specific menus and options linked to each function. (Note: With the Professional Extension, a fifth function called Table Edit is added to Ventura, as explained in Part IV, "The Professional Extension.")

Selecting Functions

Because only one of Ventura's functions can be active at a time, it's important to learn when to use each mode. In some cases, certain menus or options are only accessible when a specific function is selected; in other instances, you also need to choose a particular item on a page before additional features become accessible. When menus and menu options are not accessible, they are displayed in gray rather than black type.

Ventura provides three different methods for choosing one of the program's functions:

- Choose a function selector (i.e., one of the four icons shown on the left) in the side-bar.
- Choose a function menu option in the View menu.
- Use a function selector keyboard shortcut.

To pick a function, you can click on one of the function selectors or use the View menu options (shown on the right) or keyboard shortcuts. The latter two methods are handy when you use the Hide Side-Bar command to make more room for the work area.

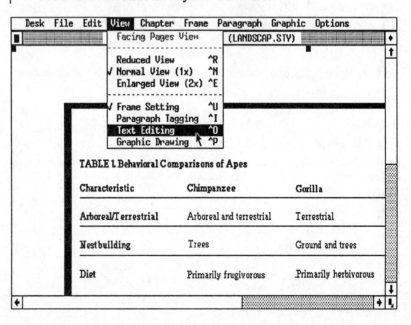

In most cases, the fastest way to select a function is to move the cursor on top of one of the side-bar's function selectors and click the mouse button. However, the other two methods provide alternative ways to select functions when the side-bar isn't displayed on the screen — for example, when you use the Hide Side-Bar command (Options menu) to display more of a publication page.

Whenever you change from one function to another, the contents of the side-bar's add button and assignment list also change to reflect the different controls and commands available. The appearance of the side-bar when each function is selected is shown in the illustration below, and the sections that follow explain each operating mode and its use.

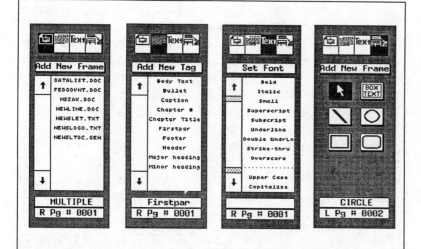

Ventura's side-bar changes as you select each function. From left to right are the side-bar contents used by the Frame Setting, Paragraph Tagging, Text Editing, and Graphic Drawing functions.

Frame Setting

The general design and layout of a Ventura document is accomplished with the Frame Setting function. This function provides you with the ability to create and manipulate rectangular areas, called *frames,* that serve as the basic building blocks for constructing a page layout. Frames are used to hold all the text and graphics files that you import, or "load," into Ventura from other programs.

When Frame Setting is selected, the cursor turns into a crossbar icon (shown on the right), the add button reads "Add New Frame," and the assignment list is used to display the names of all the text and graphics files loaded into the program.

To create a document with Ventura, you can use two types of frames: *page frames*, which the program automatically generates for each full-size page, and *added frames*, which you can manually create and place on a page. While the program provides similar control over both types of frames, there are two key distinctions between page frames and added frames. First, the dimensions of page frames are always equivalent to the height and width of the underlying page itself, but added frames can vary in size, ranging from the proportions of a full-size page to an area as small as a single character of text. And second, you cannot cut, copy, or move page frames as you can with added frames.

The main characteristic of both page frames and added frames, however, is that each can only hold a single text or graphics file. Although you can easily change the contents of any frame whenever you want, you simply cannot place more than one file in a single frame at a time. Therefore, to place additional text or graphics files on the same page, you must use added frames to hold them.

Page Frames and Automatic Pagination
One of Ventura's most impressive feats is that it can automatically paginate an entire text file for you. Because it has the ability to generate additional pages as needed, you can simply place a text file on the opening page and the program will automatically "flow" all of the text that doesn't fit in the first page frame onto as many additional pages as necessary, until all of the text is paginated.

The first step required to import a file into the program is to select the Load Text/Picture option from the File menu (above) and fill out the dialog box (right) that is provided. Ventura automatically changes the file format options (button controls) available, depending on the type of file you select. The "Destination" setting is only available when you import a text file.

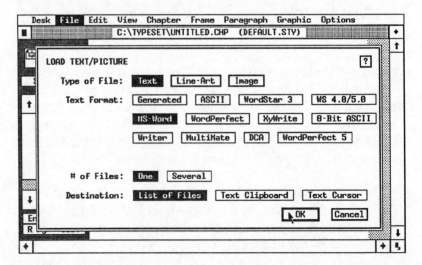

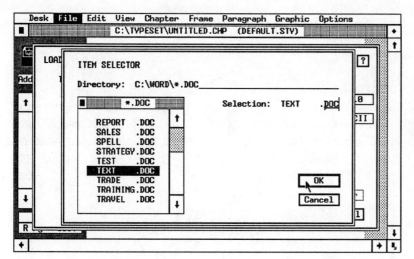

The second step required to import a file is to use an item selector to tell Ventura where to find the target file you want it to load. In this example, the file "TEXT.DOC" has been selected from the "WORD" directory. After the "OK" command is selected, Ventura will proceed to load the file.

Only four basic steps are required to load a text file into Ventura and automatically paginate it:

1. Point to the File menu and select the Load Text/Picture option. Ventura responds by providing the Load Text/Picture dialog box, which asks you for more information.

2. Apply the Load Text/Picture dialog box by clicking on the "Text" button for "Type of File" and the appropriate choice for your word processor's "Text Format" (e.g., "MS-Word" for Microsoft Word). Use the default settings for the other buttons ("# of Files: One" and "Destination: List of Files") and select "OK." Ventura provides an item selector with the appropriate file filter (e.g., ".DOC" for a Microsoft Word file).

3. Use the Load Text/Picture item selector to instruct Ventura where to find the file you want to load. Either use the directory list to locate the proper file or type in the information on the blank lines provided, and select "OK." Ventura goes to work and displays the message "Loading & Hyphenating Text File" until the main screen returns.

4. Move the Frame Setting cursor (crossbar) anywhere on the page and click to select the page frame, then move the cursor on top of the filename in the assignment list and click again to select it as the file you want Ventura to place in the page frame.

In this Facing Pages View, the base page frame is set for a three-column format. After selecting the page on the right side (marked by black boxes) and clicking on the file in the assignment list, the program immediately paginates the file.

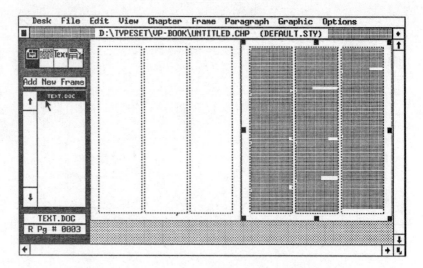

After you finish these steps, Ventura will place the text file on the first page and as many additional pages as necessary to paginate the remainder of the file. If you select the page frame before using the Load Text/Picture option, you won't even need to perform the last step because Ventura will already know where you want to place the newly loaded file.

The exact size and formatting of a text file placed in a page frame depends on the current style sheet. For example, if you use the program's default style sheet (DEFAULT.STY), the text is converted into a 12-point serif font — Times or Dutch, depending on the printer width table installed — and placed into a single-column format on a portrait-oriented, letter-size page. Other style sheet settings, such as hyphenation and justification, are also employed.

After Ventura places a file in a frame, it displays the filename in the current selection box (as shown above). If no file has been placed in a frame, the current selection box reads "EMPTY" when that frame is selected. To view the various pages in a document, use the PageDown and PageUp keys to scroll through the pages one at a time, or use the End or Home keys to go directly to the last or first page of your document, respectively. You can also go to a specific page by using the Chapter menu's Go to Page option.

Because page frames can be easily used to automatically paginate entire text files, they are often used to produce books, manuals, and other lengthy documents that require design consistency from page to page. If you want to include graphics files as illustrations along the way, you can add new frames wherever you want, fill them with graphics, and the program will automatically reformat the text so that it flows around them. Best of all, as more frames for graphics are added, Ventura will keep generating as many new pages as necessary to continue paginating the text.

Also, at any time, you can print pages by using the File menu's To Print option. That's all it takes to produce a document using page frames. Since you can use Ventura in this way to quickly paginate and print a text file, it isn't necessary to master all of the program's features just to print simple pages. But by learning how to use more of the features available, you can turn those simple pages into a dynamic document, full of design and formatting flourishes.

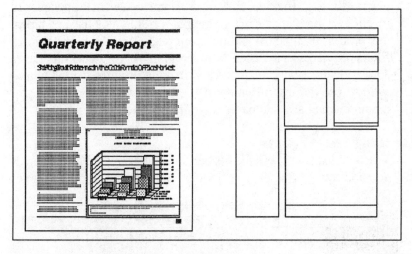

To create the newsletter on the left (shown as it appears on screen), the Frame Setting function was used to add a series of frames (shown on the right) to hold the text and graphics files.

Added Frames and Manual Pagination

For some publications, page frames alone do not provide enough design flexibility. With newsletters and magazines, for example, it's often necessary to use additional frames of different dimensions to hold various text and graphics files on each page. To produce these and other design-intensive publications, you can easily add new frames to augment or replace the use of page frames.

To add a new frame to a document, click on the "Add New Frame" button, and move the cursor to the work area where you will begin drawing the top left corner of the frame. Inside the work area, the crossbar cursor changes into the letters "FR" and the top corner of a box (shown on the left). Click and hold down the mouse button, and the cursor changes into a pointing finger (shown on the left), the cursor shape for drawing and resizing frames. To draw the frame, drag the cursor to the bottom right corner where you want the frame to end, and release the mouse button. A frame in the shape you've drawn is immediately inserted on the page. This frame remains active and is affected by the next action you take until you pick or draw another frame or change functions.

For example, you can apply the same steps described earlier and place a text file inside an added frame. Unlike page frames, however, when you place a text file in an added frame, any remaining text will not automatically flow beyond that frame. Instead, you must manually select the next frame (or page) and instruct Ventura to continue placing the text. To do so, click on the frame you want the text placed in, click on the filename in the side-bar's assignment list, and repeat this process until all text has been placed in as many additional frames as necessary. Because the program doesn't generate pages automatically when you place text in added frames, you may also need to use the Insert/Remove Page option, found in the Chapter menu, to manually add pages to your document.

Using Added Frames

When you add a new frame, its border is displayed on the screen; if you add several frames, you'll see borders around all of the frames

As the direction of the arrow indicates, you draw all frames diagonally by clicking and dragging the pointing finger cursor from the upper-left corner to the lower-right corner. After you release the mouse button, the frame is inserted on the page and the cursor changes back to the crossbar.

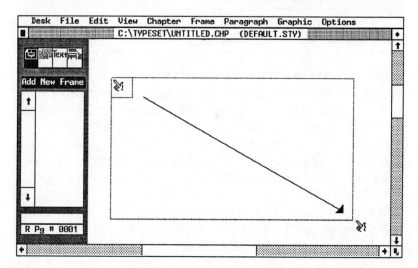

as long as the Frame Setting mode is active. A frame's border will not appear on the printed page, however, unless you add a ruling box around it or fill its background with a solid color or pattern. Ventura also displays small black boxes inside the perimeter of a frame to indicate it is currently selected. To select a different frame, move the cursor inside the desired frame, click, and the small boxes will appear inside its perimeter to indicate it is currently selected.

Once a frame is selected, you can move, resize, copy, delete, and paste it as many times as you want. To move a frame, place the cursor anywhere inside it, then click and hold the mouse button. The cursor changes into a cross with arrows on each end (shown on the right) and you can now drag the frame in any direction. Just move the frame where you want it, release the mouse button, and the frame is displayed in its new location. Ventura temporarily displays frames in both locations until you release the mouse button, which helps if you want to use the old location as a point of reference.

To resize a frame, the small boxes that indicate a frame is selected also serve as "sizing buttons." By using the mouse, you can click on a sizing button and drag it inside the frame to reduce the size or outside the frame to increase it. If you drag one of the corner sizing buttons, you can perform two-dimensional scaling — that is, you can resize a frame's width and height in a single move. To scale a frame in only one dimension, you use the other sizing buttons; to change a frame's width only, use the center sizing button on either the left or right side; to change its height only, use the sizing button on the top or bottom side. When you resize a frame with the mouse, the cursor shape changes from a crossbar to a pointing finger. If the cursor doesn't make this change, you probably haven't placed it directly over one of the sizing buttons and should try again. If you're dealing with a very small frame, it's best to enlarge the page view first before trying to use the sizing buttons.

As long as the Frame Setting mode is active, you can use the Edit menu options (shown on the right) to cut, copy, and paste any added frame. If a frame you want to copy contains a text or graphics file, Ventura will copy the contents along with the frame. The Edit menu also provides the Frame Setting mode with two other controls: the Remove Text/File option, which allows you to remove a file either from a frame or from the assignment list, and the File Type/Rename

Edit	
Cut Frame	Del
Copy Frame	↑Del
Paste Frame	Ins
Ins Special Item...	^C
Edit Special Item...	^D
Remove Text/File...	
File Type/Rename...	

When you select multiple frames, black boxes are placed inside the border of each frame selected, and the current selection box reads "MULTIPLE." The next action you take in the Frame Setting mode will affect all selected frames.

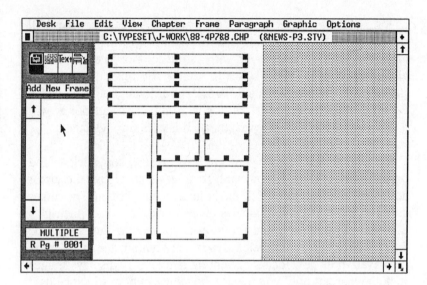

option, which lets you save a text file (but not a graphics file) under a new name and format.

Ventura also permits you to select more than one frame at a time by holding down the Shift key as you click on each additional frame. If more than one frame is selected, the current selection box reads "MULTIPLE," and you can move, cut, copy, and paste the entire group of frames all at once.

Frames and Picture Cropping

The final cursor shape used by the Frame Setting mode is an outstretched hand (shown on the left) for adjusting a picture placed in a frame. With this tool, you can crop any picture — that is, any "Line-Art" or "Image" graphics file — after it has been loaded and placed in a page frame or added frame. Cropping means offsetting or keeping portions of a picture from being displayed in a frame, as if you had cut parts of it away with scissors. Yet the portions you crop and keep from being displayed and printed are not eliminated from the original graphics file, where they remained stored.

To crop a picture, move the crossbar cursor to the center of the frame containing the graphics file to be cropped, hold down the Alternate key, and click and hold down the mouse button. The crossbar turns into the cropping cursor, and you can now move the picture in any direction to cut off part of its contents. For instance, drag the

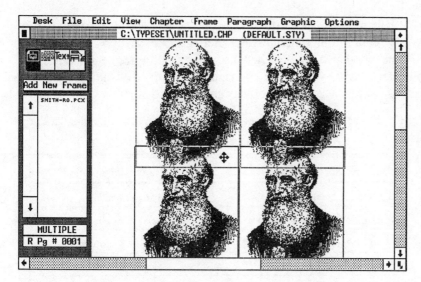

Desk File Edit View Chapter Frame Paragraph Graphic Options

C:\TYPESET\UNTITLED.CHP (DEFAULT.STY)

Add New Frame

SMITH-RO.PCX

MULTIPLE
R Pg # 0001

Using the Edit menu's cut-copy-paste features, you can quickly make copies of graphics-filled frames and place them anywhere in a document. In this screen shot, the two frames on top have been copied from the two frames below, and are now being dragged off of the source frames — where copies of frames are initially pasted by the program.

cropping cursor to the left side of the frame to cut portions of the picture's left side and reveal more of its right side; or drag the cursor to the top of the frame to show more of the picture's bottom. After you've cropped the picture the way you want, release the Alternate key and mouse button, and the picture stays in its new position.

When a picture is initially placed in a frame, its original height-to-width aspect ratio is maintained and it is scaled to fit inside the frame accordingly. But after a picture is placed in a frame, you use the Sizing & Scaling option, in the Frame menu, to increase the picture's size independent of the frame's size. You can also use the Sizing & Scaling option to crop pictures with greater precision than you can with the mouse because it lets you use numeric values to control both horizontal and vertical cropping.

Frame Attributes

Each frame has a formidable set of attributes that you can control by using the various options in the Frame menu. When you select any of the Frame menu options, Ventura provides a dialog box containing the specific frame properties you can control, ranging from frame size and placement to the use of ruling lines above, below, and around a frame. Some of these attributes pertain only to frames with contents, either text or graphics files, whereas others affect all frames, even if they are empty. However, the Frame menu options are not accessible unless the Frame Setting mode is active.

Although the focus of this chapter is to present an overview of Ventura's four functions and their general relationship to certain menus, the following chart lists many of the frame attributes you can control by using the Frame menu options. The dialog boxes you use to manage these attributes are fully explained in Chapter 6.

Frame	
Margins & Columns...	
Sizing & Scaling...	
Frame Typography...	
Anchors & Captions...	
Repeating Frame...	
Vertical Rules...	
Ruling Line Above...	
Ruling Line Below...	
Ruling Box Around...	
Frame Background...	
Image Settings...	

Frame Setting Function

Frame Attributes	Frame Menu Option*
Size (width, height)	Sizing & Scaling
Placement (X-Y coordinates)	Sizing & Scaling
Margins (top, bottom, left, right)	Margins & Columns
Columns (up to 8)	Margins & Columns
Column balance within frame	Frame Typography
Widows and orphans within frame	Frame Typography
Pair kerning within frame	Frame Typography
First line distance from column top	Frame Typography
Flow text around frame	Sizing & Scaling
Holding channel (white space) around frame	Sizing & Scaling
Scale picture contents	Sizing & Scaling
Crop picture contents	Sizing & Scaling
Vertical rules (up to 2) inside frame	Vertical Rules
Intercolumn rules (up to 7) inside frame	Vertical Rules
Horizontal rules (up to 3) above frame	Ruling Line Above
Horizontal rules (up to 3) below frame	Ruling Line Below
Surrounding box rules (up to 3)	Ruling Box Around
Fill color and pattern	Frame Background
Repeating frame	Repeating Frame
Frame anchor name	Anchors & Captions
Caption frame	Anchors & Captions
Gray-scale halftone control	Image Settings

* A frame must be selected before menu options are available.

Paragraph Tagging

After placing a text file in a frame, you can proceed to format the text by using the Paragraph Tagging function. Paragraph Tagging, as the name suggests, is based on the use of a series of *tags*, or labels, that can be applied to any paragraph in a document.

To use the Paragraph Tagging mode, you can click on the second box from the left in the function selector, pick the Paragraph Tagging option in the View menu, or use the Ctrl-I (^I) keyboard shortcut. When Paragraph Tagging is active, the cursor changes into an icon resembling a paragraph of text (as shown on the right), the only cursor shape used by this function.

The process of formatting text in the Paragraph Tagging mode involves assigning a number of typographic attributes to tags, and assigning the tags to various paragraphs of text in your document. With Ventura, a paragraph is defined as any single letter, word, line of text, or several lines of text followed by a paragraph return. Paragraph returns are created by pressing the Enter key.

To assign typographic characteristics to a tag, you use the Paragraph menu options and fill out a series of dialog boxes to select such attributes as typeface, type size, line spacing, word spacing, text alignment, tab settings, and special effects. You can also choose to put a ruling box around a paragraph, or place ruling lines above or below it. Ventura offers an extensive amount of typographic control

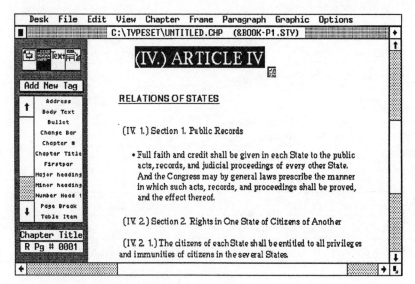

To use the Paragraph Tagging function, you place the cursor on top of a paragraph and click the mouse button to select it. Then click on a tag in the side-bar's assignment list to assign that tag's typographic attributes to the paragraph.

over the text in a document, but what's even more impressive is the speed at which you can assign all these specifications to any selected paragraph or group of paragraphs. This is accomplished by the use of style sheets with powerful formatting capabilities. The Paragraph Tagging chart below provides a general overview of the major

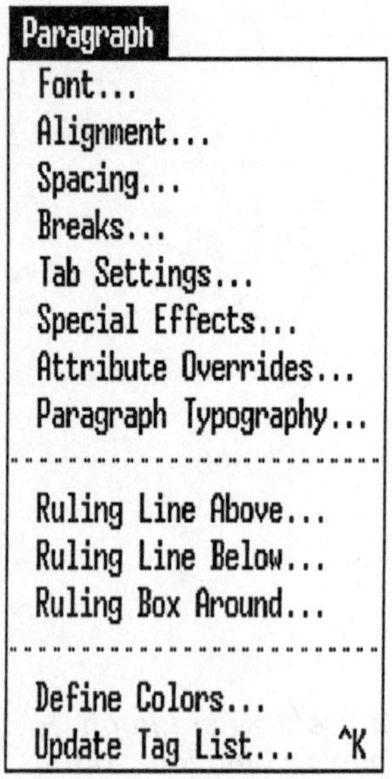

```
┌──────────────────┐
│ Paragraph        │
├──────────────────┤
│ Font...          │
│ Alignment...     │
│ Spacing...       │
│ Breaks...        │
│ Tab Settings...  │
│ Special Effects...│
│ Attribute Overrides...│
│ Paragraph Typography...│
│ ·················│
│ Ruling Line Above...│
│ Ruling Line Below...│
│ Ruling Box Around...│
│ ·················│
│ Define Colors... │
│ Update Tag List...  ^K│
└──────────────────┘
```

Paragraph Tagging Function

Paragraph Attributes	Paragraph Menu Option*
Typeface, type size, type style, type color	Font
Hyphenation and justification	Alignment
Text rotation	Alignment
First line indent/outdent	Alignment
Line and paragraph spacing	Spacing
Temporary margins	Spacing
Hanging indents	Breaks
Paragraph lead-ins	Breaks
Vertical tabs	Breaks
Horizontal tabs (up to 16)	Tab Settings
Tab characters	Tab Settings
Large initial capital letter	Special Effects
Bullet characters	Special Effects
Automatic kerning	Paragraph Typography
Letter spacing and word spacing	Paragraph Typography
Tracking	Paragraph Typography
Line height and shift for underline, double underline, strike-thru, overscore	Attribute Overrides
Horizontal rules above paragraph	Ruling Line Above
Horizontal rules below paragraph	Ruling Line Below
Surrounding box rules	Ruling Box Around
Rename or remove style sheet tags	Update Tag List

* A paragraph must be selected before menu options are available.

typographic attributes you can control; Chapter 6 will continue to discuss these features in detail.

Style Sheets and Tags
A Ventura style sheet is a file that tells the program how to format a document. A style sheet contains page layout and typographic specifications you define by using various menu options and dialog boxes. The page layout controls, such as page size and orientation, can be changed at any time — regardless of which function is active — by using various options in the Chapter menu. But in order to assign a style sheet's typographic specifications to the text in a document while using Ventura, you must first select the Paragraph Tagging function.

Once you activate the Paragraph Tagging function, all tags available within the current style sheet are shown in alphabetical order in the side-bar's assignment list. When you use the DEFAULT.STY file, for instance, only one tag — Body Text — appears in the assignment list. But if you load other style sheets that Ventura provides, you'll see a longer list of tag names, such as the following tags provided in the program's &BOOK-P1.STY file:

- Body Text
- Caption
- Chapter Title
- Footer
- Major Heading

- Bullet
- Chapter #
- Firstpar
- Header
- Minor Heading

You can use any of the tags that are already incorporated with the program's sample style sheets to format your own documents. To load a sample style sheet use the Load Different Style option in the File menu. After you've loaded one of these sample style sheets, you can modify its tags or add new tags with different attributes.

If you want to rename or delete a tag, you can do so with any tag except Body Text. Although you can change the typographic attributes associated with the Body Text tag, you cannot change or remove the tag name itself because it is reserved by Ventura to provide the program with default settings for formatting text when it is first placed in a document. When you place a text file in a page frame, for instance, Ventura uses the Body Text specifications as the default settings for formatting the contents of the file if no other tags are present.

Using Tags

To use the Paragraph Tagging function, first select a paragraph from a page of your document by moving the cursor on top of the paragraph and clicking. Ventura responds by highlighting the paragraph you select — black text changes to white text, for example. To de-select a paragraph, click on another paragraph or on another part of the page that contains no text at all.

After you've selected a paragraph you want to tag, move the cursor on top of a tag name in the assignment list — the tag name will be highlighted — and click to assign the tag to the selected paragraph. The program responds by formatting the paragraph according to the typographic attributes associated with that tag. If you proceed to click on a different tag name in the assignment list, the same paragraph will be reformatted according to the new tag's attributes.

When a paragraph is selected, the tag name assigned to it will be displayed in the side-bar's current selection box. As you continue to work with the Paragraph Setting function, every time you select a paragraph with an assigned tag, the tag name will appear in the current selection box. By holding down the Shift key as you use the Paragraph Tagging cursor, you can select more than one paragraph

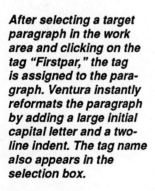

After selecting a target paragraph in the work area and clicking on the tag "Firstpar," the tag is assigned to the paragraph. Ventura instantly reformats the paragraph by adding a large initial capital letter and a two-line indent. The tag name also appears in the selection box.

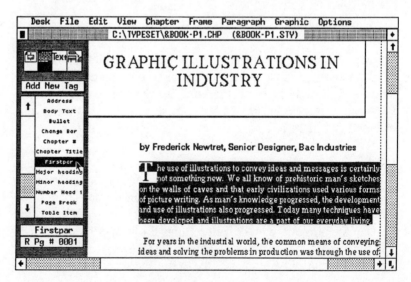

to assign the same tag. As with multiple frames, when you select several paragraphs the current selection box reads "MULTIPLE." To de-select a paragraph, click on it again and it's no longer highlighted.

Using the Function Keys

In addition to selecting multiple paragraphs as a shortcut for assigning type attributes to all of the paragraphs in a document, Ventura also lets you expedite the process by assigning tag names to the 10 keyboard function keys, F1 through F10. To assign tag names to each of these keys, you select the Assign Function Keys command in the Update Tag List option, found in the Paragraph menu, and fill out the dialog box provided. After you've selected a paragraph (or group of paragraphs), pressing the appropriate function key will cause that tag to be assigned to the highlighted paragraph(s).

The best part of using the function keys to tag paragraphs is that you can use them when either the Paragraph Tagging or the Text Editing function is enabled. By tagging paragraphs in the Text Editing mode, you can significantly decrease the amount of time it takes to both edit and format a document. To use the function keys with the Text Editing function, the typing cursor must first be inserted in the target paragraph before you press the function key to assign the tag.

Generated Tags

With the Paragraph Tagging function, you can not only select and tag text placed in a frame, but also the text used in headers and footers, section numbers, footnotes, and captions. When you use various menu options to automatically add these additional text items to a document, Ventura tags the text with *generated tags*. All generated tag names are preceded by the letter "Z," for example, "Z_HEADER," "Z_FOOTER," and "Z_CAPTION."

Although the typographic specifications for generated tags are initially taken from the attributes assigned to the Body Text tag, you can modify and change these tags just like any other tag. But since generated tags are not normally assigned to regular paragraphs in a document, the program does not automatically display these tags in the assignment list. Therefore, if you want all generated tags displayed in the assignment list so that you can tag any paragraph with them, use the Set Preferences option in the Options menu and select "Generated Tags: Show" in the dialog box provided.

In order to change a tag's specifications, you first assign the tag to a target paragraph, then select a Paragraph menu option, such as Ruling Box Around.

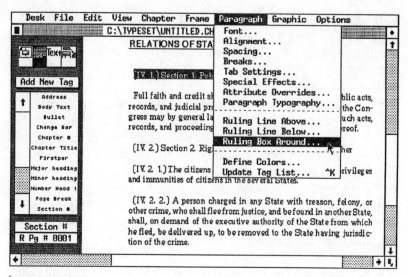

Adding Tags

To create a new tag with different specifications, use the side-bar's add button, which reads "Add New Tag" when the Paragraph Tagging mode is active. If desired, you can select a paragraph before clicking on the add button so that the new tag will be assigned to the selected paragraph automatically, though you can also use the Add New Tag button without first selecting a paragraph.

After you click on the Add New Tag button, Ventura provides a dialog box which you fill out by using the keyboard to type in the

The next step is to fill out the dialog box that the program provides. In this example, a solid ruling box is being selected to apply to all paragraphs that are tagged with the name "Section #."

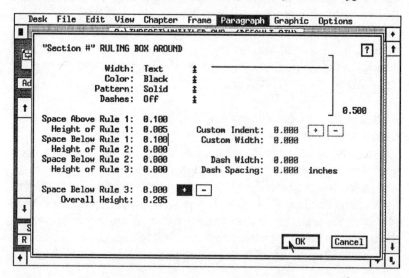

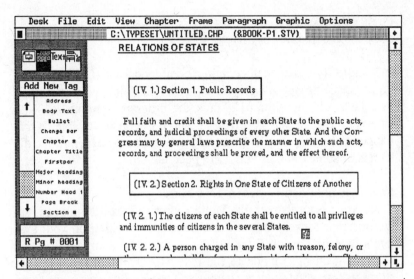

After clicking "OK" in the dialog box, the program instantly reformats all paragraphs assigned the "Section #" by placing a ruling box around the paragraph. You may need to repeat this process a few times until you're satisfied with the results.

new tag name and then click "OK." The new tag name immediately appears in the alphabetized assignment list and, if a paragraph is already selected, the new tag is automatically assigned to it. Better still, if you select a paragraph before using the Add New Tag button, Ventura will place the old tag name on the "Tag Name to Copy From" line in the dialog box and copy all of its existing attributes over to the new tag's typographic specifications.

It usually saves time to use an old tag as the basis for creating a new tag when only a few characteristics will be changed. To assign or

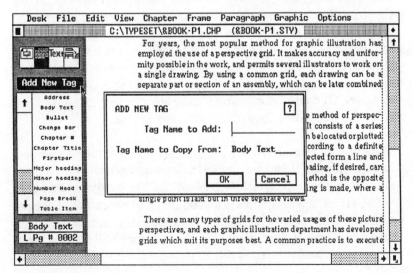

When you click on the "Add New Tag" button, a dialog box appears and enables you to enter a new tag name. In this example, the new tag will be assigned the same typographic characteristics as the "Body Text" tag.

modify the specifications of any tag, you'll use the Paragraph menu options, as explained in Chapter 6.

A Ventura style sheet can contain a combined total of 128 different tags, consisting of the tags you've added plus all generated tags. If you try to add more than 128 tags, the program prompts you with an error message that says there are no more tags available. If this happens, the only way you can add new tags is to first remove the names of some old tags you don't need anymore.

Saving Embedded Codes in Text Files

When you save a chapter file, Ventura stores all text files loaded into the program back in their original locations — either on your system's hard disk or on floppy disks — along with any editing and formatting changes made to the text. However, because Ventura stores its own style sheet tag names and other references in the same files, you'll also see the program's embedded codes the next time you open these text files in your word processor. The actual codes that Ventura uses are explained in the "Working with Text" section in Chapter 7.

If you intend to use your text files with Ventura again, do not delete any of the tags, codes, or extra line returns that Ventura has inserted or you'll have to reformat the file the next time you use it with the program. Since Ventura's tags and codes are inserted in your text files after using the program, you may find it inconvenient to use the same files for other purposes or with other programs. To maintain a "clean" copy of a text file that doesn't contain this formatting information, make a copy of the file before you use it with Ventura. However, if you edit the text inside Ventura, you'll also have to repeat those changes in the file copy if you want both files to be identical. Of course, if you don't make any changes to the file, you won't have to worry about this potential problem.

Ventura automatically creates backup files of all text files you import into the program if you use the Set Preferences option in the Options menu and select "Keep Backup Files: Yes" in the dialog box provided. Keeping backup files is a good protective measure in case of a system failure. However, since these backup files are updated each time you save a chapter file within Ventura, they will only be clean copies after the first time you save your work.

Text Editing

In order to insert, delete, cut, copy, and paste text in a Ventura document, you use the Text Editing function. With this mode, you can also change certain typographic attributes of single characters or blocks of text, and you can insert what Ventura refers to as "special items," including box characters, footnotes, fractions, index entries, frame anchors, and references for page or chapter numbers.

To select Text Editing, either click on the third function selector box, click on the Text Editing option in the View menu, or use the Ctrl-O (^O) keyboard shortcut. When Text Editing is active, the cursor changes into an icon called an "I-beam" (as shown on the right). Once the I-beam is inserted in the text, it turns into a typing cursor, the same thin vertical line used in dialog boxes and item selectors.

When Text Editing is selected, the side-bar's add button changes to read "Set Font," and the assignment list displays various text attributes, such as bold and italic, which you can assign to a selected character or block of text. Like the other modes, Text Editing is also directly related to one of the program menus — in this case, the Edit menu. However, unlike the others, this relationship is not exclusive since both the Frame Setting and Graphic Drawing modes also make use of Edit menu options. The following chart presents a general overview of the operations you control using the Text Editing function in conjunction with the side-bar and Edit menu.

Text Editing Function

Text Attributes or Insertions	Side-bar or Edit Menu Option*
Type style (e.g., normal, bold, italic, underline, overscore)	Assignment List (Side-bar)
Special font properties (e.g., shift, kern, overscore, underline)	Set Font button (Side-bar)
Add box characters, footnotes, and fractions in text	Insert Special Item (Edit menu)
Add references in text for index entries, page/chapter numbers, and frame anchors	Insert Special Item (Edit menu)

* The text cursor must be inserted in text before options are available.

Using the Mouse and Keyboard

After selecting the Text Editing function, you can easily edit existing text or type in new copy from scratch. To accomplish these tasks, Ventura provides a built-in text editor which uses both the mouse and the keyboard. To edit existing text, such as a text file you've loaded and placed in a frame, move the mouse (I-beam) cursor to the point in the text where you want to type and click to insert the typing cursor in the text.

You can now use the keyboard as you would with a word processor. The Backspace key deletes characters directly to the left of the typing cursor, and the Delete key deletes characters directly to the right of it. The Tab key adds a tab, the Enter key adds a paragraph return, and the Caps Lock and Num Lock keys also perform their usual function. To move the cursor a short distance, use the keyboard cursor keys; to move the cursor a greater distance, use the mouse to again move the I-beam cursor and click to reinsert the typing cursor. As you use the mouse and the keyboard in this way, both the I-beam and typing cursors will be displayed on screen.

Selecting Text

In order to use the cut, copy, and paste features available in the Edit menu or to change text attributes by using the side-bar's add button and assignment list, you first need to select the target text. Ventura offers two methods for selecting text: by using the mouse and the keyboard or by using the mouse only.

To select text using the mouse and keyboard, move the I-beam cursor in front of the first character you want to select, click the mouse button, move the cursor to the end of the last character you want to select, hold down the Shift key, and click again. The text between the first and last characters you selected is now highlighted in reverse video (i.e., black text changes to white text or vice versa). You can also select text if you click at the end of the last character you want, hold down the Shift key, and click in front of the first character. To extend or shorten any selected text, move the I-beam cursor to a new insertion point, hold down the Shift key, and click.

To select text using the mouse only, move the I-beam cursor in front of the first character you want to select, click and drag the cursor to the end of the last character, and release the mouse button — the text you selected is now highlighted. You can also select text by reversing this procedure: click and drag the I-beam cursor from the back of the last character to the front of the first character.

Using either of these methods, however, you cannot select text from one frame to another or across pages; you can only select text on a frame-by-frame or page-by-page basis. For example, if you're in the middle of selecting text and you press the PageDown or PageUp key and go to a different page, the first insertion point is lost as soon as you leave that page. To cut, copy, or paste large blocks of text that extend several pages or make other major changes to text, it's much easier to use a word processor rather than Ventura.

Cut, Copy, and Paste Text

Once you've selected a character or block of text in the Text Editing mode, there are several operations you can perform. First, you can use the Edit menu options (shown on the right) or the keyboard to cut or copy the selected text. To cut the text, click on the Cut Text option or press the Delete key; to copy the text, click on the Copy Text option or hold down the Shift key and press the Delete key.

```
┌─────────────────────────────┐
│ Edit                        │
├─────────────────────────────┤
│ Cut Text              Del   │
│ Copy Text            ↑Del   │
│ Paste Text            Ins   │
│ ............................│
│ Ins Special Item...    ^C   │
│ Edit Special Item...   ^D   │
│ ............................│
│ Remove Text/File...         │
│ File Type/Rename...         │
└─────────────────────────────┘
```

After you cut or copy the text you've selected, you can insert it back in the same spot or paste it in a new location. Text can be pasted in this manner to different text files in other frames throughout your document, or it can also be placed in an empty frame. To paste text, use the mouse to insert the typing cursor wherever you want the selected text to be placed, and click on the Paste Text option in the Edit menu or press the Insert key. A copy of the selected text is immediately inserted wherever the typing cursor is located.

When you use the cut-copy-paste text options, Ventura keeps the selected text in an offscreen holding area (data buffer) called the *clipboard.* The clipboard will continue to keep the last character or block of text you cut or copied even if you leave Text Editing and change to one of the other functions. If you quit using Ventura, however, any text that remains in the clipboard is lost. It is not saved in the chapter or any other program file.

Assigning Text Attributes

In addition to the cut-copy-paste text options, you can perform a series of formatting operations with selected text. By using the assignment list, you can apply 13 different text attributes to any selected text as follows:

- Normal
- Italic
- Superscript
- Underline
- Strike-thru
- Upper Case
- Lower Case
- Bold
- Small
- Subscript
- Double Underline
- Overscore
- Capitalize

The procedure to assign any of these attributes to selected text is the same as the method used for tagging selected paragraphs. Move the cursor on top of the attribute in the assignment list that you want to apply to selected text — the attribute name becomes highlighted — and click the mouse button. Ventura immediately reformats the selected text and gives it the new attribute you picked.

Various combinations of the attributes in the assignment list can also be applied to selected text. For instance, if you click on "Bold," "Underline," and "Capitalize," you will apply all of these attributes to the selected text, as shown in the following example:

Before: text attributes   After: **Text Attributes**

If you were to continue clicking on "Italic," "Small," "Overscore," and "Upper Case," the same selected block of text would change accordingly, as follows:

Before: **Text Attributes**   After: *TEXT ATTRIBUTES*

As these examples show, the "Capitalize" attribute converts selected text to initial capital letters, "Upper Case" changes all letters to upper case, and "Small" reduces text to the next smallest point size.

The text attributes you set using the Text Editing mode take precedence over the attributes assigned by a style sheet tag in the Paragraph Tagging mode. In other words, if a tag assigns italic to a paragraph but you want the first few words to appear in bold italic, use the Text Editing mode to add bold to the selected words. To restore the attributes assigned by a paragraph tag, click on the "Normal" attribute, located at the top of the assignment list, and the text will return to the original specifications assigned by the tag. The "Normal" attribute will not, however, undo any case conversions created by using "Capitalize," "Upper Case," or "Lower Case." To restore case conversion, you must click on the opposite case attribute or delete and retype the letters.

As you use the Text Editing function to change the attributes of selected text or insert and delete text, you may occasionally continue to see part of a character or ruling line you've already changed or deleted still displayed on the screen. If you press the Escape key, however, Ventura will redisplay the page in the work area and eliminate this extra on-screen "ink."

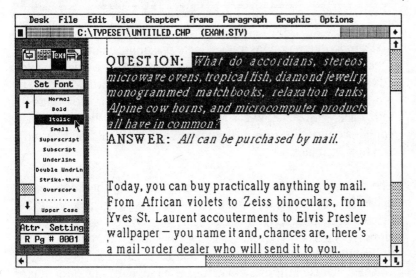

Using the Text Editing cursor, you can select a single character or block of text, then click on any of the text attributes in the assignment list, and the selected text will take on the characteristic you pick, such as italic or bold.

The Set Font Button

When the Text Editing function is active, the side-bar add button reads "Set Font" and you can use it to change the typeface, type size, style, color, and vertical and horizontal position of any selected text. You can also override certain text attribute settings previously established by the paragraph tag. The font changes you make in the Text Editing mode will affect only the characters or blocks of text you've selected, whereas the font changes you make in the Paragraph Tagging mode will affect an entire paragraph and are kept as part of a tag's specifications.

After selecting a single character or block of text in the Text Editing mode, clicking on the "Set Font" add button produces a dialog box that you can use to assign a specific typeface, type size, style, and color to the target text. You can also control the vertical (shift) and horizontal (kern) placement of the selected text.

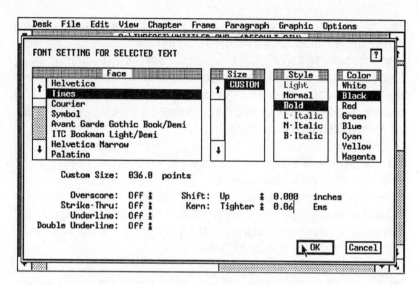

To exercise these options after selecting a single character or block of text, click on the Set Font button, and Ventura provides a dialog box (shown above) labeled "Font Setting For Selected Text." The top half of this Font Setting dialog box contains directory lists for the "Face," "Size," "Style," and "Color" options; the bottom half contains option lines for custom type sizes, text shift and kerning, and text attributes.

The actual typefaces and type sizes available in the Font Setting dialog box will depend on the printer width table installed in the Set Printer Info option (Options menu). If your system uses more than eight typefaces or type sizes, use the vertical scroll tools on the left of the "Face" and "Size" directory lists to locate additional choices. To select items in the directory lists, you move the cursor on top of an item and click to highlight it in the usual manner. Ventura will proceed to implement your selections after you click "OK."

Type sizes are always shown in points (72 points equals 1 inch). If your printer only supports specific type sizes, these sizes will be displayed automatically in the "Size" directory box. For PostScript and Interpress printers, which are capable of creating their own sizes from outline fonts, you can select the type size by typing any integer size between 1 and 254 points on the "Custom Size" line. But if your printer only supports discrete sizes from bit-mapped fonts, such as a PCL printer, the "Custom Size" option is not available.

The "Style" choices for various typefaces and type sizes are also dependent on the printer and fonts installed, and choices that are not available are displayed in gray. The "Color" choices (red, green, blue, yellow, magenta, and cyan) enable you to change text from black to any other colors supported by your printer (e.g., white text in a black box). Or, if you used the Define Colors option to create other color names, those names will appear as choices. Also, if you installed Ventura for color operation, the font colors you use for various text elements will be displayed in color on your screen.

Overriding Text Attributes

With the next set of options in the Font Setting dialog box, you can override four text attributes assigned to a paragraph tag. Specifically, you can turn "Overscore," "Strike-Thru," "Underline," and "Double Underline" on or off for any selected text within a paragraph.

For example, in legal contracts and voter pamphlets, strikeout type is often used to format paragraphs that contain existing provisions proposed to be deleted. With Ventura, you can create a paragraph tag to do this automatically by specifying "Strike- Thru: On" in the Paragraph menu's Font option. However, what if some of these paragraphs also contain new provisions proposed to be inserted? The Font Setting dialog box provides a fast solution: you can indicate the selected text is new by specifying "Strike-Thru: Off" and, at the same time, change the type "Style" option — from normal, for instance, to bold italic.

Text Shift and Kerning

With the Font Setting dialog box, you can easily manipulate the vertical placement of any selected text. For example, if your document contains mathematical or scientific data, you may want to raise or lower parts of a formula. To adjust selected text in this manner, use the "Shift" option's pop-up menu to select "Up" or "Down" and type in the amount by which you want to move the text. To change the unit of measurement, move the cursor on top of the current unit — inches, centimeters, picas and points, or fractional points — on the "Shift" option line, and click until the unit desired appears.

With the large type sizes often used in titles, headlines, and advertisements, you may find it necessary to adjust the horizontal placement of various characters to produce more pleasing results. In

To manually kern a character pair, such as "Vo," first use the mouse to select the character you want to shift to the left. As shown here, the highlighted text is reversed as black type on a white background. Next, select the "Set Font" button and enter a kerning value for the "Kern Tighter" option in the dialog box provided.

commercial typesetting, for example, ligatures (such as ff, fl, and fi) and certain upper case and lower case character pairs (such as Va, Wo, and AV) are automatically moved closer together. This horizontal adjustment is called *kerning,* and Ventura offers both automatic and manual kerning.

Automatic kerning is controlled by using options in the Paragraph menu and Chapter menu: the Paragraph Typography option allows you to turn pair kerning on/off for paragraph tags; the Chapter Typography option lets you turn pair kerning on/off on a global (chapterwide) basis, which overrides the tag settings for kerning. Manual kerning is controlled by using the Font Setting dialog box,

Here are the printed results before (top) and after (bottom) kerning the character pair "Vo" and "Te." The type is 44-point Times and the respective settings used are "Kern Tighter: 0.16 Ems" and "Kern Tighter: 0.08 Ems."

which is only available when the Text Editing function is active. When you use manual kerning, the action you prescribe takes effect regardless of whether automatic kerning is turned on or off.

To apply manual kerning to selected text (i.e., a character pair or group of characters that you've already highlighted with the Text Editing cursor), click on the Set Font button to access the Font Setting dialog box, and choose the "Kern: Tighter" option to move the selected text closer together or "Kern: Looser" to move it farther apart. Then type in the amount, measured in *Ems*, by which you want to kern the chosen text and select "OK." In Ventura, a full Em unit (1.00 Ems) is equal to the width of the @ character in the current font, and most kerning changes are made in small fractions of an Em (e.g., 0.10 Ems is a typical amount used for large type).

By using the program's "On-Screen Kerning" control in the Set Preferences option (found in the Options menu), you can select the minimum point size for which you want Ventura to display kerning on screen. However, because many computer screens can't display kerning accurately (especially below 18-point type), it's usually best to print sample pages and see the actual results.

Interactive Font Control

In addition to using the Font Setting dialog box to kern or change the size of a selected character or range of text, Ventura also provides handy keyboard shortcuts for both actions. To execute each of these shortcuts, hold down the Shift key and press one of the arrow keys, as follows:

- Shift key and left arrow key to kern text tighter
- Shift key and right arrow key to kern text looser
- Shift key and up arrow key to increase text size
- Shift key and down arrow key to decrease text size

If your printer supports custom type sizes, the selected text will change by one point each time you use the Shift and up/down arrow key shortcut, but if your printer only supports certain type sizes, you'll need to use the shortcut more than once to go from one type size to another. For instance, if your printer has 12 and 14 point sizes available for a given typeface, you would press the Shift and up arrow keys twice to change from 12 to 14 point.

Creating New Text in Page Frames

As mentioned earlier, you can also use the Text Editing mode to create new text in a blank page frame. To do so, place the I-beam cursor anywhere on the page and click. Ventura responds by inserting the typing cursor on the page, usually at the top, in front of the "end of the file" symbol (a hollow box). Once you start typing from the keyboard, the end of the file symbol disappears unless the Show Tabs & Returns option (in the Options menu) is selected.

The precise placement of new text on a blank page depends on various settings in the style sheet in use. For example, with Ventura's default style sheet (DEFAULT.STY), the first line of text is inserted in

With the Text Editing function, you can enter text from scratch and place it on the first empty page. To do so, move the I-beam cursor anywhere on the page and click. The program will insert the cursor in the upper-left corner of the first column on the page.

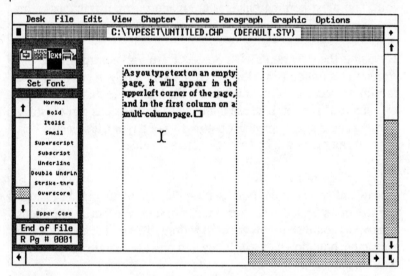

the upper-left corner of a one-column format on a portrait-oriented, letter-size page — a useful template for business correspondence. With other sample style sheets, you can enter text in such common layout formats as a two-column newsletter, three-column brochure, and so forth. And you can easily modify the sample style sheets or create new ones to meet your own needs.

When you create new text on a blank page, Ventura automatically names the text file using the same name as the chapter file, and saves it in the current text format and directory location found in the Load Text/Picture option. For instance, if the last text file you loaded into the program was an ASCII file and you start typing on a blank page in a chapter named "TEMPLATE.CHP," Ventura automatically names the text file "TEMPLATE.TXT" for you. If desired, you can also change the name of any text file by using the Edit menu's File Type/Rename option.

If you manually add a page to your document by using the Chapter menu's Insert/Remove Page option, you can also type directly on that blank page, but Ventura will not automatically name the text file for you. Instead, as soon as you place the I-beam cursor on the page and click, the program provides a pop-up screen that asks if you intend to type text on the empty page. If you select "New File," the program automatically provides the File Type/Rename dialog box (shown below) which prompts you to enter the name, location, and

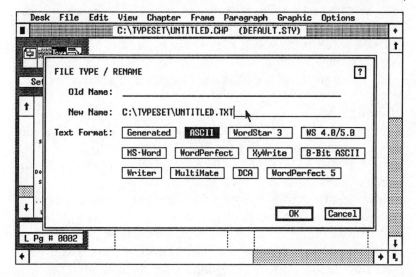

Before you proceed to add text to a blank page you insert, you must use the File Type/Rename dialog box to name the text you're creating and select a file format for the program to use when it saves the file.

text format for the new file. After you select "OK," the main screen returns and you can now begin typing.

Creating New Text in Added Frames

If you want to enter text in a specific location on a page, you can add a frame with the Frame Setting function, place it where you want it, and use the Text Editing function to type in the text directly. Whenever this frame is subsequently selected in the Frame Setting mode, the current selection box will read "FRAME TEXT." Like new text in a page frame, the new text you enter in an added frame is formatted according to the current style sheet and the attributes that you assign to the frame, such as margins and columns. However, unlike the new text created in a page frame and stored in a word processor file, frame text is automatically stored in a caption file under the same name as the chapter, but with the extension ".CAP."

Ventura also offers the option of automatically attaching a caption frame to any frame you've added. This feature is accessed by using the Anchors & Captions option in the Frame menu (discussed in detail in Chapter 6). In brief, a caption frame can be added above, below, or on either side of an added frame, and the caption can consist of text that is automatically generated, manually entered, or both. The text that you manually add to caption frames is also stored in the same caption (.CAP) file as frame text.

All Ventura caption files are saved as ASCII text files that you can later edit or check for spelling errors with any standard word processor that reads ASCII files. However, it is important that you do not change the number of paragraph returns in a caption file, or the various paragraphs of text may not appear in the correct location.

Creating Box Text
Another method by which you can enter new text on a document page — in addition to using the Text Editing mode to type text in a page frame or added frame — is by using a feature provided in the Graphic Drawing mode. This feature is the *box text* tool that, in brief, allows you to draw a rectangle and type text in it using the Text Editing mode. Box text is especially useful for creating diagram words and callouts to accompany illustrations and drawings, and for building tables and business forms. The use of box text is fully described in the "Graphic Drawing" section later in this chapter.

Special Keyboard Commands
In addition to using the standard keyboard keys already described, Ventura provides a number of special keyboard commands or short-cuts for you to use in the Text Editing mode. These commands (listed on the following page) produce line breaks, discretionary hyphens, fixed width spaces, and some commonly used typographic characters (also discussed later in this chapter).

Line breaks are used to end a line within a paragraph without breaking the text into two separate paragraphs; therefore, you can apply the same paragraph tag to a series of lines separated only by line breaks. Because line breaks add normal line spacing but do not

Keyboard Combination Commands

Character	Keyboard Command
Line break	Control key plus Enter key
Discretionary hyphen	Control key plus Hyphen (-) key
Em space	Control key plus Shift key plus M key
En space	Control key plus Shift key plus N key
Thin space	Control key plus Shift key plus T key
Figure space	Control key plus Shft key plus F key
Nonbreaking space	Control key plus Spacebar
Em dash	Control key plus [key
En dash	Control key plus] key

add paragraph spacing, they are particularly handy when preparing directory listings and database publishing applications.

Discretionary hyphens are the hyphenation points you can insert in a word in addition to those placed automatically by Ventura when it first loads a text file into the program. The discretionary hyphens you add remain within a word but only print if the word is hyphenated at the end of a line. In the Text Editing mode, you often add discretionary hyphens to tighten "loose lines" by inserting them in the first word in the line below. You can also suppress hyphenation for a single occurrence of a word by placing a discretionary hyphen at the beginning of the word.

Ventura provides fixed width spaces of four different thicknesses, including an *em space, en space, thin space,* and *figure space.* In commercial typesetting, an em space is a unit of measurement equivalent to the width of the widest character (usually the letter *M*) of the current typeface and point size. When using Ventura, the em space is equal to the width of the @ character, the en space is equal to the width of the lower case *n*, the thin space is equal to the width of a period, and the figure space is equal to the width of a number. In addition to these fixed spaces, the program also provides a character space called a *nonbreaking space,* which is used between words you want to keep together on the same line.

Hidden Characters and Attributes

When using the Text Editing function, there are two important aids you can rely on to help identify the presence of special characters and text attributes as you insert and delete text on the screen. One aid is the side-bar's current selection box, and the other is the Option menu's Show Tabs & Returns option.

The current selection box is displayed whenever the side-bar is shown. As you move the typing cursor with the keyboard cursor keys, the current selection box indicates the presence of tabs, line breaks, paragraph ends, discretionary hyphens, fixed spaces, frame anchors, footnotes, index references, cross references, box characters, fractions, text attributes, and the end of the file. The "Character Symbols and Indicators" chart below shows the words that are displayed in the current selection box when the cursor is located on one of these items. If you press the Delete key when one of these items is displayed in the current selection box, you will delete that item. To reinsert the item, press the Insert key.

Character Symbols and Indicators

Item	Screen Symbol	Selection Box Indicator
Tab	►	Horizon. Tab
Line break	◄	Line break
Paragraph return	¶	Paragraph End
Discretionary hyphen	▬	Discr. Hyphen
Em, en, thin, figure, and nonbreaking space	−	Em Space, En Space Thin Space, Figure Space, NoBreak Space
Cross reference, frame anchor, fraction, box character, index reference	○	Reference, Frame Anchor, Fraction, Box Character, Index Entry, Index-See, Index-SeeAlso
End of file	☐	End of File
Character attribute	(None)	Attr. Setting
Footnote	(User-defined)	Footnote

When the Show Tabs & Returns option is selected, Ventura displays visual markers for many of the special characters already mentioned that are otherwise hidden on the screen. The "Character Symbols and Indicators" chart also shows what each of the hidden symbols looks like when the Show Tabs & Returns option is selected. If you use the Hide Tabs & Returns option, all of the visual markers are hidden from view, but the current selection box will continue to identify the presence of hidden characters as described.

Ventura's Character Sets
Ventura provides two complete character sets for you to use with the Text Editing function. They are:

- An International character set, with English, Spanish, French, Italian, and German language characters
- A Symbol character set, with Greek letters and mathematics characters used for equations /formulas, and other symbols

The program's International character set includes standard alphabetic, numeric, punctuation, and other characters that are labeled on the keyboard's keys, plus an extended set of nonlabeled characters that you can access by using decimal codes or special commands. The extended set of characters, also called *nonkeyboard* characters, is used for adding foreign language and true typographiç characters. Foreign language characters include common diacritical marks, such as acute accent (á), grave accent (à), circumflex (â), tilde (ã), and diaeresis (ä); typographic characters — which you can easily add by using the special keyboard shortcuts mentioned earlier — include em dashes (— instead of --), open and close quotation marks (" " instead of "), and copyright (©) and trademark (™) symbols.

To add nonkeyboard characters using the Text Editing function, first insert the typing cursor in the text, then hold down the Alternate key and use the numeric keyboard to type the decimal codes for the various characters. These decimal codes, which consist of two or three digits ranging from 32 through 220, are listed on the following pages. After typing the decimal code, release the Alternate key and the nonkeyboard character is displayed on the screen.

For example, to enter the section mark used for numbering clauses, hold down the Alternate key and type the decimal code 185, then

Character Sets and Decimal Codes

Code	Internat'l	Symbol	Dingbats	Code	Internat'l	Symbol	Dingbats
1-31	Not used			63	?	?	✝
32	Space			64	@	≅	✣
33	!	!	✂	65	A	A	✿
34	"	∀	✂	66	B	B	✢
35	#	#	✂	67	C	X	✤
36	$	∃	✄	68	D	Δ	✣
37	%	%	☎	69	E	E	✥
38	&	&	✆	70	F	Φ	◆
39	'	∋	✇	71	G	Γ	◇
40	(	(	✈	72	H	H	★
41	)	)	✉	73	I	I	☆
42	*	*	☛	74	J	ϑ	✪
43	+	+	☞	75	K	K	✫
44	,	,	✌	76	L	Λ	✬
45	-	−	✍	77	M	M	★
46	.	.	✎	78	N	N	✭
47	/	/	✏	79	O	O	✮
48	0	0	✐	80	P	Π	✰
49	1	1	✑	81	Q	Θ	✳
50	2	2	✒	82	R	P	✺
51	3	3	✓	83	S	Σ	✶
52	4	4	✔	84	T	T	✴
53	5	5	✕	85	U	Y	✷
54	6	6	✖	86	V	ς	✳
55	7	7	✗	87	W	Ω	❋
56	8	8	✘	88	X	Ξ	✹
57	9	9	✙	89	Y	Ψ	✺
58	:	:	✚	90	Z	Z	✻
59	;	;	✛	91	[	[	✳
60	<	<	✜	92	\	∴	✲
61	=	=	✝	93	]	]	✱
62	>	>	✞	94	∧	⊥	❀

Character Sets and Decimal Codes

Code	Internat'l	Symbol	Dingbats	Code	Internat'l	Symbol	Dingbats
95	_	_	✿	127			
96	'		❁	128	Ç		
97	a	α	❀	129	ü	ϒ	✵
98	b	β	❂	130	é	′	✦
99	c	χ	✳	131	â	≤	✧
100	d	δ	❋	132	ä	⁄	❤
101	e	ε	✺	133	à	∞	✿
102	f	φ	✾	134	å	ƒ	❦
103	g	γ	✼	135	ç	♣	❧
104	h	η	✻	136	ê	♦	♣
105	i	ι	✶	137	ë	♥	♦
106	j	φ	✷	138	è	♠	♥
107	k	κ	✴	139	ï	↔	♠
108	l	λ	●	140	î	←	①
109	m	μ	○	141	ì	↑	②
110	n	ν	■	142	Ä	→	③
111	o	ο	❑	143	Å	↓	④
112	p	π	❐	144	É	°	⑤
113	q	θ	❏	145	æ	±	⑥
114	r	ρ	❒	146	Æ	″	⑦
115	s	σ	▲	147	ô	≥	⑧
116	t	τ	▼	148	ö	×	⑨
117	u	υ	◆	149	ò	∝	⑩
118	v	ϖ	❖	150	û	∂	❶
119	w	ω	◗	151	ù	•	❷
120	x	ξ	❘	152	ÿ	÷	❸
121	y	ψ	❙	153	Ö	≠	❹
122	z	ζ	❚	154	Ü	≡	❺
123	{	{	❛	155	¢	≈	❻
124	|	|	❜	156	£	…	❼
125	}	}	❝	157	¥	|	❽
126	~	~	❞	158	¤	—	❾

Character Sets and Decimal Codes

Code	Internat'l	Symbol	Dingbats	Code	Internat'l	Symbol	Dingbats
159	ƒ	↵	⑩	191	™	⇓	→
160	á	ℵ	①	192	„	◊	⇢
161	í	ℑ	②	193	…	〈	➡
162	ó	ℜ	③	194	‰	®	➢
163	ú	℘	④	195	•	©	➤
164	ñ	⊗	⑤	196	–	™	➤
165	Ñ	⊕	⑥	197	—	Σ	➡
166	ª	∅	⑦	198	°	(	➡
167	º	∩	⑧	199	Á	|	➤
168	¿	∪	⑨	200	Â	(	➡
169	"	⊃	⑩	201	È	⌈	⇨
170	"	⊇	❶	202	Ê	|	⇨
171	‹	⊄	❷	203	Ë	⌊	⇦
172	›	⊂	❸	204	Ì	⌈	⇦
173	¡	⊆	❹	205	Í	{	⇨
174	«	∈	❺	206	Î	|	⇨
175	»	∉	❻	207	Ï	|	⇨
176	ã	∠	❼	208	Ò	🍎	
177	õ	∇	❽	209	Ó	〉	⇨
178	Ø	®	❾	210	Ô	∫	⊃
179	ø	©	❿	211	Š	⌈	➤
180	œ	™	→	212	š	|	➤
181	Œ	∏	→	213	Ù	⌡	➤
182	À	√	↔	214	Ú	)	➹
183	Ã	·	↕	215	Û	|	➤
184	Õ	¬	↘	216	Ÿ	)	➤
185	§	∧	➡	217	ß	⌉	➹
186	‡	∨	➚	218	Ž	|	→
187	†	⇔	➔	219	ž	⌋	→
188	¶	⇐	➡	220	/	)	➤
189	©	⇑	→	221		}	➤
190	®	⇒	→	222		⌡	⇒

release the Alternate key and § appears on the screen. Or, to enter the monetary unit for the British pound, use the same process but type the decimal code 156 to obtain £. After adding nonkeyboard characters to your text, you can use the Text Editing mode to select text to cut, copy, paste, or assign text attributes (such as bold and italic), just like any other character.

Ventura's Symbol character set is well suited for scientific and mathematical publishing tasks. Scientific characters include common physics symbols, such as beta ray (β), kaon (κ), wavelength (λ), and alpha (α), xi (Ξ), and sigma (Σ) particles; mathematics characters include not equal to ($\neq$), greater than or equal to ($\geq$), less than or equal to ($\leq$), therefore ($\therefore$), infinity (∞), and many more.

Symbol characters are produced by using both the keyboard and the Symbol font, which is included in Ventura's core set of fonts, along with a serif, sans serif, and courier font. The process of adding these characters to your text involves three steps:

1. Insert the cursor in your document and type the keyboard or nonkeyboard characters (decimal codes) as you do with the International character set.
2. Use the mouse cursor to select (highlight) the characters you want to assign the Symbol font.
3. Click on the "Set Font" button and use Font Setting dialog box provided to assign the Symbol font to the selected text.

For example, to enter the pi (π) symbol, hold down the Alternate key and type the decimal code 112, then release the Alternate key and the letter "p" (from the International character set) will appear on the screen. Next, use the I-beam cursor to select the letter "p" you've just entered, click on the Set Font button, and proceed to use Font Setting For Selected Text dialog box provided to assign the Symbol font to that single letter. Click "OK," the main screen returns, and the letter "p" is replaced on screen by the π character.

If the pi symbol is part of the formula $\pi\rho^2$, follow the above steps for the number 2, and then click on the "Superscript" attribute in the assignment list to create the "second power" notation. Or, click on the Set Font button and use the "Shift" option in the Font Setting For Selected Text dialog box to raise the number.

In some cases, you may want to assign the Symbol font to an entire paragraph, and you can easily do so by using the Paragraph Tagging function. First, create a tag that assigns the Symbol font to a paragraph by using the Font option in the Paragraph menu. Then, whenever you assign that tag to a paragraph, all of the characters in the paragraph will be automatically converted to symbols. This technique is handy for adding equations to a document since both character sets use the same decimal codes for numbers (0 through 9) and several mathematics signs (plus, minus, equals, and so on), thereby eliminating a lot of additional typing.

Not all characters provided in the program's Symbol and International character sets are available on all printers. To determine which characters are supported by your system's printer, Ventura provides an example chapter file, CHARSET.CHP, which you can print to see the characters supported by your printer. The CHARSET.CHP file is automatically placed in the TYPESET directory if you elect to copy the example files when you first install Ventura on your hard disk. If you did not install the example files, copy the CHARSET.CHP file from the Ventura Publisher Examples Disk to the TYPESET directory by using the Multi-Chapter option in the Options menu. In either case, use the File menu options to open the CHARSET.CHP file and print it, just as you would with any other chapter.

Depending on your printer's fonts, you may also be able to use other character sets in addition to those provided by Ventura. For example, if you're using a Postscript printer that offers the Zapf Dingbats font (such as the Apple LaserWriter IINTX), you can assign this font to selected characters in the same way you assigned the Symbol font. Dingbats include decorative type elements, such as check marks, ballot boxes, bullets, patterns, and other shapes. For reference purposes, the Dingbats character set and decimal codes are included in the character set tables that accompany this section.

Unlike the characters in the International and Symbol character sets, Ventura can't display Zapf Dingbats on screen unless you install matching screen fonts (explained in the "System Software" section in Chapter 2). Instead, Ventura automatically displays the screen fonts for the International character set as a substitute, but the actual Dingbats font characters will appear in the printed version as long as the font is installed for your printer.

Text Editing Page Views

Depending on the resolution quality of your system's monitor, you may need to select different page views while using the Text Editing function. Unless you're using a high-resolution monitor, for example, you'll probably go back and forth between the different views as you edit the text in a document. Or, if you're working with a small type size, you may only be able to read the text in the Enlarged View.

Although the amount of text that can be shown in the Enlarged View is considerably less than in the other page views, it most accurately depicts the placement of text and other elements in your document. When you're working on text kerning and shift, alignment of a large initial capital letter, setting up tabs, or other tasks that involve some precision, you'll probably find it best to use the Enlarged View.

When the typing cursor reaches the edge of the screen, you'll need to use the scroll tools to move the off-screen part of the page into the work area in order to resume editing. However, you can sometimes cut down on excessive scrolling — particularly in the Enlarged View — by hiding the side-bar from the screen to obtain a more complete view of your document (as shown below). To do this, use the Options menu and select the Hide Side-Bar option or use the Ctrl-W (^W) keyboard shortcut.

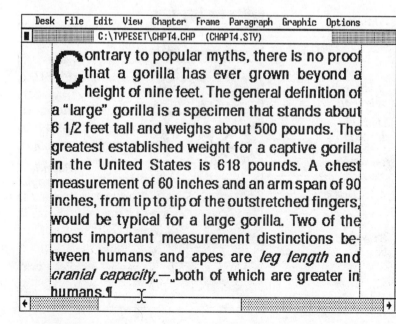

This screen shot is taken from a system using an EGA card and enhanced display. By hiding the side-bar, a full column of type (9-pt. sans serif bold) fits nicely on the screen, using the Enlarged View, and reduces the need for horizontal scrolling.

Graphic Drawing

There are two types of "graphics" you can add to your publications: *graphics files* created with other programs and loaded into Ventura, and *graphic objects* created with the Graphic Drawing function. A major distinction between these two types of graphics is that you must place graphics files in frames, but you can place graphic objects by themselves anywhere on a page.

With Ventura's built-in drawing tools, you can create such basic graphic objects as ruling lines, circles, rectangles, and squares. After creating a graphic object, you can move it, resize it, change its line thickness, fill it with a color or pattern, and perform the same cut-copy-paste operations that you can with other program modes.

To use Ventura's drawing tools, click on the fourth function selector box, click on the Graphic Drawing option in the View menu, or use the Ctrl-P (^P) keyboard shortcut. After the Graphic Drawing mode is selected, the side-bar's add button reads "Add New Frame" and the assignment list is replaced by the program's drawing tools, represented by six different icons. The function selector boxes, current selection box, and current page box remain active and are shown in their usual locations in the side-bar.

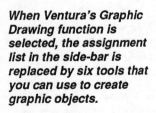

When Ventura's Graphic Drawing function is selected, the assignment list in the side-bar is replaced by six tools that you can use to create graphic objects.

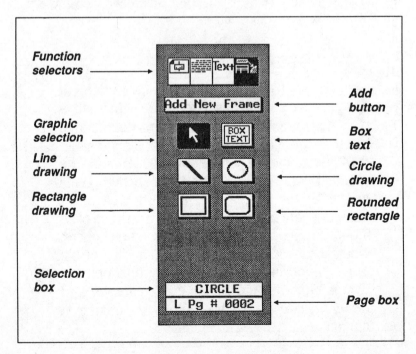

Function selectors

Add button

Graphic selection

Box text

Line drawing

Circle drawing

Rectangle drawing

Rounded rectangle

Selection box

Page box

Add New Frame

BOX TEXT

CIRCLE

L Pg # 0002

When Graphic Drawing is enabled, the cursor changes into an arrow-shaped icon known as the graphic selector. As you select different drawing tools, the program provides additional cursor shapes to indicate which tool is active, as shown below.

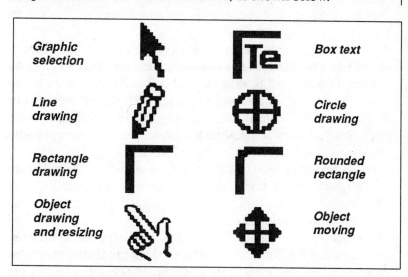

Graphic selection	*Box text*
Line drawing	*Circle drawing*
Rectangle drawing	*Rounded rectangle*
Object drawing and resizing	*Object moving*

The program's Graphic Drawing function uses several different cursor shapes to indicate which drawing tool or operation is enabled.

Frames and Graphic Objects

Earlier in this chapter, frames were introduced as the basic building blocks for constructing a page layout, provided by the Frame Setting mode. But in addition to holding all the text and graphics files that have been loaded into Ventura, frames also play a major role in using the Graphic Drawing function: all graphic objects are "tied," or linked, to frames. That is, each frame can have its own set of graphics, which can be placed inside or outside of the frame itself. Therefore, before you use the program's drawing tools, you should first select a frame that will serve as the foundation for the graphic objects you draw. Or, you can click on the Add New Frame button and draw the base frame first, then use the Graphic Drawing tools.

It makes no difference if the frame you select to link graphic objects to is empty or filled with an imported text or graphics file. If you don't want to select an added frame as the foundation, Ventura links all of the graphic objects you create to the page frame. If you link graphic objects to the page frame, you can also select the Graphic menu's Show On All Pages option and display "master" graphic objects — such as borders, margin tabs, or crop marks — throughout the pages of your document.

To indicate which frame is selected when you use the Graphic Drawing mode, Ventura makes use of the small black boxes, or sizing buttons, displayed inside the frame's perimeter. When the Frame Setting mode is active, these boxes are black, but when Graphic Drawing is active, these boxes appear gray.

After drawing a graphic object, you can resize it or move it anywhere on the page, but the frame to which it's attached will not move. As always, a frame must be selected first before it can be moved. If a frame *is* moved, all graphic objects tied to the frame are moved with it; if a frame is cut, copied, or pasted, all graphics linked to the frame are also cut, copied, and pasted. If a frame is resized, however, the graphic objects tied to that frame will not change size or shape — although they may move. Graphic objects can only be resized when the Graphic Drawing (not Frame Setting) mode is active.

Graphic Object Attributes

The Graphic Drawing function is directly related to the Graphic menu. Unless the Graphic Drawing mode is enabled, none of the options in the Graphic menu are available. The chart below presents a general overview of the graphic object attributes or operations you can control by using the Graphic Drawing mode and the Graphic menu options (described in detail in Chapter 6).

```
Graphic
┌──────────────────────┐
│ Show On All Pages     │
│ Send to Back      ^Z  │
│ Bring to Front    ^A  │
│ ......................│
│ Line Attributes... ^L │
│ Fill Attributes... ^F │
│ ......................│
│ Select All        ^Q  │
│ Grid Settings...      │
└──────────────────────┘
```

Graphic Drawing Function	
Graphic Object Attributes	**Graphic Menu Option**
Line thickness	Line Attributes*
Line color	Line Attributes*
Line end style	Line Attributes*
Fill pattern	Fill Attributes*
Fill color	Fill Attributes*
Order of stacked objects	Send to Back* (or) Bring to Front*
Graphic object placement	Grid Settings
Graphic object repetition	Show On All Pages

* A graphic object must be selected before menu option is available.

With the Graphic menu, you can control both line attributes and fill attributes for the graphic objects you create. Line attributes include thickness, color, and three types of line end styles: square ends, arrows, and round ends (as shown on the right). Fill attributes include the color, pattern, and the opaqueness or transparency of the fill pattern. However, the ability to print different colors or transparent fill patterns ultimately depends on the printer installed.

If you overlay or stack several graphic objects on top of each other, the most recently placed object will appear in front of the others. But by using the Graphic menu's Send to Back and Bring to Front options, you can rearrange the order of these graphic objects. For example, a common technique is to place a solid white box in front of a black box to create a shadow effect. Another application is to create a picture frame by placing a solid white circle or box in front of a shaded circle or box (as shown on the right).

With the Graphic menu's Grid Settings option, you can set up an invisible grid within a frame, using horizontal and vertical measurements that you define. Although this grid isn't displayed on screen and won't be printed, any graphic objects you create will automatically "snap to" this grid (i.e., the program will fasten the graphic objects to the nearest grid points to ensure perfect vertical and horizontal alignment).

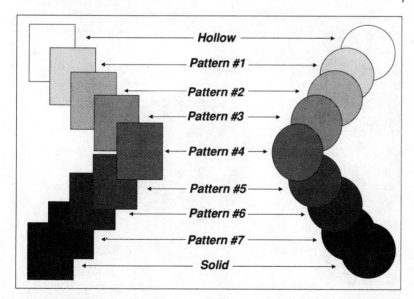

Ventura offers a selection of nine different patterns that you can use to fill graphic objects, which includes a solid and hollow pattern. These samples were output at 1,270 dots per inch on a Linotronic typesetter.

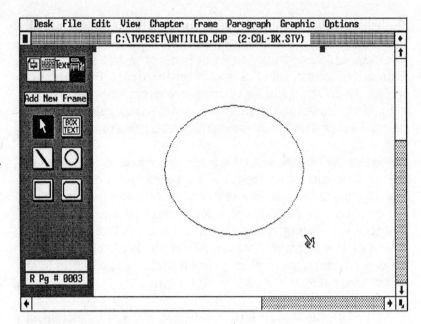

After you select a graphic drawing icon from the side-bar, such as a circle, and begin drawing a graphic object in the work area, the cursor changes into a pointing finger.

Drawing Graphic Objects

To draw a graphic object with the Graphic Drawing function, move the cursor to the side-bar and click on one of the drawing icons — line, rectangle, box text, circle, or rounded rectangle. Following the same procedure used for drawing a frame, move the cursor to the

When you release the mouse button, the object is inserted on the page, surrounded by black boxes to indicate that it is selected. The name of the type of graphic object will also be displayed in the current selection box.

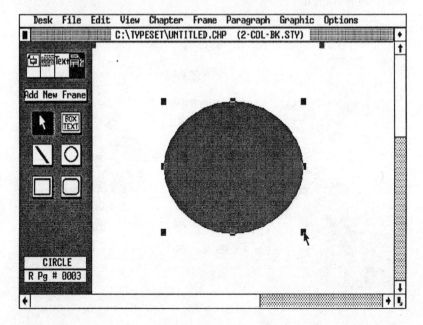

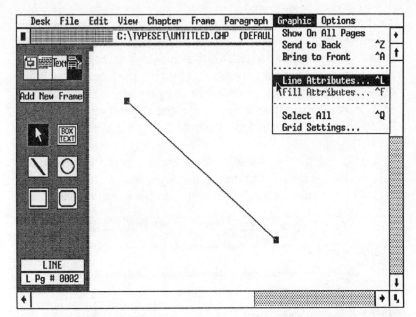

After you draw a line, it remains "selected," as indicated by the black boxes on each end of the line. To change the line's attributes, you can proceed to select the Line Attributes option in the Graphic menu.

work area where you want to begin drawing the top-left corner of the object. Inside the work area, the cursor changes into the shape associated with the graphic object you've selected. Click and hold down the mouse button, and the cursor changes into a pointing finger, the same cursor shape used for drawing and resizing frames.

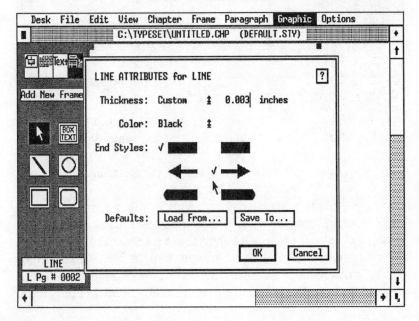

With the Line Attributes menu option from the Graphic menu, you can use a dialog box to select the line thickness, color, and end styles for each ruling line you draw with the program's Graphic Drawing function.

To draw a rectangle or circle, drag the cursor to the bottom-right corner where you want the object to end, and release the mouse button. To draw a horizontal, vertical, or diagonal ruling line, drag the cursor to the opposite end where you want the rule to stop. If you hold the Alternate key down while drawing graphic objects, they will be constrained to perfect circles, squares, and 45-degree lines. Do not use the Alternate key, however, to draw a rectangle.

When you release the mouse button, a graphic object in the size and shape you've drawn is inserted on the page, and the cursor changes back to the graphic selector. To create another graphic object, click

When you select the Fill Attributes option from the Graphic menu, Ventura provides a dialog box that you can use to choose colors and patterns for the graphic object you selected, and to see the result before you exit the dialog box.

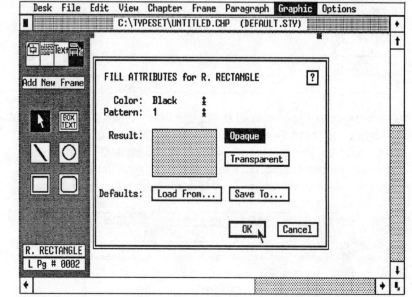

on the icon you want to draw and repeat the same process. If you want to draw several graphic objects of the same type, such as a series of rectangles, hold down the Shift key while creating each object and the same drawing tool will remain selected.

After you create a graphic object, it remains selected and is affected by the next action you take, such as using the Edit menu options to copy and paste the object. To show that a graphic object is selected, Ventura places sizing buttons around its perimeter. More specifically, with circles or diagonal ruling lines, the sizing buttons form a rectangle around the object; with horizontal or vertical ruling lines, the sizing buttons are displayed as small parallel lines at both ends and in between, depending on the line's length. The program also displays the name of selected graphic objects in the side-bar's current selection box, as follows: "RECTANGLE," "R. RECTANGLE," "CIRCLE," "LINE," or "BOX TEXT."

To select a different graphic object, move the cursor inside the object or on its edge, click, and the sizing buttons are displayed to indicate it is currently selected. Ventura also allows you to select more than one graphic object at a time by holding down the Shift key as you click on each additional object. If more than one graphic object is selected, the current selection box reads "MULTIPLE." If you want to select all of the graphic objects tied to a given frame, use the Select All option in the Graphic menu.

To select a graphic object that is covered by other graphic objects, hold down the Control key and keep clicking until the desired object is selected. For example, if you have a stack of four rectangles, hold down the Control key, move the cursor on top of the rectangle in front, and click four times to select the rectangle on the bottom.

Creating Box Text
In addition to using the program's Graphic Drawing function to draw lines, circles, and rectangles, you can also use a versatile tool called *box text* to draw a box anywhere on a page and then put text in it. Box text differs from the text you can put in frames because it can be placed on top of frames without interfering with their contents. In short, using box text is similar to using a Post-It® Note Pad, the self-adhesive note paper you can stick anywhere.

Since you have maximum flexibility in placing box text on a page, it is ideal for creating forms and tables. Unlike the text you place in frames, box text isn't controlled by margins, columns, or other frame attributes. If you want to add diagram words to an illustration, you can use box text to create each callout, or label, and use the line tool to draw arrows to point to the illustration.

To create box text, first select a frame to which the box text will be attached, as you normally do before drawing any graphic object. Next, select the Graphic Drawing function and click on the box text

In this screen shot, box text has been placed on top of a frame containing an imported graphics file. When first drawn, box text is surrounded by a line border. To eliminate this border, use the Line Attributes option in the Graphic menu and select "None" for the box's line thickness.

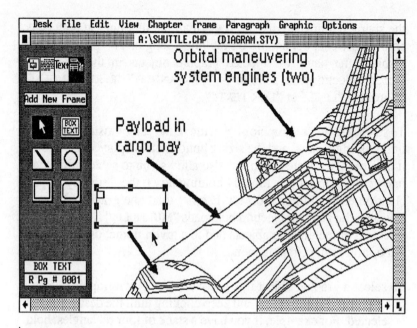

icon in the side-bar. Move the cursor to the work area where you want to begin drawing the top-left corner of the box. Inside the work area, the cursor changes into the box text cursor (shown on the left), and you can proceed to draw the box in the same way you draw a rectangle or circle.

When you release the mouse button, an empty box is immediately inserted on the page. To enter the text, use the following steps:

1. Change functions from Graphic Drawing to Text Editing.
2. Move the I-beam cursor over the box and click to insert the typing cursor.
3. Use the keyboard to type the desired text.

If you plan to type several lines of text, you may need to enlarge the box text first so all of the text can fit inside. To do this, select the Graphic Drawing mode and resize the box as necessary, then return to the Text Editing mode and continue entering the text. After you finish typing the text, you can assign text attributes to selected box text just as you can with any other text, using the I-beam cursor.

Ventura automatically assigns a tag called "Z_BOXTEXT" to all box text. The typographic specifications for "Z_BOXTEXT" will depend

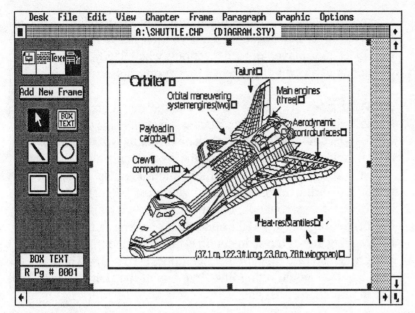

Desk File Edit View Chapter Frame Paragraph Graphic Options

A:\SHUTTLE.CHP (DIAGRAM.STY)

A shortcut for drawing multiple diagram words is to draw a "master" box text object, with any text attributes (such as bold italic) already assigned to it, and then use the Edit menu's copy and paste options to make the extra copies.

on the active style sheet. If you're using the DEFAULT.STY file, for example, the text is formatted as a 12-point serif font and will be left justified. However, you can change these specifications by changing to the Paragraph Tagging mode and using the Paragraph menu options, or you can assign different tags to any box text object.

The text you enter in all box text is automatically saved by the program in the same ASCII caption (.CAP) file where frame text and caption text are stored. As explained earlier in this chapter, you can edit this ASCII file or check it for spelling errors with any standard word processor after you exit Ventura. However, be careful not to alter the number of paragraph returns or change the location of the text within the file. If you insert or delete any paragraph returns or move blocks of text while using your word processor, the text may not appear in the correct location inside Ventura.

Manipulating Graphic Objects

After a graphic object is selected, you can move, resize, copy, delete, and paste it as many times as you want. To move a graphic object, place the cursor inside the object or on top of its edge — but not directly on top of the sizing buttons — then click and hold the mouse button. At this point, the cursor changes into the crossed arrows to indicate you can drag the object in any direction. Move the object where you want it, release the mouse button, and the object is displayed in its new location. Until you release the mouse button, the object is displayed in both locations, which lets you use the old placement as a point of reference for the object's new position.

As with frames, the sizing buttons that indicate a graphic object is selected also serve as resizing handles. To change the dimensions of a rectangle, circle, or box text, click on one of the sizing buttons and drag it inside the object to reduce the size, or outside the object to increase it. If more than four corner buttons are displayed, you can perform two-dimensional scaling (width *and* height) by dragging one of the corner buttons, or one-dimensional scaling (width *or* height) by dragging any of the middle buttons. You can resize a circle by dragging any of the sizing buttons that surround it, and the shape you create can be either circular or elliptical. To resize a horizontal, vertical, or diagonal ruling line, drag one of the sizing buttons (or line markers) on either end.

When you resize a graphic object with the mouse, the cursor changes from the graphic selector to the pointing finger icon. If the cursor doesn't make this change, you probably haven't placed it directly on top of one of the sizing buttons and will need to try again. If you're working with a very small graphic object, you may need to enlarge the page view in order to click directly on top of the sizing buttons.

Any graphic object that you select can be cut, copied, and pasted by using the corresponding options in the Edit menu. Like copies of frames, the copies of graphic objects that you make will also include any attributes or contents (i.e., line attributes, fill attributes, and the text in box text objects). By creating and formatting a "master" box text object, for instance, you can expedite the task of creating a series of callouts or diagram words. If you select multiple graphic objects, you can cut, copy, paste, and move several different objects at once. For example, you can draw an arrow to attach to a single box text callout, then copy and paste as many additional callouts and arrows as necessary. After you finish copying the callouts and arrows and moving them into position, select the Text Editing function and type the actual text for each individual callout.

Part III

Taking Command

Chapter 5

Using the Basic Menus

*B*y now you should have a fundamental understanding of how to use Ventura's four functions, or program modes. As explained in Chapter 4, these four functions (Frame Setting, Paragraph Tagging, Text Editing, and Graphic Drawing) are linked to four menus — Frame, Paragraph, Edit, and Graphic — which are called the "function menus" in this book. And, except for Paragraph Tagging, all of the functions share the use of the cut, copy, and paste options found in the Edit menu.

In addition to the four function menus, Ventura provides five other menus — Desk, File, View, Chapter, and Options — referred to here as the "basic menus." The general distinction between these two groups is that function menus are only available when a related function or function element (such as a frame, text block, or graphic object) is selected, but the basic menus are always accessible.

This chapter provides a tour of the basic menus and their options. Although each menu option is individually presented and explained, the emphasis is on understanding the features you'll use most often in preparing standard business documents. Since many of these options are also examined elsewhere in this book, use the index for additional references to specific features.

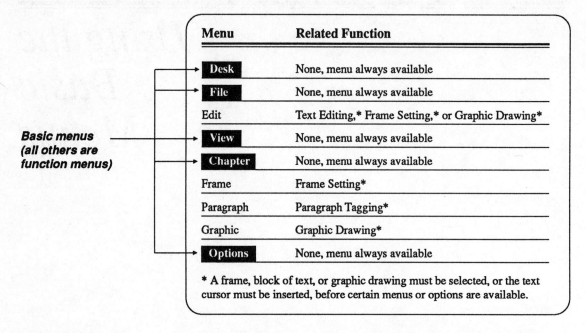

Menu	Related Function
Desk	None, menu always available
File	None, menu always available
Edit	Text Editing,* Frame Setting,* or Graphic Drawing*
View	None, menu always available
Chapter	None, menu always available
Frame	Frame Setting*
Paragraph	Paragraph Tagging*
Graphic	Graphic Drawing*
Options	None, menu always available

* A frame, block of text, or graphic drawing must be selected, or the text cursor must be inserted, before certain menus or options are available.

Basic menus (all others are function menus)

Desk Menu

Desk
Publisher Info...

First in Ventura's menu line is the Desk menu, which contains the Publisher Info option. When this option is selected, Ventura provides a pop-up screen (see top of opposite page) that shows the product version — Standard or Professional Extension, Network or Non-Network — Expanded Memory Specification (EMS) memory (if available), serial number, and copyright information. If you select the help menu (the question mark), Ventura displays a list of pop-up help screens that summarize the program's keyboard shortcuts.

The Publisher Info option also provides access to the Ventura Publisher Diagnostics screen, which supplies technical information about memory usage and certain file sizes employed by the program. To view the Diagnostics screen, click on the word "Ventura" in the lower-left portion of the Publisher Info dialog box.

The actual statistics in the Diagnostics screen depend on the contents (text and graphics) of the current chapter and page, the amount of RAM and EMS memory available, and the size of the width table, screen fonts, hyphenation dictionary, and other files used by the program. However, because the Diagnostics screen is designed for use by technical support to help diagnose memory problems, you won't need to use it during normal program operation.

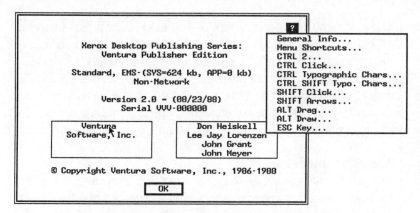

Select the help button in the Publisher Information dialog box and you can access help messages that list keyboard and mouse shortcuts. Click on the word "Ventura" (indicated by the cursor arrow) and a Diagnostic screen (shown below) will pop up.

Although you cannot directly change any of the factors listed in the Diagnostics screen (shown below), the information provides you with a status report on various memory factors. The top part of the screen lists the different amounts of RAM and EMS memory, paragraphs, and line elements currently in use, as well as the total amount available; the middle part shows how much of the document is being stored on disk; and the bottom part displays the amount of memory taken up by six more program functions. Whenever you reach the various limits placed on certain items, Ventura issues an error message and provides a possible solution. However, you can also use the Diagnostics screen to find other factors that may be responsible for affecting Ventura's performance.

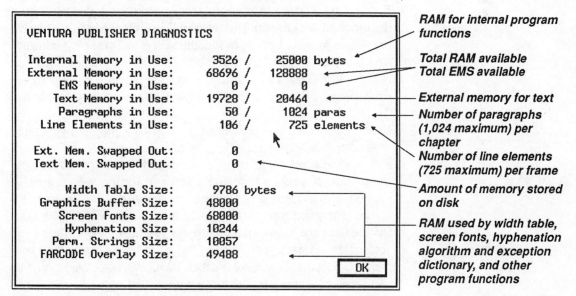

File Menu

```
┌─────────────────────────┐
│ File                    │
├─────────────────────────┤
│ New                     │
│ Open Chapter...         │
│ ----------------------- │
│ Save              ^S    │
│ Save As...              │
│ Abandon...              │
│ ----------------------- │
│ Load Text/Picture...    │
│ Load Diff. Style...     │
│ Save As New Style...    │
│ ----------------------- │
│ To Print...             │
│ DOS File Ops...         │
│ Quit                    │
└─────────────────────────┘
```

The first menu used during a typical Ventura session is the File menu, as its primary purpose is to control the flow of data into and out of the program. Of course, if you begin by creating text or drawing graphic objects within the program, you may not need to use the File menu at first. But even then, you should always save your work regularly to protect against accidental erasure, and the options for saving a document involve the File menu.

About Chapter Files

The documents you create with Ventura can include text and graphics files from other applications as well as text and graphic objects created with the program's Text Editing and Graphic Drawing modes. To save and retrieve all of this information, Ventura creates a file called a *chapter*. The File menu provides options that are used to open, save, and abandon chapter files.

A chapter file contains the instructions that tell the program how you combined the various text and graphics elements to fit together on the final layout. Chapter files do not contain the actual text and graphics, however, but merely "pointers" that tell the program where to place the various elements in a document when you open a chapter and where to store them when you save it. All of the text and graphics files you load into the program and use in a document are, in fact, stored back in their original files on your system's hard disk or on floppy disks. If you edit or reformat an imported text file from within the program, all changes are saved in the original file. If you resize or crop an imported graphics file, the sizing and cropping information is stored in the chapter file but the original graphics files are saved intact. The beauty of this technique is that it eliminates the need to store extra files and saves a substantial amount of disk space.

Each chapter file also provides a pointer to a program-generated *style sheet* file, *caption* file, *graphics* file, and *chapter information* file. A style sheet contains page layout and typographic specifications that tell Ventura how you want it to format a document. A caption file contains any text you create within the program for frame captions, frame text, and box text. A graphics file contains information about any graphic objects you draw, such as lines and rectangles. A chapter information file provides a record about your Ventura document (original creation date, date last saved, and date last archived) for use by other programs.

Ventura saves chapter and style sheet files using names that you choose and automatically adds the extensions .CHP and .STY to them, respectively. The caption, graphics, and chapter information files share the same name as the chapter file, but with the extensions .CAP, .VGR, and .CIF added, in that order.

Storing and Retrieving Chapters

The File menu options used for storing and retrieving chapter files are New, Open Chapter, Save, Save As, and Abandon. When you select New, the program provides an empty work area and places the name UNTITLED.CHP in the title bar. Whatever style sheet file is in use when you select New will remain active. If you're using the program for the first time, UNTITLED.CHP and DEFAULT.STY are already listed in the title bar and you can begin working on a document immediately without selecting the New option.

If a chapter is already loaded when you select New, it is removed from the screen and from memory. However, if you made any changes to the chapter since it was last saved, Ventura will prompt you with a pop-up screen (shown above) offering two choices: "Save" or "Abandon." If you don't want to save the changes, select "Abandon" and the last copy previously saved will be the version of the chapter used the next time you open it. If any changes have been made to the style sheet since it was last saved, the program will prompt you with a second pop-up screen (shown below) offering the same "Save" or "Abandon" choices for the style sheet file.

If you pick the Open Chapter option, Ventura provides an item selector with a default file filter for the .CHP extension. Using this

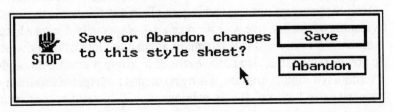

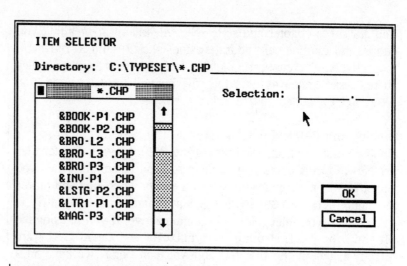

Whenever you use the File menu's Open Chapter and Save As options, the program automatically provides an item selector with a .chp file filter.

item selector, you can locate and retrieve a chapter file from Ventura's TYPESET directory — such as one of the example chapters provided with the program — or from any other location on your hard disk or on a floppy disk. Each time you pick the Open Chapter option, the item selector conveniently displays the last location from which a chapter was loaded.

The Save option is used to store a chapter file under the current name that appears in the title bar. When you select this option, the style sheet in use is also saved if you've made any changes to it since the last time you saved the chapter. If you pick the Save option before you've given the chapter a name, the program automatically provides an item selector for you to use to specify a chapter name. You can either use the keyboard to type a new name or select an existing name to assign to the chapter. If you choose an existing name, the program prompts you with a pop-up screen asking you to confirm that you want to overwrite the old file.

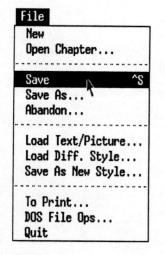

The Save command is the only option in the File menu that includes a keyboard shortcut — in this case, Ctrl-S (^S) — which underscores the importance of using this command, and on a regular basis. Of all the program tips and techniques offered in this book, the most valuable advice is: *save your work often* — especially during a long session. Not only is this a safeguard against the loss of data due to a power failure, but also in the event of a program crash. Although Ventura is a robust program, it is by no means bulletproof and it may occasionally lock up. If this happens, you'll have to reboot your computer, reload the program, and continue working with the last previously saved copy of your chapter file.

If you load a text file first before using the Save option, the program will automatically give the chapter the same name, using the .CHP extension. For instance, if you load a text file called TRAINING.DOC, the program will name the chapter TRAINING.CHP and display it in the title bar. By using the Save command, you can officially assign that name to the chapter. Whenever you save a chapter in this manner, the program also saves the .CAP, .VGR, and .CIF files in the same location as the text file. If you prefer to keep those files in another location, use the Save As command, which lets you control a chapter's storage location as well as its name.

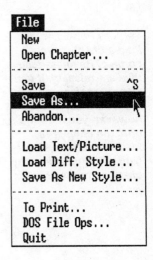

To save a chapter under a new filename, select the Save As option and the program provides an item selector for specifying a new name. After you indicate what name to use and select "OK," the new name is placed in the title bar along with the current style sheet. The Save As option is particularly useful if you aren't sure whether or not to save the changes you've made to a chapter or to keep the old version. By saving it under a new name, you can preserve *both* versions and decide later which chapter to keep and which to erase. The Save As option also provides an effective means for producing different versions of a previously saved chapter, such as a master newsletter format. For instance, you can open a previous issue of a newsletter, change the text and graphics contents as needed, and use the Save As option to specify a different name for the new issue.

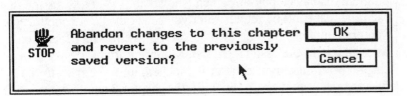

However, if you don't want to save the changes you've made to a chapter, you can select the File menu's Abandon option. When you pick Abandon, the program produces a pop-up screen (shown above) prompting you to confirm that you want to revert to the previously saved version of the chapter. If you select "OK," the program removes the current chapter from the screen and from memory and replaces it with the last saved version of that chapter.

In effect, the Abandon option is like an "undo" command since it offers you a means of recovering from major mistakes. However, the use of the Abandon option in this manner is only effective if you regularly use the Save option. That is, if you haven't saved the chapter for over half an hour and you make a serious error, selecting Abandon will also result in the loss of all other work you completed during that same period of time. The best way to avoid this, of course, is to keep saving your work as often as possible.

Ventura Publisher will load a chapter even if some of its referenced files are missing. If you want to replace a file that could not be found, however, you must wait until the chapter is loaded and then select Quit without saving any changes to the chapter.

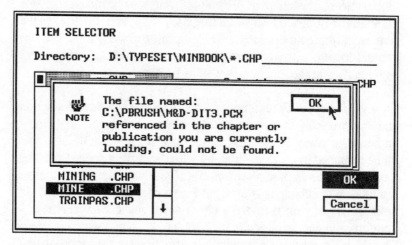

As mentioned earlier, all of the text and graphics you load into Ventura are stored in their original files whenever you save a chapter. The next time you load that chapter, Ventura retrieves each file from the location where it was saved, and if any files are missing, the program displays a pop-up screen (shown above) to inform you of each file that can't be found. After you select the "OK" command, Ventura continues loading the chapter, but the missing files won't be available in the assignment list. More important, if you save a chapter with missing files after it's loaded, all references to those files are lost from the new version of the chapter. Therefore, to avoid erasing references to missing files that you may have inadvertently misplaced but still want to use in a document, choose the Quit option and leave the former chapter intact *without* saving it.

After you locate the missing files and place them back where Ventura expects to find them, the program will load the files and place them in their correct positions in your document the next time you load the chapter. Of course, you can always start over and simply reload any missing files from other locations, but you can often avoid redoing a lot of work by simply placing the files back in their original referenced locations and using the last saved version of a chapter.

Loading Text and Graphics Files

The File menu's Load Text/Picture option is the gateway to importing text and graphics files from other programs into Ventura. As explained in the "Frame Setting" section in Chapter 4, selecting the Load Text/Picture option is a two-part process that involves using a dialog box and an item selector — both of which are provided automatically by the program.

The Load Text/Picture dialog box (shown below) lets you pick the type of file and format as well as the number of files ("One" or "Several") you want to load into the program. As you click on each of the "Type of File" options — "Text," "Line-Art," or "Image" — the program automatically changes the file format options to show the choices available. When "Type of File: Text" is selected, the dialog box also displays a "Destination" option, which permits you to send a loaded text file to one of three locations: the assignment list, the clipboard, or directly into a file at the text cursor location.

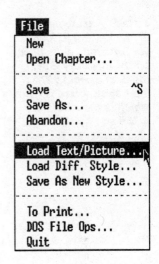

Using Ventura's Load Text/Picture option, you can import 12 types of text file formats and 12 types of graphics file ("line-art" and "image") formats.

```
┌─────────────────────────────────────────────────────────┐
│ LOAD TEXT/PICTURE                                    [?] │
│                                                          │
│   Type of File:  [Text]  [Line-Art]  [Image]            │
│   Text Format:   [Generated] [ASCII] [WordStar 3] [WS 4.0/5.0] │
│                  [MS-Word] [WordPerfect] [XyWrite] [8-Bit ASCII] │
│                  [Writer] [MultiMate] [DCA] [WordPerfect 5] │
│                                                          │
│   # of Files:    [One]  [Several]                        │
│   Destination:   [List of Files]  [Text Clipboard]  [Text Cursor] │
│                              [▸ OK]   [Cancel]           │
└─────────────────────────────────────────────────────────┘
```

After you make your selections in the Load Text/Picture dialog box and click "OK," Ventura provides an item selector (shown on following page) that enables you to designate the location of the file (or files) you want to load. As soon as you click "OK" in the item selector, Ventura loads the file(s) selected and places the filename(s) in the assignment list. At any time during a work session, you can

To help you locate the files you want to load, Ventura adds a file filter on the directory line in the item selector. The file filter shown here is *.TXT, which is the default for ASCII and XyWrite files.

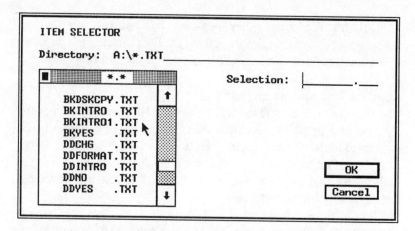

use the Load Text/Picture option to import additional text and graphics files into your chapter. If you attempt to load a text or graphics file that isn't compatible with Ventura, or try to import a file that is stored in a different format than the one you selected, the program will indicate the problem by displaying a pop-up screen (shown below) and you must cancel your attempt to load the file.

Ventura cannot load a text or graphics file unless it matches the file format you select in the Load Text/Picture dialog box.

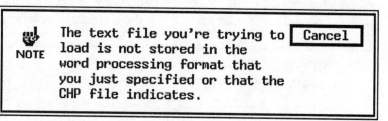

To expedite the process of locating files and loading them into a document, Ventura uses a default file filter for each type of file you select. In most cases, these defaults match the file extensions used by the source programs (e.g., *.DOC is used for Microsoft Word files, *.PIC is used for 1-2-3 graph files, and so on). A list of all the default file extensions used by Ventura's Load Text/Picture option is provided in the chart on the following page.

If you want to change the file filter in an item selector, you can delete the existing file extension and type a new one. For example, you can use DOS wildcard characters (* and ?) in the file filter to search through the files in a directory. However, an item selector cannot show more than 128 files in the directory list, and your computer will "beep" if more than 128 files match the file filter. If you

Compatible Programs, Formats, and File Extensions

Text programs or formats	File extension
ASCII format, 8-Bit ASCII	*.TXT
Document Content Architecture format	*.DCA
Generated text	*.GEN
Microsoft Word	*.DOC
MultiMate	*.DOC
WordPerfect 5, WordPerfect (4.1/4.2)	*.WP
WordStar (4.0/5.0), WordStar 3	*.WS
Xerox Writer	*.XWP
XyWrite	*.TXT

Line-Art (draw) programs or formats	File extension
GEM (GEM Artline, GEM Draw Plus, GEM Graph)	*.GEM
AutoCAD	*.SLD
Lotus 1-2-3, Symphony	*.PIC
Mentor Graphics	*.P*
VideoShow	*.PIC
Macintosh PICT format	*.PCT
Computer Graphics Metafile format	*.CGM
PostScript (Encapsulated format)	*.EPS
Hewlett-Packard Graphics Language format	*.HPG
Microsoft Windows Metafile format	*.WMF

Image (paint) programs or formats	File extension
GEM Paint, GEM Scan	*.IMG
Halo Desktop Publishing Editor	*.IMG
PC Paintbrush Plus, Publisher's Paintbrush	*.PCX
Macintosh Paint	*.PNT
TIFF (black-and-white or gray-scale images)	*.TIF

```
File
New
Open Chapter...
- - - - - - - - - - - - - - - -
Save              ^S
Save As...
Abandon...
- - - - - - - - - - - - - - - -
Load Text/Picture...
Load Diff. Style...
Save As New Style...
- - - - - - - - - - - - - - - -
To Print...
DOS File Ops...
Quit
```

encounter this limitation and want to see the files that aren't displayed, you must change the file filter to restrict the number of files shown or delete some files in the directory by using the File menu's DOS File Operations option (explained later in this section).

Any changes you make to the default file filters used for the various file formats remain in effect until you change them again. Ventura also keeps track of the location from which various types of file formats have been retrieved, and the directory line in the item selector will automatically display the previous location for a selected file format. For example, if you load a WordPerfect *.WP file from a "WORDPERF" subdirectory on drive C, Ventura displays the same "C:\WORDPERF*.WP" information in the item selector the next time you want to load a WordPerfect file. Or, if the same file was loaded from drive A, the program automatically displays "A:*.WP."

Types of Text Files

With the Load Text/Picture option, you can load text files from the word processing programs listed in the dialog box or from any word processor that creates DCA (Document Content Architecture) files, such as DisplayWrite, Samna Word, Volkswriter, and WordStar 2000. You can also load text from different programs and mix them together in the same document — such as a newsletter that contains articles from contributors who use different word processors.

After placing different text formats in the same document, you can use the Text Editing mode to cut or copy text from one file and paste it into another file. Or, when first loading a text file into the program, you can use the Load Text/Picture dialog box's "Destination: Text Clipboard" option to send the text directly to the clipboard and paste it in another file later, or use the "Destination: Text Cursor" option to immediately insert the text file at the current text cursor location.

In addition to the specific word-processing programs listed in the Load Text/Picture dialog box, you can import text from generated files and from ASCII files. *Generated files* are created by Ventura when you use the program's Multi-Chapter option to produce a table of contents or an index for a publication. As the program generates these files, they automatically receive the .GEN file extension, which is the default file filter used by the item selector when you pick "Generated" in the Load Text/Picture dialog box.

File
New
Open Chapter...
Save   ^S
Save As...
Abandon...
Load Text/Picture...
Load Diff. Style...
Save As New Style...
To Print...
DOS File Ops...
Quit

If you select "ASCII," you can load *ASCII files,* which are text files that contain displayable letters, numbers, and punctuation marks, as opposed to unreadable characters or program instructions. For non-English users of Ventura, an "8-Bit ASCII" text format which supports non-English text characters, that is, characters above decimal code 128, is also available in the Load Text/Picture dialog box.

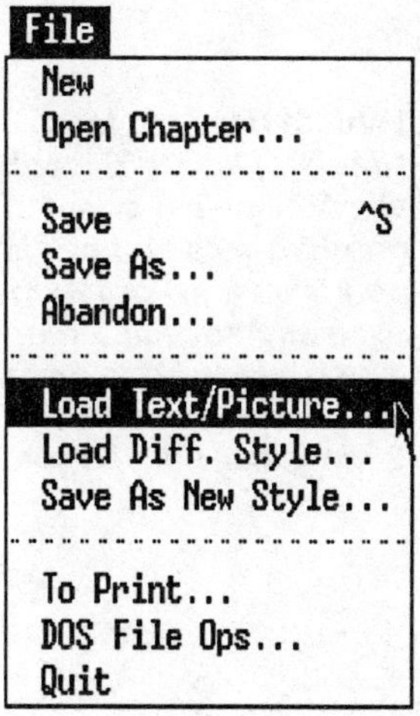

Products that create ASCII files include most word processors, database programs, spreadsheet programs, and utility programs with text editors. For example, you can generate an address or phone directory by using various dBASE commands to extract information from a database, and then save it as an ASCII text file. With 1-2-3, you can use the program's printing options to create a .PRN file, which is a spreadsheet saved in ASCII format.

ASCII files can be loaded into Ventura by using the "ASCII" or "WordStar 3" text format option in the Load Text/Picture dialog box, depending on how you want the program to handle single carriage returns. If you select "ASCII," Ventura ignores single carriage returns when it loads the file (i.e., separate lines of text will be placed together on the same line if not separated by more than one carriage return). However, if you pick "WordStar 3," Ventura treats each carriage return as a paragraph break. For example, 1-2-3 print (.PRN) files should be loaded as WordStar 3 rather than ASCII files since each row in a 1-2-3 spreadsheet is separated only by a single carriage return.

```
File
New
Open Chapter...
---
Save              ^S
Save As...
Abandon...
---
Load Text/Picture...
Load Diff. Style...
Save As New Style...

To Print...
DOS File Ops...
Quit
```

```
ITEM SELECTOR

Directory:  C:\TYPESET\TESTDATA\*.PRN_____

   ■  *.PRN                Selection:  PROFIT87.PRN

   GRAPH1  .PRN  ↑
   GRAPHOFF.PRN
   GRAPHTUL.PRN
   PROFIT-A.PRN
   PROFIT87.PRN
   _____.___
   _____.___           ┌────────┐
   _____.___           │   OK   │
   _____.___ ↓         └────────┘
                        ┌────────┐
                        │ Cancel │
                        └────────┘
```

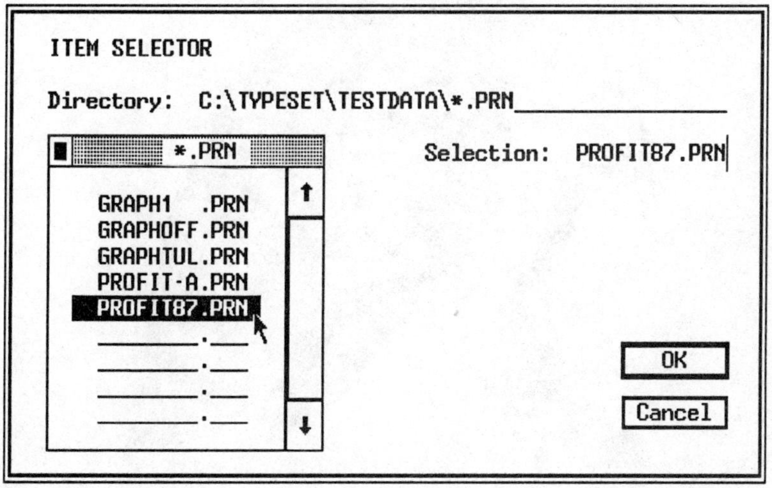

Lotus 1-2-3 spreadsheets can be saved as ASCII text (.PRN print files) and placed in a document. To load the file, you need to change the file filter to match the .PRN extension.

Ventura uses the term "line-art files" to describe all of the object-oriented graphics files you can import from draw programs, such as Adobe Illustrator, which was used to create the encapsulated Post-Script (.EPS) file shown here.

Types of Graphics Files

Ventura uses the term *picture files* to refer to the graphics files you can load into the program from graphics software and from image scanners. In addition, the program divides picture files into *line-art files,* which are object-oriented graphics created with draw or computer-aided design (CAD) programs, and *image files,* which are bit-mapped graphics produced with paint programs or scanners.

The bit-mapped graphics files you can create with scanners or with paint programs, such as Halo DPE and Publisher's Paintbrush, are referred to as "image files" by Ventura.

Whenever Ventura loads picture files, it converts those stored in a non-GEM or non-PostScript graphics format into GEM-formatted files. These converted files are actually copies of the originals and they take up a similar amount of space. When Ventura names a converted file, it gives it the same name as the original but uses a different file extension: ".GEM" is used for line-art and ".IMG" or ".IML" for image files. The source files remain intact in their original locations and Ventura stores its converted copies in the same directory on your hard or floppy disk. If you change an image file that has already been converted and placed in a chapter, Ventura automatically converts the file again the next time the chapter is opened.

Because Ventura converts certain picture files when they are loaded, you must have enough storage space on your disk to hold both versions of the file. For example, if you load two picture files and each is 25K in size, you'll actually need about 50K additional space on your disk for the program to store its converted copies of both files. If your disk doesn't have enough storage space or if the picture file you're trying to load isn't compatible with the format you selected, the program produces a pop-up error message (shown below) that indicates the file cannot be loaded.

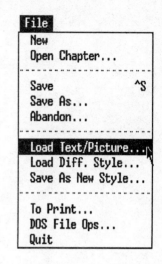

NOTE

The picture file you tried to load couldn't be converted. Either it wasn't in the proper format or there wasn't enough disk space for the conversion.

Cancel

If you don't choose the proper format or have enough disk space for the file conversion when you load a picture file, Ventura prompts you with an error message.

With Ventura, you can import picture files from a wide variety of software programs representing several different graphics standards that have gained acceptance in the microcomputer, minicomputer, and mainframe world. These programs include computer-aided drafting, design, and engineering products, analytical and presentation graphics, and a number of draw and paint programs. Because some of these programs can store files in more than one of the picture formats supported by Ventura, you may want to experiment to determine which format provides the best results. For more information on using graphics files with Ventura, see the "Working with Graphics" section in Chapter 7.

Storing and Retrieving Style Sheets

The next two options in the File menu, Load Different Style and Save As New Style, provide two of the most important and powerful features offered by Ventura. These options give you the ability to create, store, and retrieve style sheets, which contain page layout and typographic specifications that tell Ventura how you want it to format a document. A list of all the items stored in a style sheet and the menus that you use to control them is provided in Chapter 7.

Using the Load Different Style option, you can retrieve and apply any number of existing style sheets to see how your document looks with different margin and column settings, page layout specifications, paragraph tags, and other style sheet variables. When you select the Load Different Style option, the program provides an item selector with the file filter automatically set for style sheet (.STY) files. Locate and select the style sheet file you want to use, click "OK," and Ventura will load the style sheet and display its name in the title bar.

After a style sheet is loaded, the program immediately applies the margins, columns, and other general page formats defined by that style sheet. If a text file is already loaded and placed in a document, the program also applies the typographic specifications of the style sheet's tags to your text. If your document hasn't been tagged, all paragraphs receive the attributes of the "Body Text" tag, which is a universal tag name used by all Ventura style sheets. If the paragraphs in your document are already tagged and they share the same tag names used by other style sheets, the paragraphs will always be reformatted to take on the attributes assigned to those same tags in the current style sheet.

For example, you might maintain two style sheets for formatting a business report. Both style sheets use the same names for paragraph tags — "Report Title," "Major Heading," "Minor Heading," "Body Text," and so forth — but one style sheet uses a serif font (such as Times or Dutch) and the other uses a sans serif font (such as Helvetica or Swiss) for all text. As you use the Load Different Style option to switch from one style sheet to the other, you can instantly change the font for the entire report, yet maintain all the same line spacing, justification, tab settings, and so forth. Or, you might load a style sheet that uses the same font but provides automatic number-

```
File
 New
 Open Chapter...
 .......................
 Save              ^S
 Save As...
 Abandon...
 .......................
 Load Text/Picture...
 Load Diff. Style...
 Save As New Style...
 .......................
 To Print...
 DOS File Ops...
 Quit
```

ing, ruling lines, and various other specifications. After you've created a library of style sheets, you can save time and effort by simply loading the best style sheet for the job.

The Save As New Style option lets you store the countless variations of style sheets you create under different names, again using the item selector provided. A style sheet can be stored under a unique name or saved under the same name as a chapter file, for instance, BROCHURE.STY and BROCHURE.CHP. Like the Save As option used to store chapter files, the Save As New Style option is especially handy if you aren't certain whether or not to save the changes you've made to a style sheet or to keep the old version. By saving the style sheet under a new name, you can preserve both versions. For example, if you make alterations to a master style sheet used for company proposals *and* save it, all proposals that use the master style sheet will also be affected — unless, of course, you use the Save As New Style option and save the altered file under a new name.

Most important about altering style sheets is that each time you use the Save option to store a chapter file, the current style sheet is also saved if any changes have been made to it. Therefore, use the Save As New Style option *first* if you don't want to permanently change the current style sheet. However, since it's so easy to save altered style sheets under new names, you may soon have an unwieldy number of style sheets. One way to avoid this is to store related style sheets in different directories identified by the publication category (e.g., CATALOGS, MANUALS, NEWSPUBS), project name (e.g., HAND-BOOK, REPORT25, QUARTER4), major company division (e.g., FI-NANCE, SALES, RESEARCH), or similar organizational system.

Printing a Document

Using the File menu's To Print option, you can output the currently loaded chapter. After you select this option, the Print Information dialog box appears and prompts you with several options. If you simply click "OK," Ventura automatically prints a single copy of the chapter, from the first to last page. In order to print less than the entire chapter, you must first change the default settings.

After you click on the "Which Pages" option, you can pick one of the pop-up controls to print out all pages, selected pages, all left pages, all right pages, or the current page (the page number that

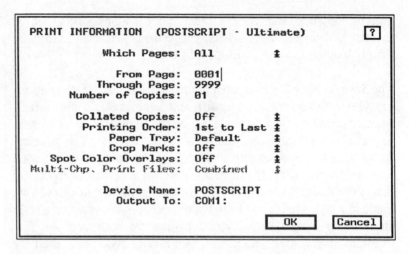

The Print Information dialog box is used by the File menu's To Print option to output single pages or chapters, and by the Options menu's Multi-Chapter option to print several chapters or publications.

appears in the current page box). If you pick "Selected," you can then use the keyboard to type the first and last page numbers after the "From Page" and "Through Page" options. You can also print selected pages when using the "Left" or "Right" options, which enables you to produce duplex (double-sided) printing. When using this option, however, print a test page first so you know which way to place the paper in the tray in order to print both sides correctly. To print multiple copies of all or selected pages, type the amount you want after the "Number of Copies" option. You can also print collated copies and set the printing order ("1st to Last" or "Last to 1st"), but it's often faster to sort the copies manually, especially if the document contains a lot of graphics.

If you plan to send master pages of your document to a commercial printer, you can use the "Crop Marks" option to provide an accurate indication of where a page is to be cut by the printer. Because a commercial printer trims the crop marks off of the printed page, however, you can only use this option if the size of the page frame is *less* than the size of the page itself, as defined by the Chapter menu's Page Size & Layout option. For example, publishers of computer product reference manuals can print crop marks on letter-size (8.5 by 11-inch) paper for the standard page size (about 5.5 by 8 inches) used for "slip-cover" style documentation packages (as shown on the following page). In order to place the crop marks correctly, you must use the Frame menu's Sizing & Scaling option to change the default size and placement of the page frame (as explained in the "Frame Menu" section in Chapter 6).

With the "Spot Color Overlays" option, you can instruct Ventura to print a separate page for each color enabled in the Paragraph menu's Define Colors option, plus a page for black. Although each color page is printed in black ink — assuming that your laser printer is using a black toner cartridge — these pages can immediately be used by a commercial printer as camera-ready masters. For example, to produce the masters for a two-color publication, you can pick "Spot Color Overlays: On" and print two separate pages: one sheet will contain the text and graphics for the first color, and the other

Automatic Publishing Editor™

The Desktop Publisher's
Style Sheet Companion
for the IBM PC

User Manual

For Version 1.0

Copyright © 1987
Tulpa Productions
P.O. Box 10185
Berkeley, CA 94709-0185
U.S.A.

This example of an 8.5 by 11-inch page (reduced here) shows how the "Crop Marks" option in the To Print dialog box can be used to produce four sets of horizontal and vertical marks, which indicate where to trim the page to produce a smaller (5.5 by 8-inch) page for a software documentation manual.

To print a standard-size software documentation manual with crop marks, you must use the Sizing & Scaling option to modify the size and placement of the base page frame. The information shown here is used to create the example shown on the previous page.

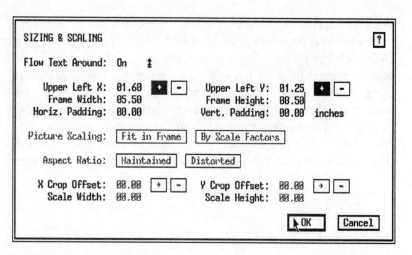

sheet will contain the elements for the second color. If the page frame is smaller than the actual page size, Ventura will print the color names you define at the top of each page, along with camera registration guides. The Print Information dialog box also contains a "Multi-Chp. Print Files" option, which is unavailable (displayed in gray) when printing single pages or chapters. This feature is only accessible when you use the "Print Information" dialog box provided with the Multi-Chapter menu option in the Options menu.

The "Device Name" and "Output To" options, which indicate the current printer and printer port, cannot be changed with this dialog box. To change the printer configuration, use the "Set Printer Info" option in the Options menu. If you're using a printer font width table designed for a printer other than the one connected to your computer, Ventura will display the word "Draft" after the name of the current device that appears at the top of the dialog box; otherwise, the word "Ultimate" will appear, which means that Ventura is using the width table that matches the current device.

If you've used the Page Size & Layout option in the Chapter menu to select a large-page format for your publication — "Double" (11 by 17 inches) or "Broad Sheet" (11 by 24 inches) — Ventura will prompt you with other dialog boxes containing a few additional choices when you print your document. First, if you're using the double-size page format but your printer can only output letter-size pages, the dialog box provided enables you to "Shrink" or "Overlap" the pages. Shrink reduces the large format to fit on an 8.5 by 11-inch

```
?    Should this 18 x 24 page be shrunk      ┌─────────┐
WAIT to fit on your 8.5 x 11 printer,        │ Shrink  │
     or be overlapped in 3, 4, or 9          ├─────────┤
     strips/pages, or be printed normally    │Overlap..│
     (without special handling)?             ├─────────┤
                                             │ Normal  │
                                             └─────────┘
```

```
?    Should these 18 x 24 pages be           ┌─────────┐
WAIT printed as 3 long 8 inch wide           │ 3 Strips│
     strips, or 4 overlapping 11 x 17        ├─────────┤
     pages, or 9 overlapping 8.5 x 11        │ 4 Pages │
     pages?                                  ├─────────┤
                                             │ 9 Pages │
                                             └─────────┘
```

When you print a broad sheet page, Ventura lets you shrink or overlap the pages if the printer you're using can't actually print 18 by 24-inch pages. If you choose to overlap the pages, Ventura provides an additional dialog box (bottom left) that lets you print the pages in strips or on smaller pages.

page and is only available with PostScript printers or typesetters. Overlap produces four 8.5 by 11-inch pages for each 11 by 17-inch page; you then paste the pages together to form one double-size page, which becomes the master copy to take to a commercial printer. If your printer actually supports this large format directly, you simply select "Nothing." If you're printing a broad sheet page, however, the dialog boxes provided (shown above) enable you to print each page normally, if the output device can actually print an 18 by 24-inch page (such as certain typesetting machines), or you can also shrink or overlap the page to fit on smaller pages.

File Management

The File menu's DOS File Operations option makes it possible to perform a number of simple file management chores from within Ventura. When you select this option, the program provides the DOS File Operations dialog box (see following page), which consists of a file directory line, called "File Spec," and four different "Operation" options. If you move the cursor to the "Select Different File Specification" option and click, Ventura provides an item selector that you use in the usual fashion. Because this operation is designed to let you identify any file or directory located on your system, the default file filter uses DOS wildcard characters (*.*). You can also use the keyboard rather than the item selector to type the appropriate information on the file specification line.

After you identify a file or directory location, you use the other three options to perform the DOS file operation indicated. Using the "Make Directory" command, you can create new directories on your

```
┌──────────────────────┐
│ File                 │
├──────────────────────┤
│ New                  │
│ Open Chapter...      │
│ - - - - - - - - - -  │
│ Save            ^S   │
│ Save As...           │
│ Abandon...           │
│ - - - - - - - - - -  │
│ Load Text/Picture... │
│ Load Diff. Style...  │
│ Save As New Style... │
│ - - - - - - - - - -  │
│ To Print...          │
│ DOS File Ops...      │
│ Quit                 │
└──────────────────────┘
```

By using the DOS File Operations menu option, you can easily delete all Ventura backup copies in a selected directory. As shown here, these back-up copies use a dollar sign for the first character of the filename extension.

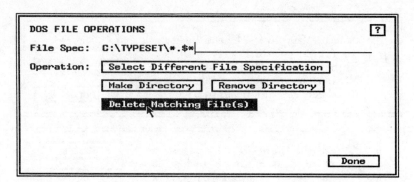

hard or floppy disks for storing the files used to produce your documents, including Ventura files (.CHP, .STY, .CAP, .VGR, .INF) and the component text and graphics files. After erasing all of the files in a directory (perhaps to make more disk space available) you can use the "Remove Directory" command to delete the directory itself.

The "Delete Matching File(s)" option box is also useful. With this command, you can easily erase unwanted files from any location on a hard or floppy disk *without* quitting the program. By the same token, you can also easily erase files that you don't want to lose, for example, if you deleted "C:*.*" you would erase *all* of the files in the root directory on your hard disk. Fortunately, to stop you from making a mistake, Ventura always prompts you with a warning message that asks for confirmation before it erases files.

If you're wondering why you're spending time erasing files from inside rather than outside Ventura, you'll quickly understand if you ever try to save a chapter or style sheet file and receive an error message that your disk is full. Without the ability to erase files from inside the program, you only have two possible choices: try to copy your files to floppy disks, or lose all changes made since the last save. But by using the DOS File Operations menu option, you can delete enough files to make room for the new files you want to save.

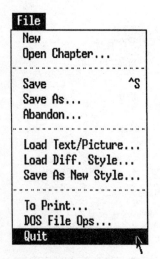

Ending a Session
Selecting the Quit option returns you to the DOS prompt. If you've made additional changes to the chapter or style sheet since the last save, the program prompts you with two dialog boxes — one for the chapter and one for the style sheet — that let you save or abandon the changes, or cancel the Quit option by selecting "Don't Quit," which allows you to continue using the program.

Whenever you quit using the program, Ventura remembers the current function (Frame Setting, Paragraph Tagging, Text Editing, or Graphic Drawing), Options menu settings (preferences, printer information, rulers, column guides, and so on), and the page view selected in the View menu. When you start your next session, Ventura automatically resumes all of these settings, which are stored in the VP.INF file in the VENTURA directory.

The View menu is the only program menu that doesn't offer any dialog boxes. Furthermore, since all but one of the View menu's options can be accessed by keyboard shortcuts, you hardly need to use this menu once you learn the shortcuts and become proficient at using Ventura. The first four options in the View menu provide different views of the publication page displayed in the work area, and the remaining four are used to activate the program functions.

The Facing Pages View option lets you see the entire left and right page of a document at the same time, using the portrait or landscape page orientation. This two-page view is only available if the style sheet is set for a double-sided (not single-sided) document, which you control with the Chapter menu's Page Size & Layout option. Instead of working with single vertical pages, the Facing Pages View

View Menu

View	
Facing Pages View	
Reduced View	^R
√ Normal View (1x)	^N
Enlarged View (2x)	^E
Frame Setting	^U
√ Paragraph Tagging	^I
Text Editing	^O
Graphic Drawing	^P

The Facing Pages View is particularly useful for checking the horizontal alignment of text or graphics elements that cross the inner space between two facing pages, which is called "jumping the gutter." However, because you can't drag elements across the gutter, you must use the Edit menu's cut-copy-paste options to move these items from one page to another.

helps you to think in terms of horizontal spreads. Therefore, this view is indispensable for checking and adjusting the basic layout design of any spread for a book, magazine, newsletter, or other double-sided publication. If you perceive that various elements — text, pictures, or graphic drawings — are too scattered or poorly balanced, you can make overall adjustments to rectify the layout, and then use the other page views to make more precise adjustments.

The Reduced View option displays an entire single page of a document and, like the Facing Pages View, is primarily used for checking and adjusting the overall layout design. Without a high-resolution display, small text is usually unreadable when using either of these page views. Therefore, Ventura displays *greeked* text instead of the actual text, which also speeds up the time it takes to display the information on screen. Greeked text consists of horizontal lines used to approximate the height and length of the actual text on a page. By using the Set Preferences option (Options menu), you can select the range of type sizes that will be greeked.

The Normal View option is used more frequently than the other page views because it provides the most accurate display of the final printed page. You'll probably do most of your text reading and editing in this view. The Enlarged View option magnifies the page twice as much as the Normal View and is usually used to check graphic placement and layout details. However, it takes the program longer to display bit-mapped graphics in the Enlarged View because the greatest amount of detail is shown. If you are simply positioning graphics, you can use the Hide All Pictures option (Options menu) to speed up the screen display time. Also, in changing from the Facing Pages or Reduced View to the Normal or Enlarged View, you can zoom in on a specific portion of the page by first placing the cursor in the upper-left corner of the area you want to magnify, and then use the keyboard shortcuts to change the view.

The other options in the View menu provide alternative methods for changing program functions, as explained in Chapter 4. Each of the four functions is represented by a menu option, along with the keyboard shortcut. Because you may want to hide the side-bar in order to see more of your publication (as shown on the previous page), these menu options provide an alternative method for selecting functions without requiring the side-bar to be present on screen.

```
View
 Facing Pages View
------------------------
 Reduced View        ^R
√ Normal View (1x)    ^N
 Enlarged View (2x)  ^E
------------------------
 Frame Setting       ^U
√ Paragraph Tagging   ^I
 Text Editing        ^O
 Graphic Drawing     ^P
```

Chapter Menu

With Ventura's Chapter menu, you can control an extensive range of page formatting options for an entire chapter. Most of the Chapter menu's options provide you with dialog boxes as soon as they are selected; others enable you to execute a single action, such as turning a header or footer on or off for a given page. It isn't necessary to use *all* of these options, however, unless the document you're publishing requires the various features provided, which include footnotes, section numbers, headers, and footers.

Some of the formatting settings you establish with the Chapter menu options are stored as part of the style sheet (.STY) file, whereas others are saved in the chapter (.CHP) file. The options containing information that is saved as part of a style sheet include:

- Page Size & Layout
- Auto-Numbering
- Chapter Typography
- Footnote Settings

When a style sheet formats a chapter, it uses all of the settings in the Page Size & Layout and Chapter Typography options (except the "Widows" and "Orphans" controls), whereas the Auto-Numbering and Footnote Settings options must first be activated before a style sheet can apply them. At any rate, because the features these four menu options control are saved as part of a style sheet, it's important to remember that any changes made using these options will not only affect the current chapter, but all other chapters that use the same style sheet. Therefore, when you change the settings for any of these four options, always use the File menu's Save As New Style option to save the style sheet under a new name if you don't want to alter all other chapters that use the same original style sheet.

Chapter

Page Size & Layout...
Chapter Typography...

Update Counters...
Auto-Numbering...
Renumber Chapter   ^B
Re-Anchor Frames...

Headers & Footers...
Turn Header On
Turn Footer On
Footnote Settings...

Insert/Remove Page...
Go to Page...   ^G

PAGE LAYOUT   [?]

Orientation: Portrait ↕
Paper Type & Dimension: Letter,   8.5 x 11 in. ↕
Sides: Double ↕
Start On: Right Side ↕

[OK] [Cancel]

The Page Layout dialog box enables you to create the layout for the base page. Shown here are the default settings used for most common business documents.

```
Chapter
 Page Size & Layout...
↖Chapter Typography...
.............................
 Update Counters...
 Auto-Numbering...
 Renumber Chapter   ^B
 Re-Anchor Frames...
.............................
 Headers & Footers...
 Turn Header On
 Turn Footer On
 Footnote Settings...
.............................
 Insert/Remove Page...
 Go to Page...      ^G
```

Laying Out the Basic Page

The Page Size & Layout option provides the general page layout settings that Ventura Publisher uses to format all of the pages in a chapter. When this option is selected, the dialog box provided lets you pick either portrait (vertical) or landscape (horizontal) for the page "Orientation," and one of seven different sizes for "Paper Type & Dimension," which include the following:

- Half (5.5 by 8.5 inches)
- Letter (8.5 by 11 inches)
- Legal (8.5 by 14 inches)
- Double (11 by 17 inches)
- B5 (17.6 by 25 centimeters)
- A4 (21 by 29.7 centimeters)
- Broad sheet (18 by 24 inches)

If you choose the double or broad sheet size, the program offers you additional choices on how to output the page at print time (explained earlier in the "Printing a Document" section in this chapter).

Choices for single- or double-sided formatting and starting page side (left or right) are also provided in the Page Size & Layout dialog box. You must select "Sides: Double" if you want to use the Facing Pages View option (in the View menu) or if you want to use different settings for recurrent items on each left and right page, such as margins, column widths, headers, footers, vertical rules, repeating frames, and spacing indents. For example, you might want a left-aligned header on the left page and a right-aligned header on the right page. If you select "Sides: Single," however, the headers and footers settings for all pages will be identical.

Typographic Control by Chapter

To give you maximum control and flexibility over the various typographic attributes in your document, Ventura provides several different typographic features throughout the program. The primary typographic controls are found in three separate menu options, which all use the word "Typography" in their titles, but are located in three separate menus. Once you understand the hierarchical relationship of these menu options, however, you are well on your way to mastering typographic control of the program.

In brief, the typography menu hierarchy works like this: At the lowest but most complex level, the Paragraph Typography option controls pair kerning, letter spacing, word spacing, and other typographic features, all on a paragraph tag-by-tag basis. At the next level up, the Frame Typography option sets parameters for widows and orphans, pair kerning, column balance, and baseline spacing for the first line in each column, all on a frame-by-frame basis. At the highest level, the Chapter Typography option controls the same parameters as the Frame Typography option, but all on a global, or chapterwide, basis. (For more information on the Paragraph Typography and Frame Typography options, see Chapter 6.)

In practice, this menu hierarchy often saves time by letting you control certain features at higher levels. For example, you can turn automatic pair kerning on at the paragraph level (for some tags) and on at the frame level (for some frames), but you can also turn pair kerning off for the entire chapter *all at once* by changing only one control: select "Pair Kerning: Off" in the Chapter Typography dialog box and it immediately overrides both of the other settings. Because features like pair kerning and column balance take longer for Ventura to display on screen and to print, the ability to turn these features on/off in one move lets you save time in the interim stages required before producing the final version of a chapter.

The first two controls in the Chapter (Default) Typography Settings dialog box (shown below) are the "Widows" and "Orphans" options, which let you set the minimum number of isolated lines of text that can appear at the top (widow) and bottom (orphan) of a page or column. The program's default value of "2" (two lines) reflects the standard setting for widows and orphans, but you can also select no less than one, three, four, or five lines of a paragraph to appear alone

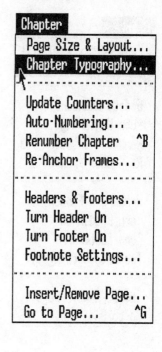

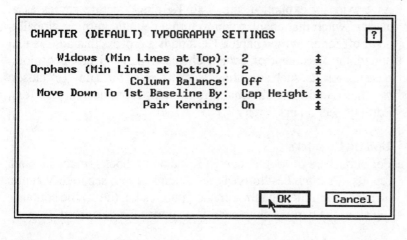

Except for widows and orphans, the settings you define in the Chapter Typography dialog box are applied by the current style sheet whenever it formats the text files in a chapter.

Chapter
Page Size & Layout...
Chapter Typography...
Update Counters...
Auto-Numbering...
Renumber Chapter   ^B
Re-Anchor Frames...
Headers & Footers...
Turn Header On
Turn Footer On
Footnote Settings...
Insert/Remove Page...
Go to Page...   ^G

at the top or bottom of a page. The settings for widows and orphans are stored in the chapter (.CHP) file, while the other options in this dialog box are saved as part of the style sheet (.STY) file.

The "Column Balance" option adjusts the number of lines in multi-column formats so that all column text ends on the same line within a frame or on the base page. For instance, if you produce a three-column newsletter and in the middle of the page you use a framewide headline, that is, text that extends across all columns within a frame, you can use the "Column Balance: On" option to ensure that all columns above the headline are equally distributed. However, because column balance is also affected by the settings you use for widows/orphans and for the "Keep With Next" feature in the Paragraph menu's Breaks option (explained in Chapter 6), one column may occasionally be shorter than the rest.

With the "Move Down to 1st Baseline By" option, the program provides two different systems for determining the distance from the baseline of the first line of text on the page (or column) to the top margin. "Cap Height" places it on the page so the distance is equal to the ascender height for that font; and "Inter-Line" makes the distance equal to the text's inter-line spacing, as specified in the Paragraph menu's Spacing option for that particular tag. The advantage of using inter-line spacing for this distance is that you can always get an integral number of text lines on a page, which provides a more uniform-looking document when, for example, different type sizes are used at the top of different columns or facing pages.

As previously explained, the "Pair Kerning" feature serves as a master switch that enables you to turn automatic kerning globally on or off for an entire chapter. Kerning is a process that adjusts the horizontal placement of certain character pairs to produce more pleasing results, such as pulling the characters "Vo" and "Te" closer together. (Additional information on kerning is provided in the "Text Editing" section in Chapter 4.)

Update Counters
For publishers of long documents, including books, manuals, and reports, it's often best to break the document into separate Ventura chapter (.CHP) files and then create a publication (.PUB) file containing all of the various chapters that comprise the document. In such

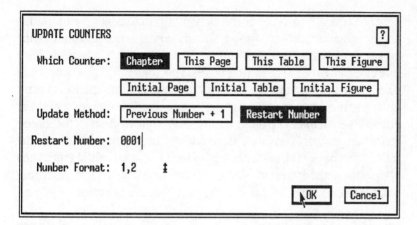

The numbers you specify in the Update Counters dialog box can be automatically inserted in headers, footers, table of contents, and indexes. The Chapter counter is also used for numbering sections and captions.

cases, Ventura's ability to manage automatic numbering and reset the numbers for various types of elements is extremely handy.

With the Chapter menu's Update Counters option, you can control the chapter, page, table, and figure numbering at any point in a chapter. When you select this feature, the dialog box provided (shown above) offers seven types of counters, two ways to update the counting method, a restart number control, and eight types of number formats. The main control is the "Which Counter" option, which is like picking the "Type of File" in the Load Text/Picture option. To apply the "Which Counter" option boxes for "This Table" and "This Figure," you must first use the Frame Setting mode and select a frame already numbered as a table or figure before using the Update Counters option — otherwise, the option boxes are unavailable (displayed in gray). As an added convenience, the "Initial Page," "Initial Table," and "Initial Figure" option boxes allow you to reset the counting for the first occurrence of that item (page, table, or figure) from any page in the current chapter.

The "Update Method" option lets you link the numbers in one chapter with those in other chapters or simply reset the numbers in the current chapter. If you select the "Previous Number + 1" option box, you must also use the "Renumber" feature in the Options menu's Multi-Chapter option in order for the renumbering to actually take place. If you pick the "Update Method: Restart Number" option box, however, the "Restart Number" control becomes available and you can then use the typing cursor to change the default number (0001) to the number you want.

Chapter

Page Size & Layout...
Chapter Typography...

Update Counters...
Auto-Numbering...
Renumber Chapter   ^B
Re-Anchor Frames...

Headers & Footers...
Turn Header On
Turn Footer On
Footnote Settings...

Insert/Remove Page...
Go to Page...   ^G

Chapter

Page Size & Layout...
Chapter Typography...
....
Update Counters...
Auto-Numbering...
Renumber Chapter   ^B
Re-Anchor Frames...
....
Headers & Footers...
Turn Header On
Turn Footer On
Footnote Settings...
....
Insert/Remove Page...
Go to Page...   ^G

For example, to turn the current chapter into Chapter 5 of a publication called BOOK.PUB, which already contains the first four chapters, click on the "Which Counter: Chapter" and "Update Method: Previous Number + 1" option boxes, and select "OK." Then, using the Multi-Chapter option, open the BOOK.PUB file, add the current chapter (if necessary), and use the "Renumber" feature to renumber all of the chapters, pages, tables, and figures across the entire publication. Or, if you just want to change the first page of the current chapter to page 100, click on the "Which Counter: Initial Page" and "Update Method: Restart Number" option boxes, and use the typing cursor to enter "0100" for the "Restart Number" control.

In addition to arabic numerals (1, 2, 3), the "Number Format" option includes upper or lower case roman numerals (I, II, III), letters (A, B, C), and text (One, Two, Three). If you don't apply this option, the program automatically uses the arabic numeral "1" as the default starting number for the chapter and initial page, table, and figure.

The number settings you use in the Update Counters dialog box can be placed in headers, footers, table of contents, and indexes. In addition, chapter numbers (but not page numbers) also can be placed in section numbers and frame captions. It should be noted that the page number you set in the Update Counters dialog box does not affect the number displayed in the side-bar's current page box. The page box is instead an *on-screen* page indicator that shows the page number relative to the start of the current chapter. In the previous example, for instance, the Update Counters option would number the first page of the current chapter as page 100 when printed, but the page itself is still displayed as "Pg # 0001" in the page box.

Automatic Section Numbering

If you produce technical manuals, outlines, or other materials that require section numbers (e.g., certain legal, government, and military documents), Ventura's automatic numbering system offers an excellent way of keeping all sections numbered correctly. Even if you edit the text — adding, deleting, and moving various sections, for instance — the program will automatically renumber each section according to the numbering style you specify.

The automatic numbering styles available include arabic numerals, upper and lower case letters and roman numerals, and any combi-

Automatic Numbering Systems	
I. Section topic	I. Section topic
A. Major head	I.1 Major head
1. Subhead	I.1.1 Subhead
2. Subhead	I.1.2 Subhead
B. Major head	I.2 Major head
1. Subhead	I.2.1 Subhead
2. Subhead	I.2.2 Subhead
a) Minor subhead	I.2.2.1 Minor subhead
b) Minor subhead	I.2.2.2 Minor subhead
(1) Sub-minor subhead	I.2.2.2.1. Sub-minor subhead
(2) Sub-minor subhead	I.2.2.2.2. Sub-minor subhead

Shown here are examples of two of the automatic numbering systems you can use with Ventura. In the system on the left, the previous number level is suppressed; in the system on the right, all of the previous number levels are displayed.

nation of punctuation or text attributes (bold, italic, etc.) you choose. For instance, the examples above show two different numbering systems, each containing five levels. Notice that the conventional outline scheme on the left displays only one level of numbering with each paragraph, whereas the divisional scheme on the right also shows the previous levels.

The program tools involved in applying section numbers are paragraph tags and the Chapter menu's Auto-Numbering and Renumber Chapter options. The basic procedure involves the following steps:

- Use the Auto-Numbering option to assign paragraph tags to as many as 10 levels or section divisions.
- Use the Paragraph Tagging function to tag the paragraphs you want to automatically number.
- Use the Renumber Chapter option to update all section numbers for the entire chapter.

After selecting the Auto-Numbering option, Ventura provides a dialog box (see next page) that allows you to turn on (or off) the auto-numbering feature and assign up to 10 paragraph tags to the 10 levels of section numbers available. At the bottom of this dialog box are eight option boxes that represent the number styles and other "Inserts" you can use for each level. As you click the mouse cursor on any of these boxes, that option is inserted at the typing cursor position, which is initially located on the first ("Level 1") blank line.

Chapter
Page Size & Layout...
Chapter Typography...
- - - - - - - - - - -
Update Counters...
Auto-Numbering...
Renumber Chapter ^B
Re-Anchor Frames...
- - - - - - - - - - -
Headers & Footers...
Turn Header On
Turn Footer On
Footnote Settings...
- - - - - - - - - - -
Insert/Remove Page...
Go to Page...   ^G

The bracketed paragraph tags in levels 1-5 of this Auto-Numbering dialog box were used to create the conventional outline scheme on the previous page. The parentheses before and after the Level 5 bracketed tag are added to create section numbers like (1), (2), and (3). The bracketed minus sign [-] is inserted if you select the "Suppress Previous Level" option. The insert for Level 6 includes the default words "tag name," which show you where to type the actual tag name.

```
AUTO-NUMBERING                                    ?

  Usage:   [On] [Off]

  Level 1:  [*Section topic,I]._____
  Level 2:  [-][*Major Head,A]._____
  Level 3:  [-][*Subhead,1]._____
  Level 4:  [-][*Minor subhead,a])_____
  Level 5:  [-]([*Sub-minor sub,1])_____
  Level 6:  [-][*tag name,i]_____
  Level 7:  _____
  Level 8:  _____
  Level 9:  _____
  Level 10: _____

  Inserts:  [Chapter #] [1,2] [A,B] [a,b] [I,II] [i,ii]

            [Suppress Previous Level] [Text Attr.]
                                          [OK] [Cancel]
```

Chapter

Page Size & Layout...
Chapter Typography...

Update Counters...
Auto-Numbering...
Renumber Chapter   ^B
Re-Anchor Frames...

Headers & Footers...
Turn Header On
Turn Footer On
Footnote Settings...

Insert/Remove Page...
Go to Page...   ^G

For instance, to create the first level for the sample outline shown on the previous page, select the upper case roman numerals ("I, II") box, and the program responds by inserting the bracketed command [*tag name, I] on the "Level 1" blank. Next, use the typing cursor and backspace keys to replace the words "tag name" — but not the asterisk (*) character — with the actual tag name of the highest-level paragraphs you want numbered. In this example, the tag name "Section topic" is used and a period is added just *outside* the right bracket so the section number will end with a period. The completed command will read: [*Section topic, I]. This command tells the program to add the roman numeral "I." before the first occurrence of a paragraph tagged with "Section topic," to add "II." to the next paragraph with that tag, and so on, throughout the entire chapter.

To complete the other levels in this example, move the typing cursor to each level and click on the appropriate option boxes. However, since the numbering scheme in this example only displays one level of numbering with each paragraph, you must first click on the "Suppress Previous Level" option for each of the other levels. This places a bracketed minus sign [-] on the blank, which suppresses the display of the higher levels. Then click on the upper case letters option box for the "Level 2" blank and replace the words "tag name" with the actual tag name of the second highest level paragraphs you want numbered. In this case, the tag name "Major head" is used and a period is again added outside the right bracket. The final command for Level 2 now reads: [*Major head, A]. This command will subsequently create an enumeration of A., B., C., and so forth.

Repeating the same procedure, the options used for the remaining levels in this example are arabic numerals for Level 3, lower case letters for Level 4, and arabic numerals for Level 5. If a number requires a character to proceed the section number, such as the left parenthesis for Level 5, type in the character before inserting the numbering style option. Thus [-]([*Sub-minor subhead, 1]) is the command you would use for Level 5 to create an enumeration style of (1), (2), (3), and so forth.

Two other "Inserts" you can add to any level of section numbering are chapter numbers and text attributes. If you pick the "Chapter #" option box, the bracketed command [C#] is placed on the blank line at the cursor position, and a chapter number is automatically inserted in the section number for that level. If you pick the "Text Attr." option box, the angle-bracketed code <D>, which must be placed outside the numbering style brackets, is placed at the cursor position. You then delete the letter "D" and replace it with a Ventura text attribute code to add bold, italic, and so on, or with a spacing code to add an em space, en space, figure space, or thin space (examples of these codes are shown on the right). You can also replace the letter "D" with a decimal code to add nonkeyboard characters, such as <185> for section marks (§), <187> for daggers (†), and many others. (Note: Ventura text codes are discussed in Chapter 7; decimal codes are discussed in Chapter 4.)

For example, a <185><U>[C#]<196>[*Section topic, I] command would result in a numbering system of §1–I, §1–II, §1–III, §1–IV, and so forth, for paragraphs bearing the "Section topic" tag.

After you fill out the Auto-Numbering dialog box, Ventura adds the section numbers you specify to all paragraphs that are assigned the corresponding tags. To do this, the program automatically generates and attaches a separate tag to each level: "Z_SEC1" for Level 1, "Z_SEC2" for Level 2, "Z_SEC3" for Level 3, and up to "Z_SEC10" for Level 10. Like other generated tags, Z_SEC tags initially share the same attributes as those assigned to the "Body Text" tag, but you can change them by using the Paragraph Tagging mode (described in the "Paragraph Tagging" section in Chapter 4).

Chapter

Page Size & Layout...
Chapter Typography...

Update Counters...
Auto-Numbering...
Renumber Chapter   ^B
Re-Anchor Frames...

Headers & Footers...
Turn Header On
Turn Footer On
Footnote Settings...

Insert/Remove Page...
Go to Page...   ^G

*Text codes
(a partial listing)*

Text attributes
Bold   <B>
Italics   < I >
Overscore   <O>
Resume Normal   <D>
Small   <S>
Strikethrough   <X>
Subscript   <V>
Superscript   <^>
Underline   <U>

Spaces
Em space   <_>
En space   <~>
Figure space   <+>
Thin space   < | >

For example, most "Body Text" tags include a line break after each paragraph, which means the section number itself may initially be placed on the line *above* the paragraph it is supposed to enumerate. However, by selecting the Paragraph menu's Breaks option (discussed in Chapter 6), you can change the "Line Break" setting for each Z_SEC tag from "After" to either "None" or "Above" and place the section number on the same line as the numbered paragraph. Or, to center a section number above the paragraph or place it out in the margin, use the Paragraph menu's Alignment option to establish a center alignment or to create an outdent for each Z_SEC tag.

If the Z_SEC tags don't appear in the assignment list when using Paragraph Tagging, use the Options menu's Set Preferences option and select "Generated Tags: Shown" in the dialog box provided.

As a reminder, the settings you specify in the Auto-Numbering option become part of the current style sheet, which means that Ventura will look for paragraphs bearing the same tag names when assigning automatic section numbers to other chapters. Therefore, if the same tags are not used for automatic numbering in other chapters, save the style sheet under a new name before saving the chapter itself.

As you proceed to edit the text or retag paragraphs, you'll find that the various section numbers do not change automatically. Instead, you must instruct the program to update section numbering for the entire chapter by selecting the Renumber Chapter option, or by using the Ctrl-B (^B) keyboard shortcut. Because this option involves a single-action command, no dialog box or pop-up screen is provided.

Re-Anchoring Frames

The Chapter menu's Re-Anchor Frames option works in conjunction with the Edit menu's Insert Special Item option and the Frame menu's Anchors & Captions option. These options are designed for documents in which illustrations — pictures, tables, and figures — should appear on the same page as any references to them in the text.

In general, you first insert a hidden frame reference, called an *anchor,* in a text file; then, whenever the text moves during editing or document reformatting, you must use the Re-Anchor Frames option to move the illustrations with it. Before you can apply this

Chapter
Page Size & Layout...
Chapter Typography...
Update Counters...
Auto-Numbering...
Renumber Chapter   ^B
Re-Anchor Frames...
Headers & Footers...
Turn Header On
Turn Footer On
Footnote Settings...
Insert/Remove Page...
Go to Page...   ^G

option, however, you must first use the other two anchor-related menu options. In the Text Editing mode, you select the Edit menu's Insert Special Item option to place the anchor name in a text file. In the Frame Setting mode, you use the Frame menu's Anchors & Captions option to assign the same anchor name to a specific frame.

Once an anchor is inserted in the text and assigned to a frame, you can use the Re-Anchor Frames option. When you select this command, the program produces a dialog box (shown below) that allows you to choose if you want to re-anchor frames only on the current page or for the entire chapter. If an anchor name in the text does not match the anchor name given to a frame, an error message appears and you must correct the discrepancy — by using the other anchor-related options — before the re-anchor process can continue.

After the Re-Anchor Frames operation, you'll still need to check the document to see that frames are positioned correctly on the various pages. In some cases, the frames may be moved into the top and bottom margins and you must relocate them manually. (For more information on using frame anchors, see the "Edit Menu" and "Frame Menu" sections in Chapter 6.)

The Re-Anchor Frames dialog box allows you to re-anchor frames a page at a time or re-anchor them for an entire chapter.

```
  ?      Do you wish to re-anchor      ┌──────────────┐
  •      just this page's frames,      │  This Page   │
WAIT     or all page's frames, or      └──────────────┘
         cancel the request?           ┌──────────────┐
                                       │  All Pages   │
                                       └──────────────┘
                                       ┌──────────────┐
                                       │   Cancel     │
                                       └──────────────┘
```

Adding Headers and Footers

With the Headers & Footers option, you can use simple or complex references at the top and bottom of each page of your document. Each header and footer can contain up to three separate entries in three different locations in the header and footer area — left flush, center, and right flush — and each of these entries can occupy two lines. If you pick a double-sided page format, via the Page Size & Layout option, you can also use different headers and footers for left and right pages. If your document uses a single-sided format, the headers/footers for left/right pages will be identical. Finally, with the Turn Header Off/On and Turn Footer Off/On options, you can control the inclusion of each header/footer on a page-by-page basis.

This Headers & Footers dialog box shows how the left page header for this book was created. The <B> is the program's text attribute code for bold, [P#] represents the current page number, <D> resumes normal type (turns bold off), and < I > adds italics to the section title that follows. Since this book uses different left and right headers, however, the "Copy to Facing Page" option is not used.

```
┌──────────────────────────────────────────────────────────────┐
│  HEADERS & FOOTERS                                        [?]  │
│                                                                │
│  Define:  ▐ Left Page Header ▌  │ Right Page Header │          │
│                                                                │
│           │ Left Page Footer │  │ Right Page Footer │          │
│                                                                │
│  Usage:   ▐ On ▌  │ Off │                                      │
│                                                                │
│  Left:    <B>[P#]   <D><I>TAKING  COMMAND_____   │
│                                                                │
│  Center:  _____       │
│                                                                │
│  Right:   _____       │
│                                                                │
│  Inserts: │ Chapter # │  │ Page # │  │ 1st Match │ │ Last Match │ │
│                                                                │
│           │ Text Attr. │  │ Copy To Facing Page │              │
│                                           │ OK │  │ Cancel │    │
└──────────────────────────────────────────────────────────────┘
```

After you select the Headers & Footers option, Ventura provides a dialog box (shown above) that lets you define whether you want to create a header or footer on the left or right page. Click the mouse cursor on the "Define" option box you want and then select the "Usage: On" option. At this point, the blank lines in the dialog box change from gray (unavailable) to black (available) and you can proceed to fill them out in the same way you completed the Auto-Numbering dialog box. That is, as you click the mouse cursor on the "Inserts" option boxes (at the bottom of the dialog box), those options are inserted at the typing cursor position, initially located on the first ("Left") blank line. Or, you can also type the information directly by using the keyboard.

Chapter

Page Size & Layout...
Chapter Typography...

Update Counters...
Auto-Numbering...
Renumber Chapter   ^B
Re-Anchor Frames...

Headers & Footers...
Turn Header On
Turn Footer On
Footnote Settings...

Insert/Remove Page...
Go to Page...   ^G

If you click the mouse cursor on the "Chapter #" and "Page #" option boxes, the bracketed commands [C#] and [P#] are inserted at the typing cursor position and Ventura automatically places the chapter and page numbers in the header or footer you're defining. Or, if you use the Update Counters option to restart the numbering, the program uses those numbers accordingly. To add a text attribute like bold or italic to a header or footer, click on the "Text Attr." option box and the angle-bracketed code <D> is inserted at the typing cursor position. Following the same procedure used with the Auto-Numbering option, you can then delete the letter "D" and replace it with a Ventura text code or decimal code.

The "1st Match" and "Last Match" options provide a unique header and footer feature that is extremely useful for publishing directories, catalogs, inventories, dictionaries, and encyclopedias. This feature is called a *live header* or *live footer* because it changes from page to page. Here's how it works: When you click on the "1st Match" option, the bracketed command [<**tag name**] is inserted on the blank at the typing cursor position, and when you select the "Last Match" option, the command [>**tag name**] is likewise inserted. After you replace the words "tag name" with the name of an actual tag in each bracketed command, Ventura looks for the first and last occurrence of that tag on each page and places the tagged text in the position you've defined in the header or footer.

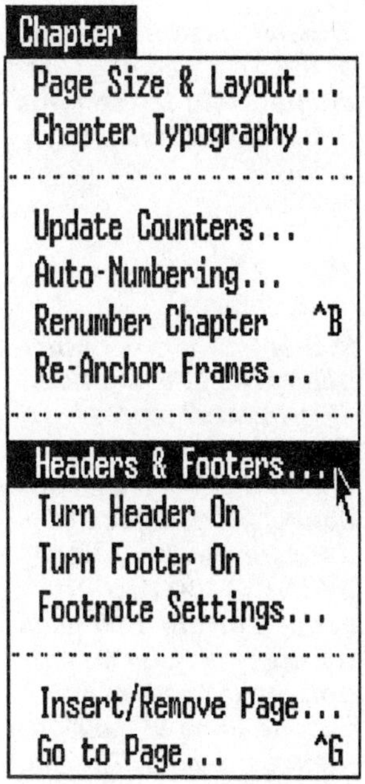

For example, if you used the tag name "Main Entry" as both the "1st Match" and "Last Match" for a bold centered header, separated by a forward slash, the command <**B**>[<**Main Entry**]/[>**Main Entry**] would be entered on the blank line. If you used this command as the live header for a hyphenation dictionary, with the text tagged "Main Entry" consisting of a single word, the first header might read:

aardvark/abrupt

At the end of the dictionary, the header for the last page might read:

zabaglione/zymurgy

As a reference aid to help readers locate information in a telephone directory, inventory list, or parts catalog (with complex entries like AS10-27-64), the ability to create live headers/footers is a big plus.

You can also use more than one set of live headers/footers per page. For instance, you can create two-line headers and footers with different "1st Match" and "Last Match" options on each line. An example of this technique, used for an encyclopedia of fish, is illustrated on the following page. Notice that in addition to the "1st Match" and "Last Match" bracketed commands, several angle-bracketed text codes are also used in the Headers & Footers dialog box illustrated above. For example, the code <**P14**> changes the header point size for that line to 14 points, whereas <**P12**> changes it to 12 points. The code <**B**> sets the type style for that line to bold, whereas <**I**> sets it to italic. Also note that an open and close

---

Chapter

Page Size & Layout...
Chapter Typography...

Update Counters...
Auto-Numbering...
Renumber Chapter   ^B
Re-Anchor Frames...

Headers & Footers...
Turn Header On
Turn Footer On
Footnote Settings...

Insert/Remove Page...
Go to Page...   ^G

The live header at the top of this reduced page was created with the settings in the dialog box shown below.

In this Headers & Footers dialog box, the tag named "Fish Entry" represents the "1st Match" option on line one of the left-justified header, and "Species" is used for the "1st Match" option on line two. The same tags are then used for the two "Last Match" options in the first and second lines of the right-justified header. The page number is used for the centered header.

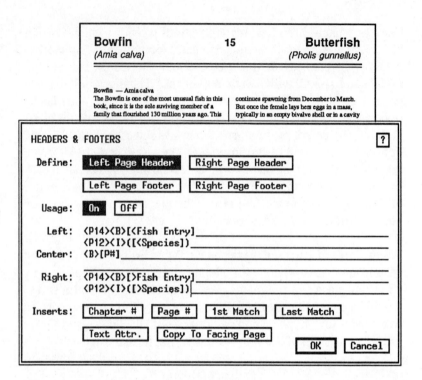

parenthesis have been added before and after the "Species" tag command so the header will appear in parentheses. The reason these codes are entered in the Headers & Footers dialog box is because you can't use the Text Editing function to edit headers or footers, or assign them text attributes with the side-bar's assignment list.

The final "Inserts" option in the Headers & Footers dialog box is "Copy To Facing Page." Unlike the other option boxes, however, selecting this item does not place a command or code at the typing cursor position. Instead, the settings you specify for the header or footer are *reflected* to the opposite page. In other words, a mirror image of those settings is automatically assigned to the alternate left or right page. For example, a left-justified header on a left page becomes a right-justified header on a right page. However, the headers used for this book are not reflected: on the left pages, the page number preceeds the name of the part title; on the right pages, the page number follows the name of the chapter title.

The "Copy To Facing Page" option is an extremely useful feature that also appears in other dialog boxes. In addition to using this feature with headers/footers, you can apply it to margins, columns widths, vertical rules, repeating frames, and spacing indents. In this book, for example, the "Copy To Facing Page" option is used for margins, columns widths, vertical rules, and spacing indents.

After you enable the Headers & Footers option, Ventura displays the headers and footers you defined at the top and bottom of the page in program-generated frames. Although you can't move or resize these frames as you can with frames you add, you can select them and use the Frame menu's Margins & Columns option to adjust the settings as desired.

Headers and footers are also automatically assigned program-generated tags, "Z_HEADER" and "Z_FOOTER," which share the same attributes assigned to the "Body Text" tag. Like other generated tags, however, you can change the settings for these Z_ tags by using the Paragraph Tagging mode (described in Chapter 4's "Paragraph Tagging" section). For example, by using the Paragraph menu's Spacing option, you can modify a header's or footer's "Above" or "Below" space in order to raise or lower it relative to the document text. Or, you can use other Paragraph menu options to add a ruling line above or below a header or footer.

The Turn Header Off and Turn Footer Off options let you remove a header or footer from the current page. These commands are commonly used on the title page of a document. In this book, for instance, the Turn Header Off option is used at the beginning of every chapter. Since both of these options involve a single-action command, no dialog box or pop-up screen is provided. If you want to add a header or footer that was previously removed, simply select the Chapter menu's Turn Header On or Turn Footer On option for that page.

Setting Up Footnotes

Applying Ventura's automatic footnote feature is a two-part process. First, you use the Chapter menu's Footnote Settings option to enable footnoting and establish the format and placement for all footnotes in the chapter. Second, you use the Text Editing function and the Edit menu's Insert Special Item option to insert footnotes in the text on the base page. It's important to note that you can only use the program's footnote feature with a text file placed in the base page frame — not with text placed in the frames you've added.

Chapter

Page Size & Layout...
Chapter Typography...

Update Counters...
Auto-Numbering...
Renumber Chapter   ^B
Re-Anchor Frames...

Headers & Footers...
Turn Header Off
Turn Footer Off
Footnote Settings...

Insert/Remove Page...
Go to Page...   ^G

This Footnote Settings dialog box is set to use the symbols on the "User-Defined Strings" line. The (#) entry on the "Number Template" line will place parentheses around the footnote number at the bottom of the page, for example, (*), (**), and (***). A 1-point ruling line, 18 picas wide (long), will be placed 1.5 (01,06) picas below the last line of text in the document and above the footnotes.

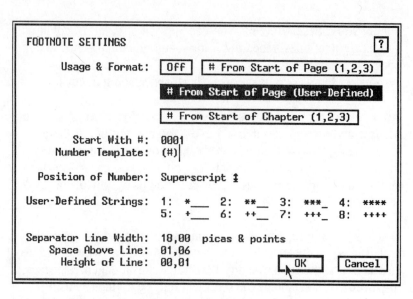

```
FOOTNOTE SETTINGS                                    [?]

    Usage & Format:   [ Off ]  [ # From Start of Page (1,2,3) ]
                               [ # From Start of Page (User-Defined) ]
                               [ # From Start of Chapter (1,2,3) ]

        Start With #:   0001
     Number Template:   (#)

   Position of Number:  Superscript ↕

 User-Defined Strings:  1:  *___   2:  **__   3:  ***_   4:  ****
                        5:  +___   6:  ++__   7:  +++_   8:  ++++

  Separator Line Width: 18,00   picas & points
      Space Above Line: 01,06
        Height of Line: 00,01            [  OK  ]  [ Cancel ]
```

Chapter

Page Size & Layout...
Chapter Typography...

Update Counters...
Auto-Numbering...
Renumber Chapter   ^B
Re-Anchor Frames...

Headers & Footers...
Turn Header On
Turn Footer On
Footnote Settings..

Insert/Remove Page...
Go to Page...   ^G

With the Footnote Settings dialog box (shown above), you control the style for all footnote reference numbers and their vertical position within the text — plus you can add a ruling line above the footnotes at the bottom of the page. To fill out this dialog box, first click the mouse cursor on one of the "Usage & Format" options, which activates the footnote process. To use arabic numbers for the reference number, you can pick either "# From Start of Page (1, 2, 3)" to restart the numbers for each separate page, or "# From Start of Chapter (1, 2, 3)" to continually increase the numbers throughout the entire chapter. If you pick "# From Start of Page (User-Defined)," you can use either the default asterisk and plus symbols provided or type in character strings (up to four characters) of your own choosing for each of the eight footnotes on each page.

As with other Chapter menu numbering options, you can change the starting number for this feature by entering a number other than one ("0001") on the "Start With #" line. You can also attach up to three extra characters to each footnote number at the bottom of the page by typing the additional characters on the "Number Template" line. For example, if you used arabic numbering and entered "10." or "(#)" as the template characters, the first footnote would be displayed as "10.1" or "(1)" respectively. And with the "Position of Number" feature, you can globally raise ("Superscript") or lower ("Subscript") the vertical position of the footnote reference numbers placed in the text itself.

The remaining dialog box options allow you to add a ruling line above the footnotes on each page. First, select the unit of measurement by clicking on the unit displayed after the "Separator Line Width" blank until the measurement system you want to use appears. Then use the keyboard to enter a setting for the line width, that is, the ruling line's length across the page. For example, if the column width for the document text is 6 inches, you would enter 6 (06.00) inches to create a ruling line as wide as the text. The "Space Above Line" controls the amount of space between the last line of document text and the ruling line above the footnotes, and the "Height of Line" enables you to designate the thickness of the ruling line.

After you use the Footnote Settings option and insert footnotes in the text (with the Text Editing function), Ventura automatically generates a footnote frame at the bottom of each page that requires footnotes. The number and length of the footnotes on each page determines the size of the footnote frame for that page; however, this frame cannot occupy more than half of the page, regardless of the length of the footnotes. If Ventura can't fit all of the footnotes inside this frame, it places the overflow on the next page. Although you can't move or resize this frame, you can select it and use the Frame menu's Margins & Columns option to adjust its margin settings (but not the number of columns). For example, if you don't want the footnote text to extend as far across the page as the document text, you can increase the footnote frame's right margin until the text ends where you want it.

Two program-generated paragraph tags are assigned to all footnotes: "Z_FNOT" for the footnote number and "Z_FNOT ENTRY" for the footnote text. As with other generated tags, these Z_ tags are initially given the same settings as those assigned to the "Body Text" tag, but you can change those settings by using the Paragraph Tagging function (described in Chapter 4). For instance, by using the Paragraph menu's Font or Spacing options, you can change a footnote's type size or decrease its "Above" or "Below" space in order to fit more text inside the footnote frame.

As a final reminder, the settings you define in the Footnote Settings dialog box and the attributes you assign to the footnote Z_ tags are all stored as part of the style sheet — not as part of the chapter file. Therefore, always save the style sheet under a new name before you

Chapter
Page Size & Layout...
Chapter Typography...

Update Counters...
Auto-Numbering...
Renumber Chapter   ^B
Re-Anchor Frames...

Headers & Footers...
Turn Header On
Turn Footer On
Footnote Settings..

Insert/Remove Page...
Go to Page...   ^G

Chapter

Page Size & Layout...
Chapter Typography...

Update Counters...
Auto-Numbering...
Renumber Chapter   ^B
Re-Anchor Frames...

Headers & Footers...
Turn Header On
Turn Footer On
Footnote Settings...

Insert/Remove Page...
Go to Page...   ^G

save the chapter if you don't want the same footnote settings and tags to be applied to all other chapters that use the same style sheet.

Adding, Deleting, and Moving About Pages

The last two options in the Chapter menu are particularly important for long documents since they enable you to add or delete pages and move quickly from one part of a chapter to another. As its name implies, the Insert/Remove Page option serves a twofold purpose: you can add a new blank page anywhere in a chapter, or you can reverse that action and remove any page you previously inserted. The Go to Page option, which you can also select with the Ctrl-G (^G) keyboard shortcut, allows you to pick any page in a document or text file and go directly to it.

The Insert/Remove Page dialog box (shown below) offers three operations, all of which are related to the current page (i.e., the page displayed in the side-bar's page box when you select this option). Therefore, if you want to add a page at the end of your document, you must go to the end before selecting the Insert/Remove Page option. When a page is inserted, it takes on the same dimensions and settings as the base page. For example, if you're working on a letter-size page layout, the inserted page will measure 8.5 by 11 inches, using either the portrait (vertical) or landscape (horizontal) page orientation. Or, if you've changed the page frame's dimensions by using the Frame menu's Sizing & Scaling option, the inserted page will incorporate those parameters as well.

A vital point to understand about using this option is how it relates to the pages that Ventura generates when you place a text file on the

The Insert/Remove Page dialog box allows you to add pages to any document or delete pages that were previously inserted. To add or delete several pages in a row, use the Control-X keyboard shortcut to quickly recall the last dialog box without pulling down the menu.

INSERT/REMOVE PAGE   [?]

Operation: | Insert New Page Before Current Page |

| **Insert New Page After Current Page** |

| Remove Current Page |

[OK]   [Cancel]

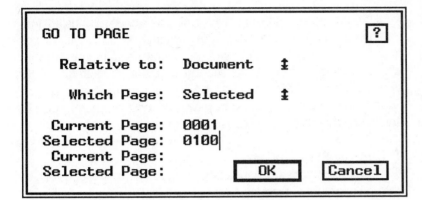

```
┌─────────────────────────────────────────────────┐
│  GO TO PAGE                                  ⌐?¬  │
│                                                   │
│     Relative to:   Document    ↕                  │
│                                                   │
│     Which Page:    Selected    ↕                  │
│                                                   │
│   Current Page:    0001                           │
│   Selected Page:   0100|                          │
│   Current Page:                                   │
│   Selected Page:          ┌──────┐ ┌────────┐     │
│                           │  OK  │ │ Cancel │     │
│                           └──────┘ └────────┘     │
└─────────────────────────────────────────────────┘
```

The Go to Page option box allows you to move quickly from one part of a document to another part. If you want to move to another page of a text file that is already placed in a document, you must first select the frame that contains the text file before using this option.

base page. As explained in the "Frame Setting" section in Chapter 4, when you place a text file on the base page, Ventura adds more pages as necessary to paginate the entire file. Because these additional pages are automatically generated, you cannot remove them by using the Insert/Remove Page option. You can only remove pages that you have manually inserted.

However, if you insert a new page within a series of automatically generated pages, Ventura simply flows the existing text around the inserted page. Even if you place a second text file on a page you insert and the program adds more pages to paginate that file, the first text file will still flow around the second file. This dynamic pagination capability often comes in handy if you need the flexibility to add new sections to an existing document — especially if those sections are being constantly changed, updated, or customized for different versions of the same basic document.

To go directly to a specific page in a document, you can use the dialog box (shown above) provided by the Go to Page option and type in the exact page after the "Selected Page" line. Or, if you select a frame that contains a text file *before* picking the Go to Page option, you can pick the "Relative to: File" option, which is otherwise unavailable (displayed in black rather than gray), and go directly to a specific page that contains that text file after using the "Which Page" pop-up options: First, Previous, Selected, Next, and Last. For example, with a magazine, newsletter, or any publication that contains multiple text files placed across noncontiguous pages, you can use this feature to find the page on which the selected text file continues rather than search for it on a page-by-page basis.

Chapter

Page Size & Layout...
Chapter Typography...

Update Counters...
Auto-Numbering...
Renumber Chapter   ^B
Re-Anchor Frames...

Headers & Footers...
Turn Header On
Turn Footer On
Footnote Settings...

Insert/Remove Page...
Go to Page...

Options Menu

The Options menu lets you set general program operations, including several single-action commands, which serve as hide/show and on/off "switches." Each time you use Ventura, the program applies the settings from the previous session, which it stores in the VP.INF file. Because most of the single-action commands have already been introduced, this section's primary focus is on the other options in this menu that use dialog boxes and item selectors.

Setting the Basic Options

The Set Preferences dialog box (shown below) provides controls for several operational features, some of which affect Ventura's performance speed. For example, if you want the program to draw text faster on screen, select "Text to Greek: All" (greeked text substitutes horizontal lines for text in certain page views) and "On-Screen Kerning: None." Neither setting affects printed output, but they can speed things up a bit. Selecting "Double Click Speed: Fast" ensures the fastest execution time when you click on "OK" in the item selectors. However, if you prefer to click twice on the filename rather than once on "OK," this setting may be too fast.

If you select the "Keep Backup Copies: Yes" option, Ventura creates backup files of the chapter (.CHP), caption (.CAP), style sheet (.STY), graphic (.VGR), and all text files (loaded into the chapter) each time you use the File menu's Save or Save As option after making any changes to a chapter. Backup files are stored in the same location and under the same name as the originals, except that a dollar ($) sign is used as the first character in the filename extension. For

Options

Set Preferences...
Set Ruler...
Set Printer Info...
Add/Remove Fonts...
- - - - - - - - - - - - - - - - - - - -
Hide Side-Bar   ^W
Show Rulers
Show Column Guides
Hide All Pictures
Hide Tabs & Returns ^T
Hide Loose Lines
- - - - - - - - - - - - - - - - - - - -
Turn Column Snap Off
Turn Line Snap Off
- - - - - - - - - - - - - - - - - - - -
Multi-Chapter...

The Set Preferences dialog box uses common default settings, so it isn't necessary to use this option unless desired. The "Text to Greek" and "On-Screen Kerning" settings shown here enable the program to speed up the screen drawing time.

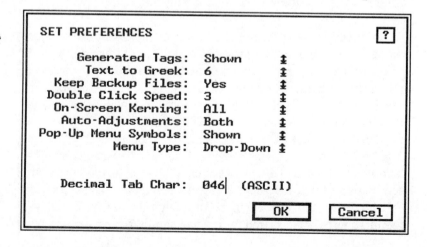

```
SET PREFERENCES                                    [?]

        Generated Tags:   Shown      ↕
         Text to Greek:   6          ↕
     Keep Backup Files:   Yes        ↕
     Double Click Speed:  3          ↕
      On-Screen Kerning:  All        ↕
       Auto-Adjustments:  Both       ↕
    Pop-Up Menu Symbols:  Shown      ↕
             Menu Type:   Drop-Down  ↕


   Decimal Tab Char:  046|  (ASCII)

                           [  OK  ]   [ Cancel ]
```

example, backup files of SALES-89.CHP and SALES-89.DOC would be labeled SALES-89.$HP and SALES-89.$OC. Although backup files require additional disk space and increase the amount of time it takes the program to save a chapter, you might need them if anything happens to the latest version of your chapter. For example, in the event of a power failure or system crash, you could lose the current version of a chapter; but by using the DOS RENAME command to rename the backup files using their original names, you could continue working with the last saved version of the chapter.

Selecting "Generated Tags: Shown" displays the "Z_tags" (for headers, footers, captions, box text, and so on) in the assignment list when the Paragraph Tagging function is active. The default character the program uses as the decimal tab for the Paragraph menu's Tab Settings option is a period (ASCII code 046), but you can change this value to a comma, slash, equal sign, or other character by typing a different numeric value on the "Decimal Tab Character" line.

The "Auto-Adjustments" option lets you turn on two time-saving features: automatic inter-line spacing when a type size changes, and automatic conversion of the quote (") and double dash (--) characters into real typographic quotes and an em dash. Select the "Styles" setting to activate the first option, pick "" and --" to turn on the second option, or choose "Both." If the "Styles" option is not selected, Ventura will not automatically increase or decrease the space between lines of text whenever you change a tag's type size, which provides you with more manual control over line spacing.

With the "Pop-Up Menu Symbols" option, you can choose to hide or show the pop-up menu symbols (double arrows) in all the dialog boxes. Though using this option has no affect on menu operation, you may want to hide the symbols to reduce the screen clutter once you've become proficient at using pop-up menus. With the "Menu Type" option, you can choose whether you want Ventura to use standard GEM-style "Drop-Down" menus or alternative Windows-style "Pull-Down" menus for accessing the program's menus. Drop-down menus pop down and remain on screen whenever the cursor touches the menu bar area, whereas pull-down menus remain on screen only as long as you hold down the mouse button. Frequent user of Windows programs will most likely benefit from being able to customize Ventura's interface with pull-down menus.

Options
Set Preferences...
Set Ruler...
Set Printer Info...
Add/Remove Fonts...
Hide Side-Bar   ^W
Show Rulers
Show Column Guides
Hide All Pictures
Hide Tabs & Returns ^T
Hide Loose Lines
Turn Column Snap Off
Turn Line Snap Off
Multi-Chapter...

With the Set Ruler dialog box, you can set separate units and zero points for the horizontal and vertical rulers. The zero points can also be reset interactively when the rulers are displayed by dragging cross-hairs from the zero point (0,0) box.

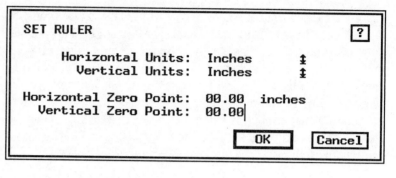

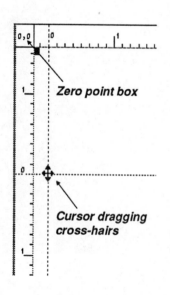

Zero point box

Cursor dragging cross-hairs

Setting the Rulers

The Set Ruler dialog box (shown above) lets you define settings — in inches, centimeters, or picas — for the program's vertical and horizontal rulers, which are displayed on screen when the Show Rulers command is selected. When displayed, a thin hairline moves inside each ruler to accurately show the current cursor position. The use of these rulers is optional, but many users find them helpful when designing the basic page layout, and setting up margins and columns, ruling lines, tab settings, and other measurement-related items.

The default zero point for both rulers is the top-left corner of the page, but you can change these settings at any time. When setting indents or tabs, for instance, it's often easier to determine the exact measurements if you reset the horizontal zero point from the edge of the page to the edge of the column. To change the zero point using the Set Ruler dialog box, simply type in a different numeric value on the appropriate line. To change the zero point with the mouse cursor, click on the zero point box (shown on the left) and hold, then drag the cursor onto the screen and cross-hairs will appear. When you release the mouse button, the zero points will be reset at the cross-hairs location in each ruler.

To change only one of the zero points, click on the zero point box, drag the cursor *inside* the vertical or horizontal ruler to the desired location, and then release the mouse button. To reset the zero point to its original location, just click on the zero point box. You can also use the zero point cross-hairs to check the vertical and horizontal alignment of text and graphics elements, using any page view. Simply drag the cross-hairs onto the screen, check out the alignment, and then move the cursor back to the zero point box before releasing the mouse button.

```
┌──────────────────────────────────────────────────────────────────┐
│ SET PRINTER INFO  (POSTSCRIPT - Ultimate)                    [?]   │
│                                                                    │
│  Device Name:  [AST TURBO]  [HP LJ+, 300dpi]  [POSTSCRIPT] [XEROX 4020] │
│                                                                    │
│                                                                    │
│  Screen Fonts:  EGA│  (Use those matching this file extension.)    │
│                                                                    │
│    Output To:  [LPT1] [LPT2] [LPT3]  [COM1] [COM2]  [Direct] [Filename] │
│                                                                    │
│                                                                    │
│  Width Table:  D:\VENTURA\OUTPUT.WID_____       │
│                                                                    │
│     Command:   [ Load Different Width Table (i.e., Font Metrics) ] │
│                                                                    │
│                                          [ OK ]    [ Cancel ]      │
└──────────────────────────────────────────────────────────────────┘
```

The Set Printer dialog box allows you to change printers (four are installed in this example), width tables, and screen fonts. If you select the "Output To: Filename" option, you can print a single page, chapter, or an entire publication to a file that can then be output on another system, or at a later time.

The Printer and Fonts Options

The Set Printer Info and Add/Remove Fonts options let you print your document on different output devices and control the use of different printer and screen fonts. The information displayed in the dialog boxes used by these options depends on the printer(s) selected when installing Ventura on your computer system.

If you installed the program to run with more than one printer, you can easily switch printers at any time by using the Set Printer Info dialog box (shown above). To do this, click on the "Device Name" option for the printer you want to use and on the "Output To" option that applies. For example, you may have installed an HP LaserJet Plus on a parallel port (LPT1) and a PostScript printer on a serial port (COM2). Or, you can select the "Output To: Filename" option to print a page, chapter, or publication to a file rather than to a printer. This file can be kept on a disk and output later or sent another location, such as a typesetting service bureau.

As a general rule, the filename in the "Width Table" line should match the output device selected. A *width table* is a special file that contains font metric (shape, height, width) information for a specific printer. Ventura uses width tables to print individual characters for various printers and to configure the font-related dialog boxes that display typefaces, type sizes, and styles. For each line, paragraph, and page displayed on screen to match the actual printed output, Ventura must use the width table that matches the output device.

To change the width table, click on the "Command" option and the program provides an item selector, with the width table file filter

```
┌────────────────────────────┐
│          Options           │
│  Set Preferences...        │
│  Set Ruler...              │
│  Set Printer Info...  ▶    │
│  Add/Remove Fonts...       │
│  ..........................│
│  Hide Side-Bar        ^W   │
│  Show Rulers               │
│  Show Column Guides        │
│  Hide All Pictures         │
│  Hide Tabs & Returns  ^T   │
│  Hide Loose Lines          │
│  ..........................│
│  Turn Column Snap Off      │
│  Turn Line Snap Off        │
│  ..........................│
│  Multi-Chapter...          │
└────────────────────────────┘
```

```
┌─────Options─────┐
│ Set Preferences...│
│ Set Ruler...      │
│█Set Printer Info...│
│ Add/Remove Fonts..│  ↖
├∙∙∙∙∙∙∙∙∙∙∙∙∙∙∙∙∙∙∙┤
│ Hide Side-Bar    ^W│
│ Show Rulers       │
│ Show Column Guides│
│ Hide All Pictures │
│ Hide Tabs & Returns ^T│
│ Hide Loose Lines  │
├∙∙∙∙∙∙∙∙∙∙∙∙∙∙∙∙∙∙∙┤
│ Turn Column Snap Off│
│ Turn Line Snap Off│
├∙∙∙∙∙∙∙∙∙∙∙∙∙∙∙∙∙∙∙┤
│ Multi-Chapter...  │
└───────────────────┘
```

(.WID), and displays all of the width tables available in the VENTURA directory. These files include width tables for each installed printer, plus an extra width table called OUTPUT.WID, which initially serves as the default width table in the Set Printer Info dialog box.

The OUTPUT.WID file is a duplicate of the width table for the *first* output device you selected during the installation process. For example, if the first printer you installed is a PostScript printer, the font metric information in the OUTPUT.WID file is identical to the information contained in the POSTSCPT.WID file. The reason the program creates an OUTPUT.WID file is because the width table setting in the Set Printer Info dialog box is saved as part of the style sheet. Thus, when the OUTPUT.WID file is used as the current setting, you can transfer style sheets between systems that use Ventura with different printers and the style sheet will specify the OUTPUT.WID file for each system, which automatically matches the printer. For instance, if you output the sample chapters provided with the program, they should all match your system's printer — without requiring any help on your part — because each of the sample style sheets uses the OUTPUT.WID table in the Set Printer Info dialog box.

Another useful feature provided by the Set Printer Info option is the ability to produce a document on one printer while using the width table for another printer. For example, if you want to print a draft version of a document on an HP LaserJet but intend to print the final version on a PostScript printer, you can use the PostScript width table (POSTSCPT.WID) with the HP LaserJet printer. Although the word spacing on the draft version won't be accurate, the number of characters on each line, paragraph, and page should correctly match the version ultimately printed on the final printer. When the width table matches the selected output device, the word "Ultimate" is displayed after the name of the selected device at the top of the dialog box; otherwise, the word "Draft" is shown.

You can also load and use new screen fonts with Ventura by typing the extension of the screen font files on the "Screen Fonts" line in the Set Printer Info dialog box. First, you must copy the new fonts to the VENTURA directory before starting the program, and all of these fonts must have the same file extension, for example, .PSF for PostScript screen fonts. Consult the "Font Utilities" appendix in the *Ventura Publisher Edition Reference Guide* (supplied with the program) for more information on adding printer and screen fonts, as well as on using the the font conversion utilities provided.

Add/Remove Fonts is the other printer-related option in the Options menu. When selected, this option provides a dialog box (shown below) that displays the current width table and includes three directory lists (for faces, sizes, and styles) and three "Command" options. With this dialog box, you can add or remove printer fonts, and disable automatic downloading for each font. In order to add fonts, you must first copy the new width tables, and usually the fonts, to the VENTURA directory before using the program. Generally, these fonts must be designed for use with the printer you've installed, although you can convert some fonts for use by other printers.

To use the Add/Remove Fonts dialog box, click on the "Save As New Width Table" option and an item selector showing the width tables in the VENTURA directory is provided. By saving the current width table under a new name, you can still use the original file if desired. Next select the "Merge Width Tables" option and use the item selector provided to pick the width table with the new fonts you want to add to the current width table. Click "OK" and the program performs the file-merge operation or displays an error message if the current and merge width tables are intended for different devices.

As soon as the merge is completed, the new combined set of faces, sizes, and styles is displayed in the corresponding directory lists and you can begin using them. If you don't want to use a given face, size, or style displayed in the current width table, select it and then click on the "Remove Selected Font" option. When finished, click on the

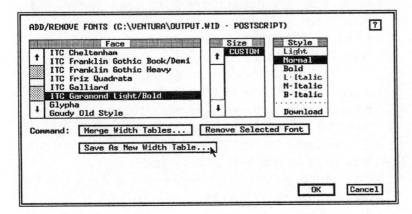

*In this **Add/Remove Fonts** dialog box, the OUTPUT.WID file will be saved under a new name before a new PostScript font is merged. Since the new font will be stored on the hard disk, the "Download" (rather than "Resident") switch will be used.*

```
┌─────────────────────────┐
│ ▐Options▌                │
├─────────────────────────┤
│ Set Preferences...       │
│ Set Ruler...             │
│ Set Printer Info...      │
│ Add/Remove Fonts...      │
│ ┄┄┄┄┄┄┄┄┄┄┄┄┄┄┄┄┄┄┄┄┄┄┄ │
│ Hide Side-Bar       ^W   │
│ Show Rulers              │
│ Show Column Guides       │
│ Hide All Pictures        │
│ Hide Tabs & Returns ^T   │
│ Hide Loose Lines         │
│ ┄┄┄┄┄┄┄┄┄┄┄┄┄┄┄┄┄┄┄┄┄┄┄ │
│ Turn Column Snap Off     │
│ Turn Line Snap Off       │
│ ┄┄┄┄┄┄┄┄┄┄┄┄┄┄┄┄┄┄┄┄┄┄┄ │
│ Multi-Chapter...         │
└─────────────────────────┘
```

"Save As New Width Table" option once again and use the item selector to save the width table under the same or a different name.

Depending on the printer type, printer fonts are either stored on your PC's hard disk or made *resident* in the printer's memory. At print time, Ventura automatically *downloads*, or sends to the printer, the font files stored on the hard disk that are required by the document. The resident or download status for each Ventura font is automatically configured during installation, but you must set this control for the fonts you add by clicking on the word "Download" or "Resident" in the bottom of the "Style" directory list. Select the right combination of "Face," "Size," and "Style" for each font you've added and click on the "Download/Resident" toggle switch to set the proper configuration. For the fonts you've copied onto your PC's hard disk, select the "Download" switch; for the fonts you've permanently installed in the printer (using utilities from the printer manufacturer, prior to running Ventura), select the "Resident" switch.

The Single-Action Commands
The Options menu's single command switches are as follows:

- Hide (Show) Side-Bar — allows more room for a document to be displayed in the work area
- Show (Hide) Rulers — displays the horizontal and vertical rulers above and on the left side of the work area
- Show (Hide) Column Guides — displays the nonprinting dashed lines that can outline up to eight columns on the base page and can be used to help place frames
- Hide (Show) This Picture or Hide (Show) All Pictures — replaces pictures placed in frames with screen tints to speed screen drawing time; at print time, you choose whether to print the actual picture or the screen tint only
- Show (Hide) Tabs & Returns — displays hidden characters (see chart on page 76) when using the Text Editing mode
- Show (Hide) Loose Lines — highlights text (white letters on black bar, or vice versa) if it exceeds the maximum space width setting in the Paragraph Typography option
- Turn Column Snap On (Off) — forces frames to align with the sides of the base page's column guides
- Turn Line Snap On (Off) — forces frames to line up with the inter-line spacing for body text on the base page

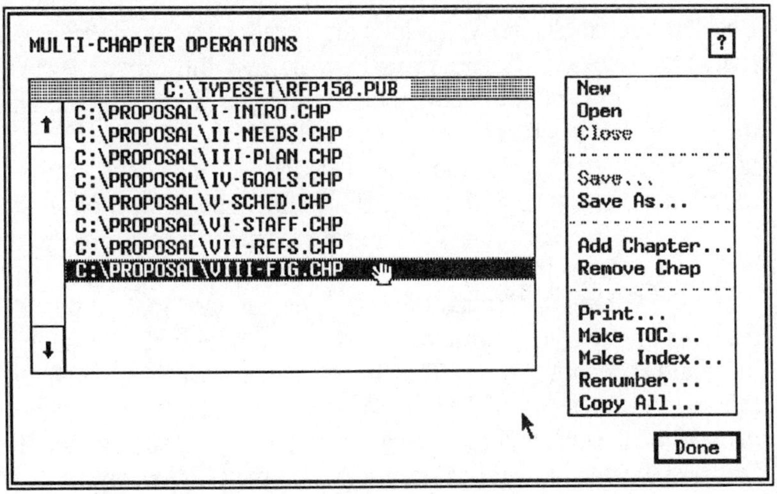
MULTI-CHAPTER OPERATIONS
?
C:\TYPESET\RFP150.PUB
C:\PROPOSAL\I-INTRO.CHP
C:\PROPOSAL\II-NEEDS.CHP
C:\PROPOSAL\III-PLAN.CHP
C:\PROPOSAL\IV-GOALS.CHP
C:\PROPOSAL\V-SCHED.CHP
C:\PROPOSAL\VI-STAFF.CHP
C:\PROPOSAL\VII-REFS.CHP
C:\PROPOSAL\VIII-FIG.CHP
New
Open
Close
Save...
Save As...
Add Chapter...
Remove Chap
Print...
Make TOC...
Make Index...
Renumber...
Copy All...
Done

In this Multi-Chapter Operations dialog box, the order in which the various chapter files for a publication (RFP150.PUB) are listed is rearranged when a selected chapter file is moved to a new location by dragging it with the hand cursor.

Using the Multi-Chapter Option

The Multi-Chapter option in the Options menu provides several of Ventura's most powerful features, including the ability to create a publication (.PUB) file, which is essentially a *list* that can link as many as 128 separate chapter (.CHP) files. Using the Multi-Chapter option, you can also generate a table of contents or an index for an entire publication, and you can create archive copies (usually on floppy disks) of any or all chapter and publication files.

After selecting this option, the program provides the Multi-Chapter Operations dialog box (shown above), which contains two elements: a directory list with title bar and scroll tools, and a menu containing the options available. When you first use this feature, the directory's title bar reads: "C:\TYPESET\UNTITLED.PUB" and only a few options are accessible (shown in black). As you select and use the available options, the other features will also become accessible.

To create a publication, select the "Add Chapter" option and use the item selector provided to pick chapters, one at a time, to add to the publication file you're creating. If you select "New," all existing chapter files are removed from the directory list — but not erased or altered in any way — and you can create a new publication from scratch. If you select "Open," an item selector with the file filter set for .PUB files is provided and you can select an existing publication to load. When a .PUB file is open, the filename appears in the directory list's title bar.

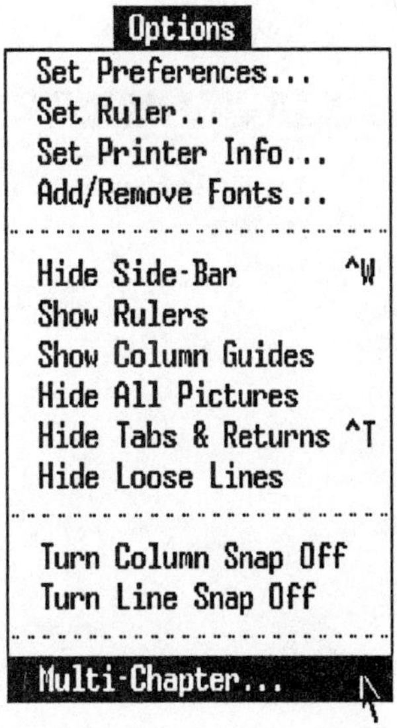
Options
Set Preferences...
Set Ruler...
Set Printer Info...
Add/Remove Fonts...
Hide Side-Bar ^W
Show Rulers
Show Column Guides
Hide All Pictures
Hide Tabs & Returns ^T
Hide Loose Lines
Turn Column Snap Off
Turn Line Snap Off
Multi-Chapter...

Options

Set Preferences...
Set Ruler...
Set Printer Info...
Add/Remove Fonts...

Hide Side-Bar   ^W
Show Rulers
Show Column Guides
Hide All Pictures
Hide Tabs & Returns ^T
Hide Loose Lines

Turn Column Snap Off
Turn Line Snap Off

Multi-Chapter...

New
Open
Close

Save
Save As...

Add Chapter...
Remove Chap

Print...
Make TOC...
Make Index...
Renumber...
Copy All...

Each additional chapter you add is displayed in the directory list in the order selected. If you want to rearrange the order of these chapters, click and hold on the chapter file you want to move, and the cursor changes into the outstretched hand icon. Drag this cursor up or down to the new location you want the selected chapter moved to, release the mouse button, and the chapter file is inserted in the new location, plus the other chapters are rearranged accordingly. To remove a chapter from a publication, click on the chapter title and select the "Remove Chapter" option. You can also look at the file contents of any chapter you've added to the directory list by selecting it and choosing "Open." The chapter title is then displayed in the title bar and the names of the individual files it contains are displayed in the directory list, including style sheet, text, and graphics files. To return to the current publication file, select the "Close" option.

After adding the chapters you want and arranging them in the proper order, select the Multi-Chapter option's "Save As" command and use the item selector provided to save the publication under any name you choose. The publication extension (.PUB) is automatically added. After you create a publication file, you can open it at any time and perform multi-chapter print or copy operations or generate a table of contents or index.

To print an opened publication file, select the Multi-Chapter option's "Print" command and the program provides the same dialog box used for the File menu's To Print option. However, if you're printing the publication to a disk file — by having previously selected the "Output To: Filename" feature in the Set Printer Info dialog box — the "Multi-Chp. Print Files" line (in the Print Information dialog box) is displayed. With the "Multi-Chp. Print Files" feature, you choose whether you want to print the entire publication as a single file or as several separate files. If you choose "Combined," the entire publication is printed into one big file, under the name you specify, and automatically assigned the .C00 extension; but if you choose "Separate," each chapter is saved under the same name but with a different extension (.C00, .C01, .C02, etc.) for each chapter.

Multi-Chapter Operations

To archive a publication or chapter file, select the "Copy All" option and the program provides an additional dialog box (shown on following page) that displays the *source* (publication or chapter) file

```
┌──────────────────────────────────────────────────────┐
│ ┌────────────────────────────────────────────────┐   │
│ │ COPY ALL                                    [?]  │   │
│ │                                                  │   │
│ │                 SOURCE (from this file)          │   │
│ │                                                  │   │
│ │   PUB or CHP:  D:\TYPESET\REFERENC.CHP_____   │   │
│ │                                                  │   │
│ │                                                  │   │
│ │             DESTINATION (to these directories)   │   │
│ │                                                  │   │
│ │   PUB & CHPs:  A:\REFPUB89_____      │   │
│ │   STYs & WIDs: A:\REFPUB89_____      │   │
│ │    Text Files: A:\REFPUB89_____      │   │
│ │ Graphic Files: A:\REFPUB89_____      │   │
│ │   Image Files: A:\REFPUB89_____      │   │
│ │                                                  │   │
│ │     Command:  │Make All Directories the Same As the First│ │
│ │                                                  │   │
│ │                          ┌────┐   ┌────────┐     │   │
│ │                          │ OK │   │ Cancel │     │   │
│ │                          └────┘   └────────┘     │   │
│ └────────────────────────────────────────────────┘   │
└──────────────────────────────────────────────────────┘
```

The Copy All dialog box appears after you select "Copy All" in the dialog box for Multi-Chapter Operations. With this tool, you can archive a chapter or an entire publication to another location, such as floppy disks. As shown here, the source file (REFERENC.CHP) is ready to be copied to a directory (REFPUB89) on a disk in drive A.

in the first line and provides blank lines for specifying the *destination* of the source file's component files. If the destination is drive A, you can type "A:\" on the first blank, click on the "Make All Directories the Same As the First" option, and "A:\" is automatically placed on the other destination lines for you. Or, if the source is located in drive A, you would need to specify your hard disk or another floppy disk drive as the destination. As an added convenience, you can also copy a chapter's or publication's component files to different directories, by simply typing different destinations on the blanks provided for .PUB and .CHP files, .STY and .WID files, text files, graphic (draw program) files, and image (paint program or scanner) files. Select "OK" and Ventura copies all of the files associated with the source file to the destination(s) indicated.

When copying files on a floppy disk, Ventura prompts you if all the component files won't fit on the disk. This enables you to use additional disks, as necessary, to complete the copying process. When you reverse this procedure and copy a source file archived on several disks back to Ventura, the program prompts you with a message indicating that it cannot find a referenced file, which is your cue to insert the next disk(s) to continue the copying process.

Contents and Index Generation

To create a table of contents (TOC) for the current publication in the Multi-Chapter dialog box, select the "Make TOC" option. Ventura

```
┌────────────────────┐
│ New                │
│ Open               │
│ Close              │
│ . . . . . . . . .  │
│ Save               │
│ Save As...         │
│ . . . . . . . . .  │
│ Add Chapter...     │
│ Remove Chap        │
│ . . . . . . . . .  │
│ Print...           │
│ Make TOC...        │
│ Make Index...      │
│ Renumber...        │
│ ██Copy All...██    │
└────────────────────┘
```

```
New
Open
Close
. . . . . . . . . . . . . .
Save
Save As...
. . . . . . . . . . . . . .
Add Chapter...
Remove Chap
. . . . . . . . . . . . . .
Print...
Make TOC...
Make Index...
Renumber...
Copy All...
```

responds by providing the Generate Table of Contents dialog box (shown below), which allows you to assign paragraph tags to the 10 levels of contents available. The "TOC File" line indicates the name of the text file that will be generated, which is the name of the current publication with the last three letters and extension changed to TOC.GEN. The "Title String" line shows the title that will appear on the first page of the TOC file. If necessary, you can edit these lines.

Filling out the other blank lines for the Table of Contents dialog box is similar to using the Chapter menu's Auto-Numbering option (described earlier in this chapter). At the bottom are five options that represent the various "Inserts" available for each level. If you select one of these options, it is immediately inserted at the typing cursor position, initially located on the "Level 1" line. For example, select the "Tag Text" option and Ventura inserts the bracketed command [*tag name] for "Level 1." Using the keyboard, you can then replace the words "tag name" (but not the asterisk *) with an actual tag name, such as "Chapter Title." Repeat this process and enter tag names for all the other levels you want to use. Select the "Tab" option to insert a tab character (represented by an arrow), or pick the "Chapter #" or "Page #" options to insert the bracketed command [C#] or [P#] on the line, which instructs Ventura to insert the page or chapter number for that level when it generates the TOC file. When the "Text Attr." option is selected, the angle-bracketed code <D> is inserted, and you can then replace the letter "D" with a Ventura text attribute code, spacing code, or decimal code to add nonkeyboard characters.

The settings in this Table of Contents dialog box produced the Table of Contents for this book. For the first two levels, two tag names are used so that part and chapter numbers appear on the same line as the part and chapter titles.

```
GENERATE TABLE OF CONTENTS                                    [?]

      TOC File:  C:\VP-BOOK\VP-BKTOC.GEN_____
   Title String: Table of Contents_____
       Level 1:  <B>[*Part #]→[*Part Title]_____
       Level 2:  <B>[*Chapter #]→[*Chapter Title]→[P#]_____
       Level 3:  [*Major Subhead]→[P#]_____
       Level 4:  [*Minor Subhead]→[P#]_____
       Level 5:  _____
       Level 6:  _____
       Level 7:  _____
       Level 8:  _____
       Level 9:  _____
       Level 10: _____

       Inserts:  [ Tag Text ]  [ Tab ]  [ Chapter # ]  [ Page # ]

                 [ Text Attr. ]                        [ OK ]  [ Cancel ]
```

```
┌──────────────────────────────────────────────────────────┐
│ GENERATE INDEX                                        [?]  │
│                                                            │
│     Index File:  C:\TYPESET\REFERIDX.GEN_____   │
│                                                            │
│    Title String: Index_____   │
│                                                            │
│  Letter Headings: On      ‡                                │
│                                                            │
│       Before #s:  ↓|_____  │
│      For Each #:  [C#]-[P#] - [C#]-[P#]_____   │
│     Between #s:   ,_____ │
│       After #s:   _____   │
│         "See ":   See _____  │
│     "See Also":   See also _____  │
│                                                            │
│        Inserts:  [ Tab ] [ Chapter # ] [ Page # ] [ Text Attr. ] │
│                                                            │
│                              [  OK  ]  [ Cancel ]          │
└──────────────────────────────────────────────────────────┘
```

Using the default settings in the Generate Index dialog box, both chapter and page numbers are used for each reference (e.g., 2-10 - 2-15) and they are separated from each index entry by one horizontal tab, as shown in the "Before #s" line. The "Between #s" line places a comma and a space between each numbered reference (e.g., 2-10 - 2-15, 3-20, 3-25, 4-10 - 4-12).

Using the Multi-Chapter option to generate an index for the current publication is similar to creating the TOC file. After you select the "Make Index" option, the program provides the Generate Index dialog box (shown above), which you use to create an index based on references inserted in the text with the Edit menu's Insert Special Item option (discussed in Chapter 6). The "Index File" line indicates the name of the text file that will be generated, which is the name of the current publication with the last three letters and extension changed to IDX.GEN. The "Title String" line shows the actual title that will appear at the top of the first page of the index file. If desired, you can edit either of these lines.

When the "Letter Headings: On" option is enabled, each group of index entries sorted under a different letter of the alphabet will use that letter as a heading (A, B, C, etc.). The rest of the box contains default settings that you can use or modify. The term "#s" refers to the page references for each entry. For an example of an index made with all the default settings except the "Before #s" tab, look at the index in the *Ventura Publisher Edition Reference Guide*.

```
┌──────────────────┐
│ New              │
│ Open             │
│ Close            │
│ . . . . . . . .  │
│ Save             │
│ Save As...       │
│ . . . . . . . .  │
│ Add Chapter...   │
│ Remove Chap      │
│ . . . . . . . .  │
│ Print...         │
│ Make TOC...      │
│ Make Index..  ▓  │
│ Renumber...    ▨ │
│ Copy All...      │
└──────────────────┘
```

To change the default settings for any of these lines, apply the same procedure used with the Generate Table of Contents option. Select an "Inserts" option to place that item at the typing cursor position, initially located on the "Before #s" line. If you don't want the chapter number to appear in the index, delete the [C#] command (and the

Options

Set Preferences...
Set Ruler...
Set Printer Info...
Add/Remove Fonts...

Hide Side-Bar   ^W
Show Rulers
Show Column Guides
Hide All Pictures
Hide Tabs & Returns ^T
Hide Loose Lines

Turn Column Snap Off
Turn Line Snap Off

Multi-Chapter...

extra hyphens) in the "For Each #" line. The "See" and "See Also" lines display the text that will be placed before the reference (if related references are used). If you prefer, however, you can edit the default text and use different wording for such related references.

After you select "OK" in the Generate Table of Contents or Generate Index dialog boxes, Ventura loads each chapter and extracts all information required to generate the TOC or index file. To save the settings in these dialog boxes so you can reuse them, save the publication file before leaving the Multi-Chapter dialog box.

To load the resulting TOC or index text files into the program, use the File menu's Load Text/Picture dialog box and select the "Text Format: Generated" option, which automatically uses the .GEN file filter extension. After loading either of these files, you can place them in a document and format them as you would with any other text file. Each paragraph in a TOC or index file is automatically assigned a program-generated tag name — "Z_TOC TITLE," "Z_TOC LVL 1," "Z_TOC LVL 2," "Z_TOC LVL 3," and so forth for the TOC file; and "Z_INDEX TITLE," "Z_INDEX MAIN," and "Z_INDEX LTR" for the index file. Like other generated tags, these Z_ tags initially share the same attributes as those assigned to the "Body Text" tag, but you can change them by using the Paragraph Tagging function. Finally, you can also use the Text Editing mode to add or delete text in the TOC or index files. However, any changes you make will only be saved in the generated text file, not in the original chapter text files.

The Renumber option in the Multi-Chapter dialog box lets you renumber the chapter, page, table, and figure numbers across different chapters in publications that use consecutive numbering systems, such as books and technical volumes. The Renumber option works with the Update Counters option in the Chapter menu.

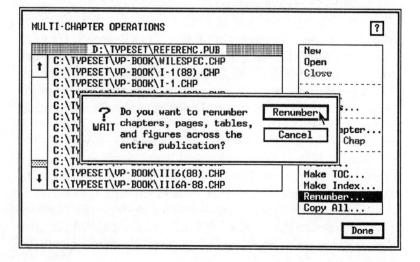

MULTI-CHAPTER OPERATIONS   [?]

D:\TYPESET\REFERENC.PUB
C:\TYPESET\VP-BOOK\WILESPEC.CHP
C:\TYPESET\VP-BOOK\I-1(88).CHP
C:\TYPESET\VP-BOOK\I-1.CHP
C:\TY
C:\TY
C:\TY
C:\TY
C:\TY
C:\TY
C:\TY
C:\TYPESET\VP-BOOK\III6(88).CHP
C:\TYPESET\VP-BOOK\III6A-88.CHP

New
Open
Close

? WAIT Do you want to renumber chapters, pages, tables, and figures across the entire publication?   [Renumber] [Cancel]

Make TOC...
Make Index...
Renumber...
Copy All...

[Done]

Chapter 6

Applying the Function Menus

*O*ne of the most creative aspects of working with a desktop publishing program as versatile and sophisticated as Ventura is the number of different approaches you can use to produce a document. For instance, one publishing group will carefully prepare and copy edit all text files before using the program, while another team will start a job with drafted copy and apply "on-the-fly" editing, as needed, using the program's text editor. With other publishing efforts, the first task is to use Ventura to create a layout design and produce a variety of sample pages, then determine how much or what kind of text and graphics elements will be required.

Different types of publications also call for varied work approaches. Publishing an in-house newsletter, for example, usually involves less stringent demands than producing an annual report or a business plan, which often requires an extensive review and approval process. Or, if you use Ventura to produce a newspaper, magazine, or other deadline-driven publication, your approach to getting the job done may be markedly different than the methods used by those who are publishing books and technical manuals. Some businesses may choose to use one of the sample Ventura chapters provided for various types of documents, replace the example files with their own files, make minor adjustments, and print the results.

However, regardless of the modus operandi you choose to use in producing your business publications, your success in working with Ventura on a day-to-day basis depends largely on how well you've mastered the program's four operating functions: Text Editing, Frame Setting, Paragraph Tagging, and Graphic Drawing. Although all of these functions have been discussed in earlier chapters, the real power of each function can be found in its associated menu.

In the following sections, each of the four function-related menus is presented and each menu option is discussed. As you read about the various options and program features, you may want to view them on your screen. Remember that if a menu option is displayed in gray rather than black, it is not available at that particular juncture; in order to access that option, you must first select the corresponding function or a function element, such as a frame, a block of text, a paragraph, or a graphic object that you've drawn.

As you use the function menus, you'll find that almost every menu option leads to a dialog box — only the Edit and Graphic menus provide single-action commands as well. Finally, all of the paragraph settings you define by using the Paragraph menu and all of the base page settings you define using the Frame menu are stored as part of the current style sheet.

Edit Menu

Ventura's Edit menu provides seven options, some of which you will use regularly and others which you will probably use less frequently, depending largely on the type of document being produced. The first three options control the cut-copy-paste operations, which make use of a data buffer, commonly called a *clipboard*. As a general rule, you'll probably use the clipboard fairly often during a typical Ventura session.

Edit	
Cut Text	Del
Copy Text	↑Del
Paste Text	Ins
Ins Special Item...	^C
Edit Special Item...	^D
Remove Text/File...	
File Type/Rename...	

The next two options enable you to insert and edit special items, which include box characters, footnotes, index entries, fractions, frame anchors, and cross references, in a document's text. These options are only available when the Text Editing function is active, and footnotes can only be used with text placed on the base page. Although each of these options is designed to help accelerate the task of producing certain types of documents, they represent specialized features and are not required to use the program.

The final options in the Edit menu are used to remove imported files from frames or from the assignment list, and to rename text files or change a text file from one word processing format to another. These options are only available when the Frame Setting or Graphic Drawing functions are active, and they are generally used after first selecting a frame whose contents you want the option to affect.

The Cut, Copy, and Paste Options

Since the use of the cut-copy-paste options, or clipboard, is covered in the "Frame Setting," "Text Editing," and "Graphic Drawing" sections in Chapter 4, the focus here is on how these three functions share the clipboard simultaneously.

Ventura's clipboard can be used to cut, copy, and paste three different types of elements — frames, text, and graphic objects — rather than a single element, from one location to another. In other words, you can place and keep copies of frames, text, and graphic objects in Ventura's clipboard without any loss of information or conflict between these different types of elements. Although you won't actually see a clipboard when using Ventura, the illustration below is provided to help show how this offscreen buffer works.

Edit	
Cut Text	Del
Copy Text	↑Del
Paste Text	Ins
Ins Special Item...	^C
Edit Special Item...	^D
Remove Text/File...	
File Type/Rename...	

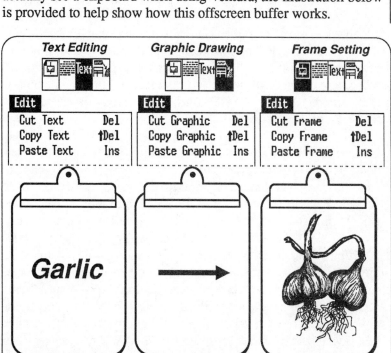

With Ventura's Edit menu, you can cut, copy, and paste text, graphic objects, and frames (empty or filled with text or graphics files) in separate operations, as if the program used three (offscreen) clipboards. Paragraph Tagging is the only mode that doesn't make use of the cut, copy, and paste options.

The type of element you can cut, copy, or paste is determined by which mode is active, and the word "Text," "Frame," or "Graphic" is displayed in the Edit menu accordingly. For example, you cannot cut or copy a text element when the Frame Setting or Graphic Drawing function is active or paste a frame when the Text Editing or Graphic Drawing function is active, and so forth.

Once a copy of a frame is sent to the clipboard, it remains there until you replace it with a copy of a different frame. Even after you paste the frame back on a page, a "master" copy of the frame remains in the clipboard's memory. Likewise, copies of text or graphic objects also remain on the clipboard until you copy a different text block or graphic object. This makes it easy to paste multiple copies of the same element on the same page or other pages throughout a document. If you copy a frame that contains a picture — either a loaded line-art or image file — everytime you paste a copy of the frame it will contain the same picture. If you copy a frame that contains a loaded text file, however, each frame is linked to the other frames containing the same file, and each successive frame will contain the remaining text until all of the text is placed within the document.

```
Edit
┌─────────────────────────────┐
│ Cut Text              Del   │
│ Copy Text            ↑Del   │
│ Paste Text            Ins   │
│ ........................... │
│ Ins Special Item...    ^C   │
│ Edit Special Item...   ^D   │
│ ........................... │
│ Remove Text/File...         │
│ File Type/Rename...         │
└─────────────────────────────┘
```

When you paste a copy of an element on a page, the location where it will be inserted depends on whether it is a block of text, frame, or graphic object. As the following discussion explains, text is pasted wherever you insert the text cursor, but frames and graphic objects are inserted in the same location on the page that they appeared *prior* to the cut or copy operation.

With text, Ventura lets you use the clipboard to paste a single character or block of text in much the same way a word processor uses block copy commands to move text. First, select the text to be copied, then move the cursor to the location in the file where you want to place the text, and finally use the Paste Text option (or press the Insert key) to insert it. With Ventura, you can not only insert text in different frames on other pages, but also in frames that contain different text files. For example, if your document includes articles from various word processors, you can copy text from a frame containing a Microsoft Word file and place it in a frame containing a WordStar, WordPerfect, or other text file format. Better yet, when you save the chapter, any text pasted in another file is saved as part of that text file and in that file's native format.

With frames and graphic objects, Ventura's paste operation works differently. If you use the Paste Frame or Paste Graphic option to paste a copy of a frame or graphic object on the same page, it is inserted directly on top of the original. You can then move the copy off of the original and place it where you want. However, if you paste a copy of a frame or graphic object on a different page, it is inserted in the same location on the new page that it occupied on the old page.

Because the graphic objects created with the Graphic Drawing mode are attached to frames (as explained in Chapter 4), they are copied to the clipboard along with the frames. This feature is particularly handy if your document calls for the repeated use of diagram words, arrows, and boxes because you can easily copy a group of graphic objects from one location to another using the clipboard. Either copy the frame to which the graphic objects are attached, or just copy the graphic objects. If you copy the graphic objects only, however, you must select a frame to which the objects can be attached on the target page before using the Paste Graphic option.

Likewise, if you use the Anchors & Captions option in the Frame menu to attach captions to a frame, the captions are also conveniently copied to the clipboard along with the frames. Better still, if you use the Chapter menu's Update Counters option to number the captions (e.g., Tables A, B, C or Figures 1, 2, 3), the program will update the caption numbers whenever the frames they are attached to are moved to other locations in a chapter.

When using the clipboard with the Text Editing function, you can also copy hidden text attributes, such as font specification, non-keyboard characters, kerning information, and so on. However, you cannot click on the Cut Text, Copy Text, or Paste Text options to do so; you must instead use each option's keyboard shortcut. In other words, you must use the Delete key to cut, the Shift and Delete key combination to copy, and the Insert key to paste text attributes from one location to another. Also, since text attributes are not displayed on the screen, you must rely on the current selection box in side-bar, which will read "Attr. Setting" whenever the cursor is positioned on these hidden characters in the text.

A final point about using the cut-copy-paste options with any of the four functions is that the elements copied to the clipboard remain

Edit	
Cut Text	Del
Copy Text	↑Del
Paste Text	Ins
Ins Special Item...	^C
Edit Special Item...	^D
Remove Text/File...	
File Type/Rename...	

there until they are replaced by new copies of each element — frames, text, and graphic objects — or until you quit using Ventura. Even after you load another chapter, the clipboard's contents will remain intact and can be pasted in another document. This feature is extremely useful since it provides you with a means of copying work from one chapter to another. For example, the clipboard illustration used earlier in this chapter consists of graphic objects (created with the Graphic Drawing tools) that are attached to a frame. By copying this frame to the clipboard and then loading a new chapter, the same illustration can be pasted into other chapters.

Inserting Special Items

The next two options in the Edit menu provide you with access to what Ventura refers to as "special items," which is a catchall term that covers several distinct and useful operations. If your publications require such references as footnotes, indexes, and illustrations that need to be linked to specific portions of the text, you can plan on using this menu option a lot.

After you select the Insert Special Item option, Ventura displays a small pop-up submenu (shown on the left) that lists all of the specific items available. To proceed, either click on the name of the submenu item you want to insert in the text or select the designated keyboard shortcut (function keys F1–F6). In brief, these special item options provide the following features:

- The Box Character option (F1) inserts a hollow or filled box (like a ballot box) in a text file
- The Footnote option (F2) puts footnote references in a text file and adds footnotes at the bottom of the base page
- The Index Entry option (F3) puts index references in a text file
- The Fraction option (F4) inserts a true fraction in a text file
- The Frame Anchor option (F5) puts frame references in a text file to keep frames linked to selected text
- The Cross Reference option (F6) places references to the current page or chapter number in a text file

In order to use these special item options, the Text Editing function must be active and the text cursor must first be inserted in the text. In some cases, you must also use options in other menus to initially activate these features.

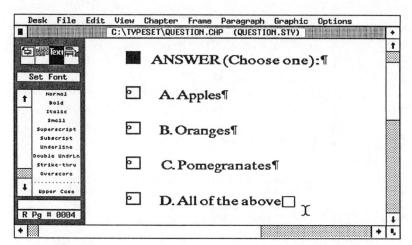

The Edit menu's Insert Special Character option includes a command that lets you insert a hollow or filled box in a text file. If the Show Tabs & Returns command is active, a degree symbol is also displayed in the text (but is not printed) to flag the location of the special item.

The easiest special item to insert is a square box, commonly used on surveys, lists, and other forms. After you select the Insert Box Character option, Ventura provides a simple dialog box that offers a choice between a hollow or filled box. Click on the box type you want and the character is immediately inserted in the text at the selected location. You can also use the Text Editing mode's Set Font button and Font Setting for Selected Text dialog box to alter the size of the box or its horizontal (kern) and vertical (shift) position.

Box Char...	F1
Footnote	F2
Index Entry...	F3
Fraction...	F4
Frame Anchor...	F5
Cross Ref...	F6

Before you can use the Insert/Footnote option, you must first select the Footnote Settings option in the Chapter menu (discussed in Chapter 5) and fill out the dialog box provided in order to activate the footnote formatting feature. The other requirement for using the Insert Footnote option is that footnotes can only be inserted in text that is placed on the base page. That means if you're publishing a document that doesn't use the base page frame to hold text, such as a newsletter in which the text is placed in added frames or in box text, you won't be able to use the footnote feature.

To place a footnote in a text file, move the text cursor where you want the footnote reference to appear, pull down the Edit menu, and select the Insert Footnote option. As soon as you click on this option, Ventura performs two actions. First, it inserts the appropriate number, symbol, or footnote character you've defined in the Footnote Settings dialog box and displays the word "Footnote" in the current selection box. (If the Show Tabs & Returns option in the Options menu is active, you will also see a degree symbol inserted in the text

Box Char...	F1
Footnote	F2
Index Entry...	F3
Fraction...	F4
Frame Anchor...	F5
Cross Ref...	F6

*When you use the Insert
Footnote option in the
Edit menu, Ventura auto-
matically inserts a foot-
note character in the text
at the current cursor position and places the words
"Text of Footnote" at the
bottom of the page.*

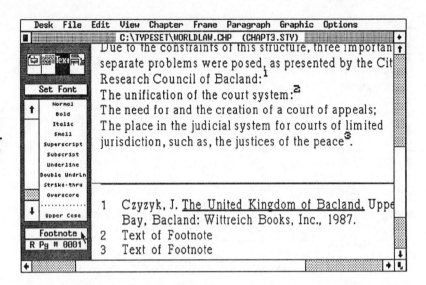

Box Char...	F1
Footnote	**F2**
Index Entry...	F3
Fraction...	F4
Frame Anchor...	F5
Cross Ref...	F6

Box Char...	F1
Footnote	F2
Index Entry...	**F3**
Fraction...	F4
Frame Anchor...	F5
Cross Ref...	F6

that indicates a footnote reference.) Second, Ventura places the footnote reference and the words "Text of Footnote" in a frame at the bottom of the page (as shown above). You can then delete the words and type the desired footnote text. Or, if the text of the footnote is already included elsewhere in the text file (at the end of the document, for example), you can use the clipboard to move the appropriate text to the footnote reference frame.

As you insert additional footnotes, the frame at the bottom of the page is automatically enlarged; however, this frame cannot exceed more than half of the page, regardless of the length of the footnotes. If you need to add a lengthy footnote or place a number of footnotes on a single page, turn off the Footnote Settings option and manually add the footnotes and footnote reference frames as needed. A final point regarding footnotes is that Ventura automatically assigns a "Z_FNOT #" tag to all footnote numbers and a "Z_FNOT ENTRY" tag to all footnote text. Although the default type specifications for both of these tags is the same as the "Body Text" tag, you can use the Paragraph Tagging function to change the attributes of footnote numbers and text to create different formatting effects.

The Insert Index Extry option is similar to the Insert Footnote option in that it enables you to place reference information in a text file during the layout process. The actual index entries are not displayed on the screen but are stored within the text file when you save the chapter. (If the Show Tabs & Returns option in the Options menu is active, you will see a degree symbol inserted in the text that indicates an index entry.) After you finish inserting all index entries, you can use the program's Multi-Chapter option in the Options menu to extract the entries in one or more chapters and generate an index as a separate file. This program-generated file lists all of the index entries under each letter heading, in alphabetical order, along with the page numbers on which they appear, and it can be loaded, edited, formatted, and printed like any other text file.

To place an index entry in a text file, insert the text cursor in front of the text you want to index, pull down the Edit menu, and select the Insert Special Item/Index Entry option. The program responds by providing a dialog box (shown below) that you use to assign an entry type — "Index," "See," or "See Also" — and up to two levels of entry headings, including an optional sort key for either level. Type major headings in the "Primary Entry" blank and minor headings in the "Secondary Entry" blank. For example, an index for a cookbook might include a major heading for "Shellfish" and minor headings for each individual shellfish recipe. These entries can be 45 characters long. Because Ventura sorts index entries alphabetically, you can assign special sort keys — "Primary Sort Key" and "Secondary Sort Key" — for each heading to ensure that certain entries, such as those beginning with numbers or articles (e.g., a, an, the), are properly located in the index. For example, in the cookbook index, the word "Seven" is used as the sort key for a shellfish recipe called "7 Seas Shellfish."

Each index entry you insert generates a reference for that page only. Therefore, if the item you're referencing is discussed on consecutive

```
+------------------------------------------------+
| INSERT/EDIT INDEX ENTRY                    [?] |
|                                                |
|    Type of Entry:  Index      ↕                |
|                                                |
|   Primary Entry:  Shellfish_____ |
|  Primary Sort Key:  _____ |
|                                                |
|  Secondary Entry:  7 Seas Shellfish_____ |
| Secondary Sort Key:  Seven_____ |
|                              [ OK ]  [Cancel]  |
+------------------------------------------------+
```

Box Char... F1
Footnote F2
Index Entry... F3
Fraction... F4
Frame Anchor... F5
Cross Ref... F6

The Insert/Edit Index Entry dialog box enables you to create two levels of index entries and special sort keys. As shown here, a sort key ("Seven") is added so an index entry beginning with a number ("7") will be listed in alphabetical order.

Shellfish
Crab Louis, 121
Crawfish Pie, 123-124
Lobster Newburg, 134
Scallops with Pine Nuts, 164
7 Seas Shellfish, 170-172
Shrimp Creole, 167-168
See also Fish

An example of part of an index for a cookbook created with Ventura. Some entries show consecutive pages.

Box Char...	F1
Footnote	F2
Index Entry...	F3
Fraction...	F4
Frame Anchor...	F5
Cross Ref...	F6

pages, you must insert the same index entry on each page in order for Ventura to list the starting and ending pages for that item. To reference an item that appears on pages 170 through 172, for instance, it is necessary to insert the same index entry on three separate pages. Since the entry itself is hidden in the text, however, you can insert it anywhere on each consecutive page, including the headers and footers text. "See" and "See Also" are two other types of index entries you can use to insert cross-reference items, which are also sorted alphabetically but without page numbers. When you use the Multi-Chapter option to generate the index, the program automatically adds the words "See" or "See Also" before the index entry, or any other text you designate.

You can also edit index entries by placing the text cursor at the location of the entry and selecting the Edit Special Item option, which produces the dialog box with the current index entry. When the cursor is at the insertion location, "Index Entry," "Index-See," or "Index-SeeAlso" is displayed in the side-bar's current selection box, which is helpful since you may have inserted a series of related entries in the same location. You can also delete the index entry at the cursor location by simply pressing the Delete key.

To ensure that this "See Also" index entry appears at the end of the major heading ("Shellfish") in the example at the top of the page, "ZZZ" is used as the sort key.

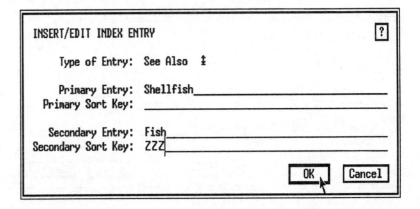

INSERT/EDIT INDEX ENTRY   ?

        Type of Entry: See Also ↕

      Primary Entry: Shellfish_____
      Primary Sort Key: _____

    Secondary Entry: Fish_____
    Secondary Sort Key: ZZZ_____

                                              OK   Cancel

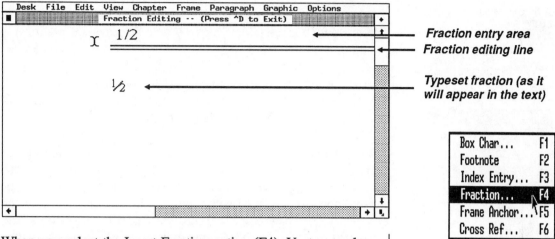

Fraction entry area

Fraction editing line

Typeset fraction (as it will appear in the text)

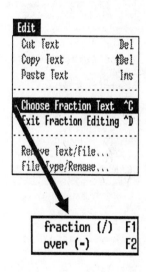

When you select the Insert Fraction option (F4), Ventura replaces the work area and side-bar with a blank screen (shown above) that displays "Fraction Editing" in the title bar and can be used in any page view (enlarged, normal, and so on). Using the keyboard, you can now type a fraction on the double line in the top part of the screen, and within seconds the typeset result appears in the area below the line. If you select the Choose Fraction Text option in the Edit menu or use the Ctrl-C (^C) keyboard shortcut, Ventura provides a pop-up menu that shows the two types of fraction bars (i.e., the line separating the numerator from the denominator) you can use. For instance, to produce ½ select the fraction (/) option (or press F1), and to produce $\frac{1}{2}$ select the over (-) option (or press F2). The only difference in implementing these bars is whether you type a forward slash (/) or the word "over" (with one space before and after the word) in the fraction entry area. Although the over bar option inserts a fraction the same size as the paragraph text, you can use the Paragraph Typography option's "Grow Inter-Line To Fit: On" setting (which automatically increases line spacing for over bar fractions) to prevent the fraction from overlapping the line above.

To edit a fraction, use the Backspace key and retype it; the typeset result changes accordingly. To insert a fraction in your text and return to the normal work area, select the Exit Fraction Editing option or use the Ctrl-D (^D) keyboard shortcut. To edit a fraction after it's inserted in the text, place the typing cursor directly in front of the fraction (the current selection box will display the word "Fraction") and select the Edit Special Item option (or press ^D) to return to the fraction editing screen.

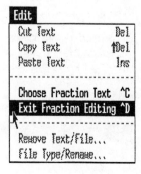

1. Insert anchors in text

2. Assign anchors to frames

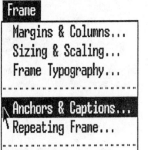

3. Move frames when anchors in text move

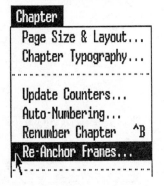

Frame Anchor (F5) is the next Insert Special Item option, and it is designed for documents in which it is crucial to keep illustrations — Ventura frames that hold pictures, tables, or figures — on the same page as their references in the text. By using this convenient option, you can insert a hidden reference, called a frame *anchor,* in the text; then, whenever the text moves, you can use another program command provided to move the illustrations with it.

For example, whenever you reformat a document, Ventura will repaginate the text but leave all illustrations in the same locations. If reformatting causes the text to flow onto more or less pages, you would normally be faced with the task of moving each illustration manually from page to page. But if you insert frame anchors first, you can use the Re-Anchor Frames option (discussed in the "Chapter Menu" section in Chapter 5) and the program will automatically move each frame to the same page as its anchor reference in the text.

The full procedure for using frame anchors involves three different options in three different menus (as shown in the left margin):

1. Insert Special Item (Ctrl-C) and Frame Anchor (F5): to place frame anchors in the text file (in the Text Editing mode)
2. Anchors & Captions: to assign anchor names to specific frames (in the Frame Setting mode)
3. Re-Anchor Frames: to move frames when anchors in text move (in any mode)

To place an anchor in a text file, first insert the Text Editing cursor in the line of text you want a frame referenced to (e.g., after words like "see Figure 1"), and then select the Insert Special Item and Frame Anchor options. Ventura responds by providing a dialog box (shown on the following page) that you use to enter the frame's anchor name and the location you want the frame moved to when using the Re-Anchor Frames option. If you choose a fixed location, the frame will occupy the same position on whatever page it moves to. If you choose a relative location, the frame will occupy a position either above, below, or within the line in the text that contains the frame anchor. For example, you can use the "Relative, Automatically At Anchor" option to move a small frame with the text whenever it moves — just like any letter, within a line of text — and a small graphic object (such as ↕) could be attached to the frame.

```
┌─────────────────────────────────────────────────────┐
│ INSERT/EDIT ANCHOR                                [?] │
│                                                       │
│   Frame's Anchor Name:   Floorplan 12|___             │
│                                                       │
│   Frame's New Location:  ┌─────────────────────────┐  │
│                          │ Fixed, On Same Page As Anchor │
│                          └─────────────────────────┘  │
│                          ┌─────────────────────────┐  │
│                          │ Relative, Below Anchor Line │ │
│                          └─────────────────────────┘  │
│                          ┌─────────────────────────┐  │
│                          │ Relative, Above Anchor Line │ │
│                          └─────────────────────────┘  │
│                          ┌─────────────────────────┐  │
│                          │ Relative, Automatically At Anchor │
│                          └─────────────────────────┘  │
│                                    ┌────┐  ┌────────┐ │
│                                    │ OK │  │ Cancel │ │
│                                    └────┘  └────────┘ │
└─────────────────────────────────────────────────────┘
```

The Insert/Edit Anchor dialog box allows you to insert a hidden reference, called an anchor, in a text file. This anchor identifies a frame — which typically contains an illustration — that you want attached to the text.

The anchor names you choose can be one or more words up to a maximum of 12 characters, for example, a name related to the illustration's caption, such as "Figure 1" or "Table II," or one that describes the illustration, such as "4thQtr Sales," "Floorplan 12," and so on. Anchor names are not displayed on the screen but are stored within the text file when the chapter is saved; however, if the Show Tabs & Returns option is used, you'll see a degree symbol inserted in the text to indicate the presence of a frame anchor.

```
┌─────────────────────┐
│ Box Char...      F1 │
│ Footnote         F2 │
│ Index Entry...   F3 │
│ Fraction...      F4 │
│ Frame Anchor...  F5 │
│ Cross Ref...     F6 │
└─────────────────────┘
```

As with index entries, you can also edit an existing anchor by placing the text cursor at the location of the entry and selecting the Edit Special Item option. When the cursor is at the right location, the term "Frame Anchor" is displayed in the current selection box. You can also delete the anchor at the cursor position by using the Delete key.

Although the program's frame anchor feature provides a powerful tool for hastening the work required in laying out such publications as computer documentation manuals that use a profusion of illustrations and screen shots, it is not a panacea for producing final layouts. After using the Re-Anchor Frames option, you still need to check each page of your document to make certain that the frames are properly placed and aligned. For example, if frames end up partially pushed off the page or overlapping each other, you'll still need to adjust the frames manually for the final layout.

```
┌─────────────────────┐
│ Box Char...      F1 │
│ Footnote         F2 │
│ Index Entry...   F3 │
│ Fraction...      F4 │
│ Frame Anchor...  F5 │
│ Cross Ref...     F6 │
└─────────────────────┘
```

The last special item Ventura provides is the Insert Cross Reference option (F6), which enables you to insert the current page or chapter number on any page in a document. While this feature is similar to the setting in the Headers & Footers dialog box (Chapter menu),

```
 ?    Do you wish to insert a      ┌──────────────┐
 •    reference to the current     │    Page #    │
WAIT  page or chapter number       └──────────────┘
      or cancel the request?       ┌──────────────┐
                                   │  Chapter #   │
                                   └──────────────┘
                                   ┌──────────────┐
                                   │    Cancel    │
                                   └──────────────┘
```

```
┌─────────────────────┐
│ Box Char...      F1 │
│ Footnote         F2 │
│ Index Entry...   F3 │
│ Fraction...      F4 │
│ Frame Anchor... F5  │
│ Cross Ref...    F6  │
└─────────────────────┘
```

which allows you to insert page and chapter numbers in headers and footers, it offers greater flexibility because it lets you place these numbers *anywhere* on a page, including frames, frame captions, and box text. For example, you can use this option to place page numbers in margin tabs (created with box text) along the edge of the page, or in customized headers and footers (created with repeating frames). After placing the typing cursor wherever you want the reference located and selecting this option, Ventura displays a dialog box (shown above) that contains choices for "Page #" and "Chapter #." As soon as you pick the type of reference you want, the current page or chapter number appears at the typing cursor's location.

```
┌─────────────────────────┐
│ Edit                    │
│ Cut Frame       Del Del │
│ Copy Frame     ⇑Del⇑Del │
│ Paste Frame     Ins Ins │
│ ......................  │
│ Ins Special Item...  ^C │
│ Edit Special Item... ^D │
│ ......................  │
│ Remove Text/File...     │
│ File Type/Rename...     │
└─────────────────────────┘
```

Removing and Renaming Files
The final options in the Edit menu are used to remove or rename files that have already been loaded into a Ventura chapter, and they are only available when either the Frame Setting or Graphic Drawing function is active. The ability to remove text or graphics files from a Ventura chapter file is essential as it provides a means of eliminating excess files from a chapter. Because all of the files loaded into a chapter are placed in the side-bar's assignment list each time the chapter is opened, it's best to remove all files that are not used in the document itself.

For example, all of the text files in a chapter are loaded in the computer system memory (RAM), so even files that aren't used decrease the amount of RAM available for loading and hyphenating other text files. Also, when you archive a chapter on floppy disks (using the Multi-Chapter option in the Options menu), the program copies all of the files in the assignment list and excess files take up more disk space than necessary.

To remove a file already placed in a frame or on the base page, first use the Frame Setting or Graphic Drawing cursor to select the frame or page containing the file, then select the Remove Text/File option.

```
┌────────────────────────────────────────────┐
│ ┌──────────────────────────────────────┐   │
│ │                                   ┌─┐ │   │
│ │  REMOVE  FILE                     │?│ │   │
│ │                                   └─┘ │   │
│ │    File  Name:    CAR        .PCX│    │   │
│ │                                       │   │
│ │    Remove  from:    Frame          ↕  │   │
│ │                                       │   │
│ │                  ┌─────────┐ ┌──────────┐ │
│ │                  │   OK    │ │  Cancel  │ │
│ │                  └─────────┘ └──────────┘ │
│ └──────────────────────────────────────┘   │
└────────────────────────────────────────────┘
```

This Remove Text/File dialog box is being used to remove a file (CAR.PCX) from a frame, but the actual file remains in the side-bar's assignment list and will still be available for use in the chapter.

Ventura responds by providing a dialog box (shown above) that lists the selected filename and gives you a choice of removing the file from the assignment list or removing it from that frame only. If you select "Frame," the file remains in the assignment list and is still available for use in the chapter, but if you select "List of Files," it is removed from the frame *and* from the chapter. If you decide later that you do want to use the file, you must reload it.

The Edit menu's File Type/Rename option enables you to change the name of any text file you've loaded into a chapter. You cannot, however, use this option to change the name of a graphics file. When a chapter is saved after selecting this option, a new text file is created, using whatever name, location, and text file format you choose, and the original text file remains intact in its original location and format.

To use the File Type/Rename option, first select the page or frame containing the text file, then click on the option. The program responds by providing a dialog box (shown on the following page) that lists the selected filename and its location in the "Old Name" and "New Name" blanks, and offers the same choice of text file formats found in the Load Text/Picture dialog box. After you delete the information on the "New Name" blank that you want to change, type the new filename (and location, if applicable) and click on the text format you want Ventura to use when it saves the file. Although the file is renamed as soon as you click "OK," the conversion operation won't take place until you actually save the chapter.

```
┌─────────────────────────────────┐
│ Edit                            │
├─────────────────────────────────┤
│ Cut Frame          Del Del      │
│ Copy Frame        ⇧Del⇧Del      │
│ Paste Frame        Ins Ins      │
│ ------------------------------- │
│ Ins Special Item...    ^C       │
│ Edit Special Item...   ^D       │
│ ------------------------------- │
│ Remove Text/File...             │
│ ▓File Type/Rename...▓           │
└─────────────────────────────────┘
```

A convenient use for this option is when you use the same text file in several different documents, but need to modify it each time it is used. After loading the file and making the changes, you can use the

In this File Type/Rename dialog box, a WordStar file (MINING.WS) is being renamed and converted into a Microsoft Word file (MINING.DOC). As soon as the chapter is saved, the new file is created and the old file remains intact in its original location.

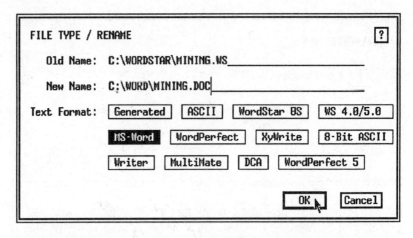

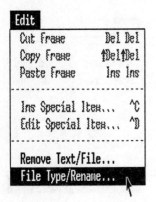

File Type/Rename option to save the file under a new name in each chapter without changing the original file. For example, you can load a master letter or legal contract into different chapters, use the Text Editing function to customize the basic text in each instance, and save the edited text file under a new name before saving the chapter.

Two other useful applications for the File Type/Rename option are to convert text files from one word processing format to another and to convert Ventura frame text into text files. To save a WordStar file as a Microsoft Word file, for example, you would type the new filename in the dialog box, select the "MS Word" text format option, and select "OK." As soon as you save the chapter, Ventura creates a new text file in the Microsoft Word format and leaves the original WordStar file unchanged in its original location.

As explained in Chapter 4, you can use the Text Editing mode to enter text directly in a frame you've added, and Ventura automatically stores the text in the chapter caption (.CAP) file. Whenever this frame is subsequently selected, using the Frame Setting or Graphic Drawing cursor, the current selection box will read "FRAME TEXT." If desired, however, you can also use the File Type/Rename option and convert the contents of a selected "FRAME TEXT" into a word processing file format, following the same procedures already described. Then, when you save the chapter, the chapter caption file will no longer contain the text that was formerly placed in that particular frame. If desired, you can repeat this process with all "FRAME TEXT" items in a chapter, converting the contents of each into a separately named word processing file.

Ventura's Frame menu provides you with extensive control over all of the frames used in a document, including the base page frame. Each frame can have its own set of formatting attributes, including margins, columns, ruling lines, background color and pattern, and certain typographic parameters. If the active style sheet calls for a double-sided page format (which you establish by using the Chapter menu's Page Size & Layout option), you can specify one set of formatting attributes for the page frame on all left pages and a different set for the page frame on all right pages. All frame settings regarding the base page are stored as part of the style sheet.

Each frame that you add can have a caption frame attached, and each caption frame can have its own set of formatting attributes as well. You can also control the margins for frames that Ventura automatically generates when you create headers, footers, and footnotes. All frame settings you define for added frames and program-generated frames are saved as part of the chapter file.

When producing simple business documents, such as letters, reports, and memos, you can usually place the text on the base page without drawing any additional frames. For these kinds of documents, you'll only need to use the Frame menu to define settings for the base page frame. When creating books, manuals, and other documents that include illustrations, you can still place the text on the base page, but you'll need to draw additional frames to contain the various pictures. For these publications, you'll use the Frame menu more often as you define settings and attributes for each frame you add.

Finally, when producing complex documents, such as magazines and news publications, that call for a variety of column widths and margins, you may decide to add frames on top of the base page and place all or most of the text inside those frames. In such cases, you'll probably find it necessary to access the Frame menu much more often as you manipulate each of the different frames in your layout.

Setting Margins and Columns

Before you can use the Margins & Columns option, you must use the Frame Setting cursor to select a frame that will be affected by the options you choose in the dialog box provided (shown on the following page). This frame can be the base page, a frame that you've added, or a program-generated frame for a header, footer,

Frame Menu

```
┌─────────────────────────────┐
│ Frame                       │
├─────────────────────────────┤
│ Margins & Columns...        │
│ Sizing & Scaling...         │
│ Frame Typography...         │
│ · · · · · · · · · · · · · · │
│ Anchors & Captions...       │
│ Repeating Frame...          │
│ · · · · · · · · · · · · · · │
│ Vertical Rules...           │
│ Ruling Line Above...        │
│ Ruling Line Below...        │
│ Ruling Box Around...        │
│ Frame Background...         │
│ · · · · · · · · · · · · · · │
│ Image Settings...           │
└─────────────────────────────┘
```

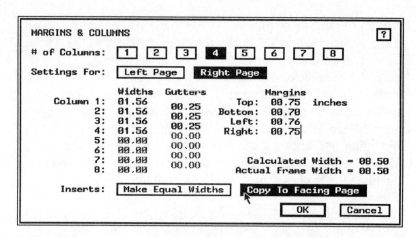

This Margins & Columns dialog box displays the settings used to create a four-column newsletter (shown on page 10). By clicking on the "Copy To Facing Page" option, a set of complementary margins and columns is created for the opposite page.

footnote, or caption. With the base page frame or added frames, you can use any measurement unit to define each frame's margins, number of columns, width of each column, and "gutters" (Ventura's term for the space between columns). With frames that are automatically generated, you can only control the margins, since the number of columns is automatically limited to one.

For example, if your document will be bound, you can add extra space to the right margin on left pages and the left margin on right pages to allow more space for three-hole punching, spiral binding, and so on. When you change the left or right margins, Ventura automatically recalculates the column widths and gutters according to the number of columns you select, and displays the total measurement of the left and right margins, column widths, and gutters in the "Calculated Width" line. This total measurement should match the same measurement value in the "Actual Frame Width" line.

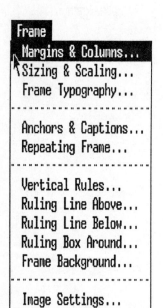

Unless you've specified the double-sided page format, Ventura will automatically use identical margins and columns for all pages. To establish different settings for left and right pages when using the double-sided format, you can either click on the opposite page in the "Settings For" option and manually reset the information as desired, or click on the "Inserts: Copy To Facing Page" option and Ventura will automatically create complementary pages for you.

When defining the columns, you can define equal or unequal column widths. To create equal column widths, click on the option box for the number of columns you want (up to eight columns per frame are allowed) and set each margin as desired. Then enter a value for the first "Gutters" space, select the "Inserts: Make Equal Widths" option, and the program will automatically make each column width and gutter space the same. To set unequal column widths, repeat the same procedure but enter each column width and gutter space manually. When finished, the "Calculated Width" line should equal the "Actual Frame Width" line; if these lines don't match, adjust the settings as necessary until the values for these two lines match.

When placing a picture inside a frame, Ventura ignores any column settings and only applies the margin settings. If no margins have been set, the picture will extend to the edge of the frame; but if margins are used, the area occupied by the picture within the frame is reduced accordingly. For example, a PostScript printer cannot print transparent overlapping images, therefore, a ruling box around a frame that contains a picture will not print. However, by setting the frame's margins to a value equal to the overall ruling box height (such as 0.001 inch), you can reduce the size of the picture and provide space for the ruling box to print. Or, if you want the picture to print closer to the top or right side of the frame, you can increase the frame's bottom or left margins, and so forth.

Sizing and Scaling Frames

The Sizing & Scaling option gives you precise control over the size and placement of any frame, including the page frame. This option also lets you reduce or enlarge the size of a picture placed within a frame, and control text formatting around an added frame. The usual procedure for adding frames is to use the mouse to draw the frame and position it as accurately as possible, using the Options menu's Show Rulers, Turn Column Snap On, and Turn Line Snap On commands. The on-screen rulers will aid you in positioning the frame more accurately, the column snap feature will force the frame to align with the sides of the base page's column guides, and line snap will force the frame to line up with the text interline spacing.

After the frame is drawn, you use the Sizing & Scaling dialog box (shown on the following page) to make precise adjustments to the frame itself by changing any of the values that control the area it occupies. The Sizing & Scaling dialog box controls include: "Upper Left X" to set the horizontal distance from the top-left corner of the frame to the left side of the page (use the plus [+] option box to move

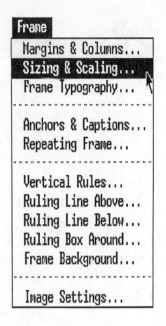

the frame to the left and the minus [-] option to move it to the right); "Upper Left Y" to set the vertical distance from the top-left corner of the frame to the top of the page (use the plus option to move the frame up and the minus option to move it down); "Frame Width" and "Frame Height" to control the horizontal and vertical size of the frame; "Horizontal Padding" to add space around the frame's left and right sides; and "Vertical Padding" to add space around the frame's top and bottom sides. For example, by reducing a frame's "Upper Left X" value, you can move it closer to the left side of the page; by using the "Padding" settings, you can create a channel of white space around a frame to keep any text from touching its sides.

When you place a picture in a frame, Ventura by default uses the "Picture Scaling: Fit in Frame" and "Aspect Ratio: Maintained" options to make the picture fit within the frame (minus any margins you've set) and maintain its original height-to-width aspect ratio. If the aspect ratio of the frame and the picture are different, however, the picture's height or width may exceed the boundaries of the frame, or it may result in producing extra white space around the picture. To fix this, you can resize the frame until its aspect ratio matches that of the picture, or select the "Aspect Ratio: Distorted" option and Ventura will disregard the picture's original aspect ratio and make it extend to all sides of the frame.

If you select the "Picture Scaling: By Scale Factors" option, you can increase or decrease the size of the picture regardless of the size of the frame in which it is placed. You can also apply the "Aspect Ratio" option to maintain or distort the picture's height and width. For

Control over text outside of frame

Control over frame size and placement

Control over size and placement of picture inside frame

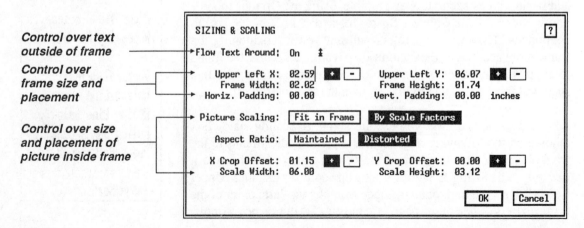

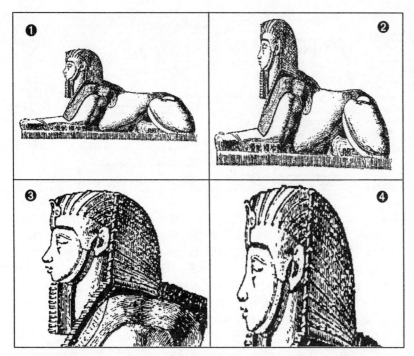

Here are four ways to apply the Sizing & Scaling dialog box in placing and positioning the same picture in the same frame.

Frames ❶ *and* ❷ *both use the "Fit in Frame" scaling option, with the aspect ratio maintained in* ❶ *and distorted in* ❷*.*

Frames ❸ *and* ❹ *both use the "By Scale Factors" and "Crop Offset" scaling options, with the aspect ratio maintained in* ❸ *and distorted in* ❹*.*

example, after selecting "Aspect Ratio: Maintained," you enter a value for the "Scale Width" line and Ventura automatically increases or decreases the picture's height, as required, to preserve the picture's original aspect ratio. If you select "Aspect Ratio: Distorted," you can enter a value for the "Scale Height" line as well.

For any picture you scale to a size larger than the frame itself, you can use the program's cropping feature to determine which part of the picture you want displayed within the frame. In some cases, if you place a large picture in a small frame, you may not be able to see the image until you pan and crop the picture. (The use of the mouse cursor to crop a picture is explained in the "Frame Setting" section in Chapter 4.) After you crop a scaled picture using the mouse, the amounts by which you've moved the picture relative to the frame are displayed in the "X Crop Offset" and "Y Crop Offset" lines in the Sizing & Scaling dialog box. If desired, you can use the keyboard to change these values to the exact amounts you want. The plus and minus option boxes both work as previously described.

The "Flow Text Around" option is a powerful feature used to make text outside a frame automatically wrap around the frame. This

Frame

Margins & Columns...

Sizing & Scaling...

Frame Typography...

- - - - - - - - - - - - - - - - -

Anchors & Captions...

Repeating Frame...

- - - - - - - - - - - - - - - - -

Vertical Rules...

Ruling Line Above...

Ruling Line Below...

Ruling Box Around...

Frame Background...

- - - - - - - - - - - - - - - - -

Image Settings...

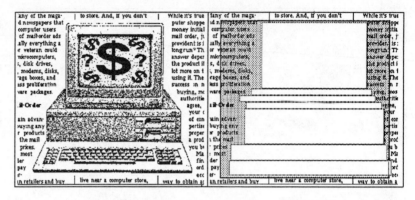

To create the runaround on the left, the frames on the right, which are set for "Flow Text Around: On," are placed on top of the picture frame, (represented by the shaded area), which is set for "Flow Text Around: Off."

Frame

Margins & Columns...
Sizing & Scaling...
Frame Typography...

Anchors & Captions...
Repeating Frame...

Vertical Rules...
Ruling Line Above...
Ruling Line Below...
Ruling Box Around...
Frame Background...

Image Settings...

feature also makes it possible to create small narrow frames that can be used to add space between paragraphs in order to help balance columns of type. This technique is similar to the old printing practice of adding thin pieces of metal, called *leading,* to make type fit properly. To ensure that each narrow frame you add is exactly one or two lines high and equal to the column or page width, use the Turn Column Snap On and Turn Line Snap On options.

The "Flow Text Around" option also plays a crucial role in enabling you to create a *runaround,* which is an area you can construct around an object — typically an irregularly shaped picture — so that text will not print in that area. To apply this technique (shown above), select the "Flow Text Around: Off" option for the frame that contains the picture. When this frame is added to the text already on a page, the text flows behind the picture rather than around it. In effect, the picture overlaps the text. However, if you proceed to draw several frames on top of the picture with the "Flow Text Around: On" option selected for each additional frame, you can force the text to wrap around the shape of the picture. Add as many different-sized frames as necessary until each portion of the picture is free of text.

Typographic Control by Frame

Ventura provides two menu options, Chapter Typography and Paragraph Typography, for controlling certain typographic characteristics of text placed on the base page of a document and automatically paginated. As explained in the "Chapter Menu" section in Chapter 5, the Chapter Typography option (Chapter menu) sets parameters for widows and orphans, pair kerning, column balance, and baseline spacing for the first line in each column on a global (chapterwide) basis, while the Paragraph Typography option (Paragraph menu)

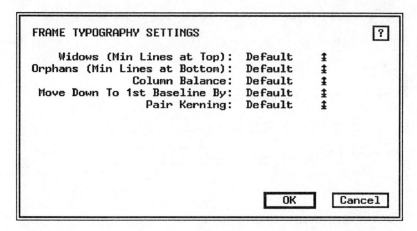

Ventura uses the same dialog box for the Frame Typography and Chapter Typography options, however, the settings you define for individual frames override those defined for the entire chapter.

controls pair kerning, letter spacing, word spacing, and other typographic features on a paragraph tag-by-tag basis. However, for documents in which text has been placed in added frames or on inserted pages, Ventura also provides a third menu option, Frame Typography, that lets you control the same settings (shown above) as those found in the Chapter Typography dialog box, but on a frame-by-frame basis and for each inserted page.

For example, in creating a sophisticated newsletter or magazine format, added frames are commonly used in addition to the base page frame for containing the text. With the Chapter Typography dialog box, you may have used the "Move Down to 1st Baseline By: Inter-Line" setting as the default for the entire chapter, but with the Frame Typography dialog box, you can use the alternate "Move Down to 1st Baseline By: Cap Height" setting for a selected frame in which you want the text to touch the top of the frame without adding any inter-line spacing. (Note: Because the controls Ventura provides for the Frame Typography and Chapter Typography menu options are identical, refer to the "Chapter Menu" section in Chapter 5 for a full explanation of how each feature works.)

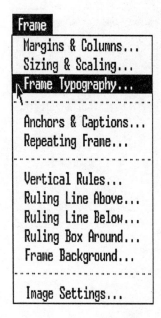

Other cases might involve using different settings for widows and orphans, column balance, and so on, for selected frames. Although this typographic fine tuning isn't used very often in producing standard business reports and many other types of documents, the ability to use the Frame Typography option to override the settings in the Chapter Typography option is a valuable feature that provides you with more on-the-fly typographic control over your documents.

This Anchors & Captions dialog box is being used to assign an anchor name ("Floorplan 12") and a caption label to a selected frame. In this case, the label will appear below the frame, in bold italic, and the chapter and figure numbers will be automatically included.

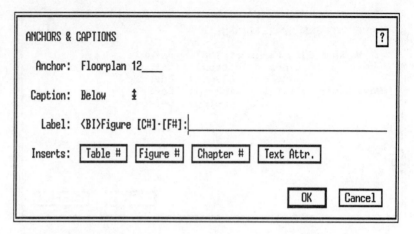

Frame

Margins & Columns...
Sizing & Scaling...
Frame Typography...
....
Anchors & Captions...
Repeating Frame...
....
Vertical Rules...
Ruling Line Above...
Ruling Line Below...
Ruling Box Around...
Frame Background...
....
Image Settings...

Anchors and Captions

As its name implies, the Anchors & Captions option serves a twofold purpose: it lets you assign anchor names and short captions, which can include automatic numbering, to any frame you add. After you select a frame and pick this option, the dialog box provided (shown above) includes two blank lines that enable you to use either or both of these features. The "Anchor" line is for you to type the name you want to assign a frame, and the "Label" line is for a caption (up to 60 characters) that you want to attach to the frame.

As explained earlier in this chapter, the anchors feature in the Anchors & Captions option is linked to the Edit menu's Insert (Special Item) Frame Anchor and the Chapter menu's Re-Anchor Frames options. In order for these three options to work together, the anchor names you assign to frames using the Anchors & Captions dialog box must match the same names you insert in the text. If you expect to use many anchors, it may be helpful to keep a written list of all anchor names inserted in the text to ensure accuracy when typing anchor names in the Anchors & Captions dialog box. After using this option, you can then use the Chapter menu's Re-Anchor Frames option whenever you need to move anchored frames to the same page as their corresponding references in the text.

To create a caption label, first pick one of the "Caption" option boxes to place the label above, below, to the left, or to the right of the frame. Next, type the desired caption on the "Label" line, using the "Inserts" options to add automatic numbering commands and text attribute codes. If you pick the "Table #," "Figure #," or "Chapter

#" option, a bracketed command — [T#], [F#], or [C#] — is inserted at the typing cursor position and Ventura calculates the correct table, figure, or chapter number when it creates the caption. Pick the "Text Attr." box and the code **<D>** is placed at the cursor position. You can then replace the letter "D" with a Ventura text attribute code (such as **<I>** for italic), spacing code (such as **<~>** for an en space), or decimal code (such as **<189>** for a copyright symbol). For instance, the "Label" entry **<I>Table [C#]-[T#]** would result in the caption "*Table 5-5*" if using arabic numerals to identify table five in chapter five. Or, **<I><189> 1989 by Graphtec** would produce the caption label "© *1989 by Graphtec.*"

After you select "OK," Ventura attaches a caption frame to the selected frame, and the caption label appears centered inside it. You can't edit this label with the Text Editing function, but you can type additional caption text inside the caption frame. To do so, insert the Text Editing cursor in front of the end-of-file symbol, which is automatically included in every caption frame. (Select the Options menu's Show Tabs & Returns command if this symbol isn't displayed.) Then type the additional caption text, which is called a *free-form caption*. This text is automatically saved in the chapter's caption (.CAP) file. If you want to type a lengthy caption but need more space, use the Frame Setting cursor to resize the caption frame as you would with any frame. If desired, you can also use the Margins & Columns option to add margins to the caption frame.

Ventura attaches two generated tags to the text in a caption frame: a "Z_LABEL FIG" tag is assigned to each caption label, and a "Z_CAPTION" tag is assigned to each free-form caption. These tags share the same settings as the Body Text tag, but the "Z_LABEL FIG" tag is initially centered regardless of the alignment used for the Body Text tag. To change the attributes for these Z_ tags, use the Paragraph Tagging function and the Paragraph menu. For example, you can change both tags so that the caption label and free-form caption both appear on the same line. To do this, first select "Left" for the "Z_LABEL FIG" Alignment dialog box and "Relative Indent: On" for the "Z_CAPTION" Alignment dialog box. Also add an "In/Outdent Width" of one pica in the "Z_CAPTION" Alignment dialog box. Finally, select "Line Break: After" for the "Z_CAPTION" Breaks dialog box, which places the free-form caption on the same line as the caption label, and adds a 1 pica space between them.

Frame
Margins & Columns...
Sizing & Scaling...
Frame Typography...

Anchors & Captions...
Repeating Frame...

Vertical Rules...
Ruling Line Above...
Ruling Line Below...
Ruling Box Around...
Frame Background...

Image Settings...

Repeating Frames

For documents that require an identical graphic or text element on every page, such as a company logo or a proprietary rights statement, the Frame menu's Repeating Frame option is quite useful. With this feature, you can place up to six recurring frames and their contents on every page in a chapter. In addition to each frame's text or graphics contents, any ruling lines or background attributes that have been added to the frame will also be duplicated on each page.

After you select the target frame and pick the Repeating Frame option, Ventura provides a dialog box (shown below) that lets you specify the pages (left, right, or both) on which you want the selected frame to repeat. If you don't want a repeating frame to appear on a certain page, go to that page and select the frame, then pick the "Hide This Repeating Frame" option in the dialog box to hide it on that page only. By using this technique, you can selectively show or hide each of the repeating frames used in a document. To make a hidden repeating frame reappear on the current page, select the frame and use the "Show All Hidden Frames" option. Then repeat the hiding procedure for any frames on that page which you want to remain hidden.

If you want a repeating frame to be reflected on the opposite page, pick the "Left & Right" option. For instance, to create complementary visual tabs in the outside margins of a double-sided publication, draw the frame in the right margin on the right page, select the "Left & Right" option, and Ventura will automatically place the frame in the left margin on all left pages. However, to create nonidentical margin tabs (like those shown on these two pages) you would need to create a separate repeating frame on both pages.

Up to six frames and their contents can be made to automatically repeat on every page of a document by using the Repeating Frame dialog box. You can also choose to hide or show each repeating frame on any current page.

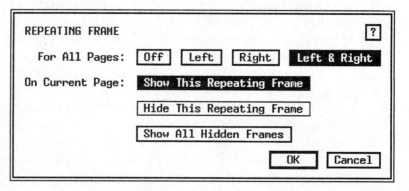

Because repeating frames can contain multicolumn text, you can also use a repeating frame to add more columns to the base page (as shown below) and apply Ventura's automatic pagination to flow text into more than eight columns per page. To use this technique, first set the margins and columns on the base page to provide space for the extra columns. For example, to create a 10 column layout on an 8.5 by 14-inch page, using the landscape page orientation, set the left margin at 0.75 inch, the right margin at 3.40 inches, each column at 1.10 inches, and each gutter at 0.15 inch. This produces eight 1.10-inch columns and a large right margin. Next, draw a repeating frame that covers the eighth column and overlaps into the right margin by about 2.5 inches to provide space for the ninth and tenth columns. Select the Turn Column Snap On and Turn Line Snap On options (Options menu) to help you completely mask the eighth column with this frame. After the frame is drawn, use the Margins & Columns option to format it for three 1.10-inch columns with 0.15-inch gutters, and then use the Repeating Frame option to turn it into a repeating frame on all pages.

The final step is to place the text file on the base page and then in the repeating frame. This will cause the text to flow into the seven columns on each base page first, and into the three columns in each repeating frame second. (Note: To use this technique on a single-sided page format, use the same repeating frame on all pages; but to use it on a double-sided format, you must manually place a second repeating frame in the exact *same position* on the facing page so that it doesn't cover the first seven columns on that page.)

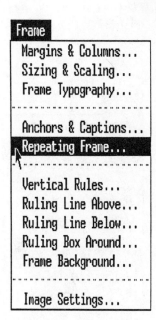

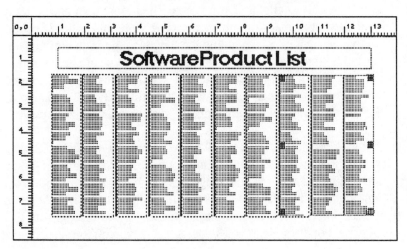

The text in this 10-column layout flows into the first 7 columns on the base page and then into the 3 columns created by a repeating frame, marked by gray selector boxes, on the right. By applying a multicolumn repeating frame in this way, you can automatically paginate a document on the base page using more than 8 columns, which is the normal limit.

This Vertical Rules dialog box for a base page frame is set to add 1-pt. vertical rules between all columns and two 3-pt. vertical rules at 0.85 and 7.90 inches from the left side of the page. By using the "Copy To Facing Page" option, these settings will also be reflected on the left page.

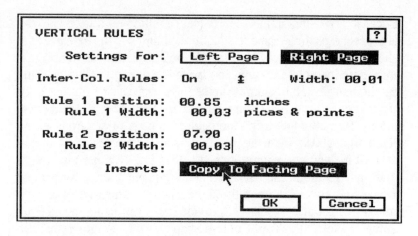

Frame

Margins & Columns...
Sizing & Scaling...
Frame Typography...
- - - - - - - - - - - - - - - - -
Anchors & Captions...
Repeating Frame...
- - - - - - - - - - - - - - - - -
Vertical Rules...
Ruling Line Above...
Ruling Line Below...
Ruling Box Around...
Frame Background...
- - - - - - - - - - - - - - - - -
Image Settings...

Frame Rules and Background

With the remaining group of options in the Frame menu, you can add a variety of ruling lines and textures to the base page frame or to any frame you've added, as well as to the frames that Ventura automatically generates, which include header, footer, footnote, and caption frames. You can also add color to the background of any frame and see the color displayed on screen if you've installed Ventura to run in a color mode. Since rules and color can play such an important role in visually organizing the information on a page, these options are valuable design aids.

When you select the Vertical Rules option, the dialog box provided (shown above) lets you use two types of vertical rules inside the base page frame or any frame you've added. First are intercolumn rules, which are only available if you've specified more than one column for the target frame, using the Margins & Columns option. Second are two vertical rules, extending the length of the frame (minus the top and bottom margins), that you can place anywhere in the frame. The measurement unit for the "Rule 1 Width" line is used to control the width of all vertical rules created with this option. To change it, click on the measurement unit until the system you want is displayed.

To add vertical rules between all of the columns in a selected frame, click on the "Inter-Col. Rules: On" option box and a default 1-point rule width is displayed. To change this value, use the typing cursor. Ventura automatically generates the intercolumn rules in the center of each column gutter and makes them the same length as the columns. For example, if you're using a two-column format and you select this option, Ventura adds one intercolumn rule to the frame; if you're using four columns, it adds three intercolumn rules (as shown on the right), and so on. If you want to add up to two vertical rules that are not connected to the columns, use the Rule 1 and Rule 2 options. (To add one rule, use Rule 1 only.) To create these rules, you first tell Ventura where to place them in relation to *the left side of the page,* then enter a value for each rule's width. The measurement unit used to place these rules is displayed on the "Rule 1 Position" line, and you can change it by clicking on it as usual. A common use for these rules is to add vertical rules to the outside edge of the left and right columns on a multicolumn page.

For example, to place a vertical rule at the outside of a left column, enter a value less than the width of the left margin itself. If you want this rule placed at precisely the same distance from the column as any intercolumn rules, subtract half of the gutter width from the left margin. Thus, for a four-column format using a gutter width of 0.30 inch, you subtract 0.15 inch from the left margin and enter that value on the "Rule 1 Position" line. If the left margin is 1.00 inch, then place Rule 1 at 0.85 inch from the left side of the page. To place Rule 2 at the outside of the right column in the same example, you subtract the right margin from the total page width, add half the gutter width to that figure, and enter the total as the value on the "Rule 2 Position" line. If a right margin of 0.75 inch is used on an 8.50-inch wide sheet of paper, place Rule 2 at 7.90 inches from the left side of the page.

When adding vertical rules to an added frame, the main point to remember is that the position of these rules is still relative to the left edge of the paper — not the left side of the frame. Therefore, use the Options menu's Show Rulers command to display the on-screen rulers as a guide to help you determine exact measurement values.

The Vertical Rules dialog box also lets you define separate settings for left and right pages, or use complementary settings for both pages by using the "Inserts: Copy To Facing Page" option. To produce the vertical rule in this book, for instance, complementary settings were used. Finally, it should be noted that paragraph tags using the "Overall Width: Frame-Wide" setting, in the Paragraph menu's Alignment option, will cause the text to interupt any rules that you create with the Vertical Rules option. In this book, this feature is used at the beginning of each chapter for the chapter title.

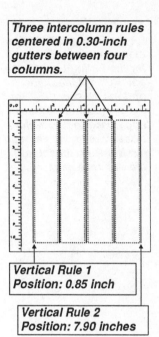

Three intercolumn rules centered in 0.30-inch gutters between four columns.

Vertical Rule 1 Position: 0.85 inch

Vertical Rule 2 Position: 7.90 inches

The dialog box provided for the Ruling Box Around menu option is also used for the Ruling Line Above and Ruling Line Below options. Shown here are the space and height settings used to create the three ruling boxes around the frame on the top of the opposite page.

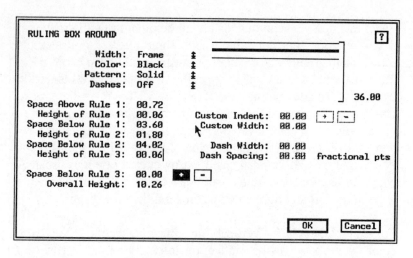

The next three options in the Frame menu let you automatically add ruling lines to any frame. When selected, each option — Ruling Line Above, Ruling Line Below, and Ruling Box Around — provides the same dialog box (shown above), referred to here as the Ruling Lines dialog box; only the menu option name at the top of the dialog box changes. You can use these options to create one, two, or three ruling lines of any thickness up to a total of 0.5 inch (36 points), including spacing above and below the rules, which you also define. You can apply either or both the Ruling Line Above and Ruling Line Below options to any frame, but the Ruling Box Around option takes precedence over the other two. Ventura also provides the same Ruling Lines dialog box when you select the Paragraph menu's Ruling Line Above, Ruling Line Below, and Ruling Box Around options. However, certain features, such as custom widths and indents, are only available when the Ruling Lines dialog box is used with the Paragraph menu (not the Frame menu) options.

To use the Ruling Lines dialog box with any of the Frame menu's three ruling line options, first, select the "Width: Frame" option. If desired, you can change the ruling line measurement unit, located just above the "OK" box, by clicking on the unit words until the unit you want to use is displayed. The figure in front of the measurement unit shows the maximum space allowed for all three ruling lines, and this value (0.500 inch, 36.00 fractional points, 03,00 picas & points, or 1.270 centimeters) cannot be changed. The maximum space for all ruling lines is also represented by the area inside the right bracket in the center of the dialog box.

```
╔═══════════════════════════════════════╗
║ ┌─────────────────────────────────────┐ ║
║ │                                     │ ║
║ │   ✦ 1990 Business Plan ✦            │ ║
║ │                                     │ ║
║ └─────────────────────────────────────┘ ║
╚═══════════════════════════════════════╝
```

This frame is set for three ruling lines, using the values in the Ruling Box Around dialog box on the previous page.

The Filmmaker's Newsletter

This newsletter logo consists of two frames: a frame containing white text and white dashes (ruling lines above and below) is placed on top of a frame with a solid black background.

Next, use the typing cursor to enter a value for the height (thickness) of each ruling line you want to add, plus the amount of spacing above and below each line, as required. For example, to simply add a 1-point ruling box around a frame, using fractional points and the Ruling Box Around option, you would leave the "00,00" value in the "Space Above Rule 1" line, move the cursor down one line and enter a value of "01,00" for the "Height of Rule 1" line. Ventura responds by displaying the resulting rule in the center of the dialog box to help you determine whether the line thickness is exactly what you want. If you enter values for the other rules and spacing between rules, or change the values already entered, the results displayed in the dialog box are automatically updated by the program. At the bottom of the dialog box, the "Overall Height" line displays the total amount of space required by the settings. Remember that this total amount should not exceed the maximum space allowed.

If you prefer to use dashes as the "Pattern" for the rules you're adding, select the "Dashes On" option and two additional option lines for dashes become available. The "Dash Width" line controls the size of all dashes, and "Dash Spacing" defines the space between them. (Note: the "Custom Indent" and "Custom Width" lines, and the plus [+] and minus [-] options following the "Space Below Rule 3" line, only apply to the Paragraph menu's ruling line options.)

The Frame Background menu option enables you to define two final attributes for any selected frame: color and pattern. The base page

```
┌──────────────────────────┐
│ Frame                    │
├──────────────────────────┤
│ Margins & Columns...     │
│ Sizing & Scaling...      │
│ Frame Typography...      │
│ ------------------------ │
│ Anchors & Captions...    │
│ Repeating Frame...       │
│ ------------------------ │
│ Vertical Rules...        │
│ Ruling Line Above...     │
│ Ruling Line Below...     │
│ Ruling Box Around...     │
│ Frame Background...      │
│ ------------------------ │
│ Image Settings...        │
└──────────────────────────┘
```

The Frame Background dialog box enables you to change the color or pattern of any frame. For example, if Ventura is installed to run in color, you can change the color of the base page frame to preview how a document will appear on colored paper stock. You can also create solid white frames that can be used to keep parts of other frames from printing.

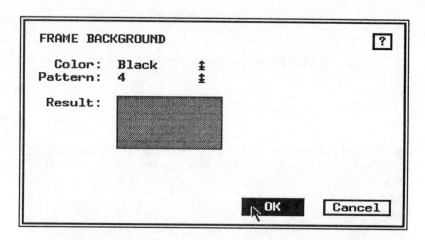

frame and all added or generated frames are initially assigned the default attributes of "Color: White" and "Pattern: Hollow," but you can change these attributes by selecting any of the other choices in the Frame Background dialog box (shown above). For example, if your printer supports white on black printing, you can change the frame background color to black and Ventura will automatically change any text placed inside the frame to white. Or, if you want to preview what your publication will look like on colored paper stock, you can change the color attribute for the base page frame or any frame you've added. This same technique can be used to preview what adding color to spot art (various graphics placed in small frames) might look like. Unless you're using a color output device, however, you'll need to change back to colors or gray shades supported by your black-and-white printer before final printing.

If you choose a background pattern other than hollow, the pattern will fill the entire frame *minus* all spacing set for ruling lines and margins. Therefore, if you created a shaded or colored frame with white ruling lines above, below, or around it, none of the rules will be visible unless you use the following technique. First, use the Edit menu's clipboard to make an identical copy of the frame and paste it on top of the original. Set the bottom frame for the desired background pattern but no ruling lines, then set the top frame for white ruling lines but no background pattern (use "Hollow"). To select the bottom frame, press the Control key while clicking on the frames. The final result of this juxtaposition is a shaded frame with white rules (as shown on the left). If you want to add text, simply place it in the frame on top.

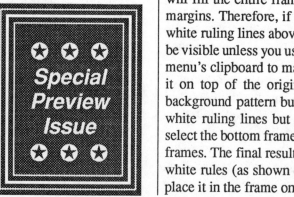

Gray-Scale Image Control

Until recently, quality-minded desktop publishers rarely included scanned images of continuous-tone pictures, such as photographs, in their Ventura publications. If such scanned images were used at all, they were usually for draft purposes or to convey position, scaling, and cropping instructions for the printer, who would then convert the original picture into a conventional halftone and strip it onto a flat for making printing plates. However, desktop scanners have made significant progress in reproducing continuous-tone pictures by incorporating the ability to capture gray-scale information and save it as a Tagged Image File Format (TIFF) graphics file, which is a digital image exchange format supported by Ventura. For professional publishers, graphics designers, and others who use photographs, paintings, and shaded drawings in their publications, it's now possible to import TIFF gray-scale images into Ventura and output them as digital halftones along with the text on the same camera-ready page or film media. Best of all, you can use Ventura's Image Settings option to control the halftone screening process for each gray-scale image you place on a page.

In order to take full advantage of this sophisticated technology, however, you need to understand the difference between conventional halftones and digital halftones. Because a printing press prints only solid tones, commercial printers use special fine-line screens to convert continuous-tone images into halftones that consist of regularly spaced patterns of variously sized small dots. From a normal reading distance, a person's eyes and brain blend the dots and background together to create a perception of grays. Although halftone dots vary in size, the number of dots printed per square inch does not; that number is measured by the lines per inch (lpi) in the screen, which is known as the *screen frequency* in printing jargon. The most commonly used conventional halftones have screen frequencies ranging from 55 to 150 lpi, with 150 lpi being the maximum frequency most commercial printing presses can handle, The greater the screen ruling, the higher the resolution and quality of the printed halftone. Newspapers generally use 65- to 85-lpi screens, while magazines and books usually choose finer 120- to 150-lpi screens.

Like conventional halftones, digital halftones simulate shades of gray by using patterns of dots and various screen frequencies. However, a 300-dpi laser printer or higher-resolution typesetter

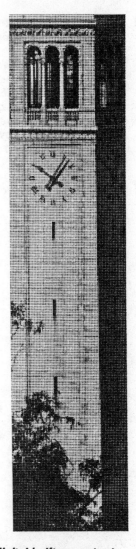

A digital halftone output on a 300-dpi PostScript laser printer, using the default settings for Ventura's Image Settings option. The original gray-scale image was scanned at 78 dpi, using a gray-scale scanner capable of capturing 256 levels of gray.

Digital halftones simulate conventional halftones by arranging the printer output dots in grids called "cells." Each cell is equal to a conventional halftone dot, which varies in size to depict different levels of gray. The cells shown here are made up of 16 printer output dots, turned on or off, and can represent 17 gray levels.

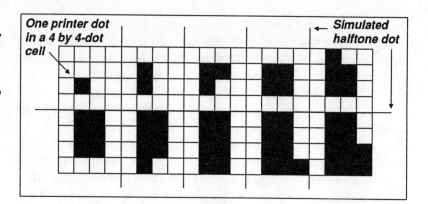

One printer dot in a 4 by 4-dot cell

Simulated halftone dot

lacks variable-size dots; therefore, digital halftones must simulate halftone dots by arranging the printer dots in grids called "cells." Each printer dot within the cell is turned on or off to produce different gray values, from completely black (all dots on) to completely white (all dots off). The more printer dots that are on, the darker the gray level; the more that are off, the lighter the gray level.

Using this technique, the number of gray levels a digital halftone can simulate depends on the number of printer dots arranged in the cell. For example, a 4 by 4-dot cell, made of up 16 printer dots (as shown above), can represent 17 gray levels (16 plus 1 extra level if the cell is empty, or white). A larger 8 by 8-dot cell can represent 65 gray levels (64 plus 1 white level). When all of these simulated halftone dots (cells) are combined, they produce the various gray-level patterns that emulate a traditional halftone.

There are two ways to produce digital halftones. The first method is to create the halftone at the time a picture is scanned, which is called *dithering*. Dithering turns a picture into a bit-mapped image that emulates shades of gray by using the simulated halftone dots (cells) technique just described. Unfortunately, once you create a dithered image, you have no further control over the screening process when you print the image. The second and preferable way to produce a digital halftone is at the time the image is sent to the printer, which requires the use of a gray-scale image and the type of controls offered by Ventura's Image Settings option. Because a gray-scale image consists of raw gray-level data rather than an inflexible pattern of black-and-white dots, you get to choose the best screen type, angle, and frequency for the printer in use. You can also scale a gray-scale image without fear of distortion, unlike a dithered image, which often produces unwanted patterns when resized. (See the "Working with Graphics" section in Chapter 7 for more information on producing gray-scale and other scanned images.)

Unless you plan to print the gray-scale images in your publication on a high-resolution typesetter, don't expect top quality from a digital halftone output on a laser printer. For example, printing a gray-scale image on a 300-dpi laser printer with a 50-lpi screen will only produce up to 37 gray levels. If you apply a screen frequency lower than 50 lpi to the same image, a 300-dpi printer can produce more gray levels, but the larger halftone dot (cell) sizes will make the image look coarse. With a higher screen frequency, the potential number of grays decreases and you may wind up with noticeable bands of gray instead of continous tone.

If you print a gray-scale image on a higher-resolution typesetter, however, you can use finer screen frequencies and still obtain a large number of gray levels. At 1,270 or 2,540 dpi, screen frequencies ranging from 90 to 150 lpi produce excellent results. For example, gray-scale images printed on a 1,270-dpi typesetter with a 133-lpi screen produce digital halftones that can simulate up to 92 gray levels. Printing the same images on a 2,540-dpi typesetter with a 133-lpi screen can produce 265 grays.

To use Ventura's digital halftone feature, first select a frame containing the gray-scale image, which can either be a TIFF or PostScript (EPS) file with gray-scale information. Next, choose the Image Settings option and Ventura displays a dialog box (shown below) with three halftone screening controls. Although you can use the defaults for most work, you can apply the "Halftone Screen Type"

The settings in this dialog box were used to create the digital halftone shown above, which was output as a film negative on a Linotronic typesetter at 1,270 dpi, and stripped onto the printing flat for this page of the book. The gray-scale file is the same image used on page 185.

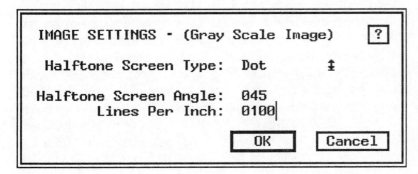

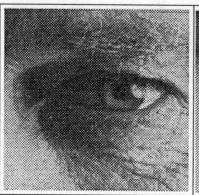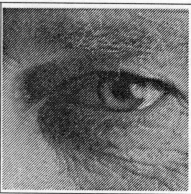

Two of the halftone screen patterns available with the Image Settings option output on a 300-dpi PostScript laser printer. The sample on the left uses "Dot" and the sample on the right uses "Line."

option to select a dot, line, ellipse, or custom (user-definable) screen pattern, the "Halftone Screen Angle" option to set the orientation of the halftone screen (measured from a vertical angle of 0 degrees), and the "Lines Per Inch" option to select the screen frequency.

For example, those familiar with PostScript code can select the "Halftone Screen Type: Custom" option and define their own screen type in the PostScript PS2.PRE file (found in the VENTURA directory). As for the halftone screen angle, a 45-degree (or 0-degree) angle usually provides the best results. The proper screen frequency depends on the printer in use; for example, 50- to 60-lpi screens generally work best on 300-dpi printers, 90- to 100-lpi screens on 1,270-dpi typesetters, and 120- to 150-lpi screens on 2,540-dpi typesetters. The best way to learn the different effects you can obtain with various settings for each of these options is to experiment and print samples of the scanned images you intend to use.

Finally, although Ventura's documentation states that you can only use the Image Settings option with a PostScript printer, you can also use it with an HP LaserJet Series II or compatible laser printer by installing a special printer control adapter that uses its own driver to ouput gray-scale images. For example, you can use Intel's Visual Edge (which works with EMS), DP-Tek's LaserPort Grayscale, or Microtek's GLZ to output TIFF gray-scale images on an HP LaserJet and also boost the printer's graphics resolution. With the Visual Edge, for instance, you can apply Ventura's Image Settings option to print a digital halftone on an HP LaserJet using a 70-lpi screen and maintain up to 64 gray levels, or you can use a 100-lpi screen and produce up to 37 gray levels.

Paragraph Menu

As a desktop publisher, your primary goal is to convey a message through print communication. Of all the tools that Ventura offers to help you meet that goal, the Paragraph menu options are among the most important since they provide extensive control over the typesetting process. All of these options are related to the tags found in every style sheet, as discussed in the "Paragraph Tagging" section in Chapter 4. Each paragraph tag contains settings for a variety of typographic characteristics, including font, alignment, line and paragraph spacing, indents, line breaks, column breaks, page breaks, tabs, word spacing, letter spacing, bullets, drop capitals, ruling lines, color, and other attributes.

```
┌─────────────────────────────────┐
│ Paragraph                        │
├─────────────────────────────────┤
│ Font...                          │
│ Alignment...                     │
│ Spacing...                       │
│ Breaks...                        │
│ Tab Settings...                  │
│ Special Effects...               │
│ Attribute Overrides...           │
│ Paragraph Typography...          │
│ - - - - - - - - - - - - - - - -  │
│ Ruling Line Above...             │
│ Ruling Line Below...             │
│ Ruling Box Around...             │
│ - - - - - - - - - - - - - - - -  │
│ Define Colors...                 │
│ Update Tag List...        ^K     │
└─────────────────────────────────┘
```

In order to use any of the options in the Paragraph menu, you must first select the Paragraph Tagging function; in most cases, you must also select a tag that will be affected by the various specifications you define. As soon as you click on a paragraph, which can consist of any number of sentences or a single character followed by a paragraph return, all of the Paragraph menu options are available.

Although you won't need to use *all* of the Paragraph menu options to prepare each document you produce with Ventura, you will normally need to use the first three options — Font, Alignment, and Spacing — to control the essential parameters common to every typeset job. However, since the dialog boxes provided with these options include more than just the most common settings, you'll need to know which features are essential and which are not. Editors and designers with experience in specifying and marking up copy for typesetting will also need to adjust to the program's method of keeping certain typographic parameters in separate dialog boxes.

This is 7-pt. Times
This is 8-pt. Times
This is 9-pt. Times
This is 10-pt. Times
This is 11-pt. Times
This is 12-pt. Times
This is 13-pt. Times
This is 14-pt. Times
This is 15-pt. Times

This is 7-pt. Helvetica
This is 8-pt. Helvetica
This is 9-pt. Helvetica
This is 10-pt. Helvetica
This is 11-pt. Helvetica
This is 12-pt. Helvetica
This is 13-pt. Helvetica
This is 14-pt. Helvetica
This is 15-pt. Helvetica

Among the many typographic decisions you'll need to make for each publication are the type sizes to be used. Most readability studies will recommend an optimum type size of 9 to 12 points for body text, with a corresponding optimum line length of 18 to 24 picas (or approximately 1.5 times the type size).

The dialog box provided by the Font option is the same as the one you use when you select the "Set Font" button in the Text Editing mode, except that the "Shift" and "Kern" options are not included. Shown here are the fonts Ventura automatically provides when you install the program for use with an HP LaserJet Series II printer.

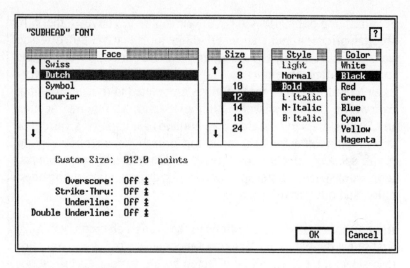

Selecting the Font

With the Font menu option, you can assign a typeface, type size, style, and color to all text assigned the same paragraph tag. When you select this option, the program provides the same dialog box (shown above) it displays when you click on the side-bar's "Set Font" button in the Text Editing mode. One important difference, however, is that the "Shift" and "Kern" features do not appear at the bottom of the dialog box since they are not available in the Paragraph Tagging mode — these options are only active when you specify font settings for a selected character or text block using the Text Editing mode. To review how to use the typeface, type size, style, and color options, consult the "Text Editing" section in Chapter 4.

The main difference in using the same basic dialog box with two separate functions is that the font settings you specify in the Text Editing mode take precedence over those you define in the Paragraph Tagging mode. For example, if you select a character with the Text Editing cursor, click on the "Set Font" button, and use the dialog box provided to increase the character's size from 10 to 12 points, it will remain 12 points unless you use the "Set Font" button again to change it. Even if you switch to Paragraph Tagging and use the Font menu option to increase all text in that paragraph to 14 points, the 12-point character will not change with the rest of the text. Therefore, you should normally use the Paragraph Tagging mode first to specify the overall font setting, and then use the Text Editing mode to make specific changes to selected text within paragraphs.

If your printer has a limited number of fonts, it may be just as well since mixing a lot of typefaces and styles on a page often looks amateurish. As a general rule, it's best to limit the number of fonts in a document to one or two typefaces and three or four combinations of sizes and styles. If you survey other publications, you'll usually find that a serif font, such as Times or Dutch, is used for large amounts of text more often than a sans serif font, such as Helvetica or Swiss, which is typically favored for headlines and display type. As for using different type sizes to distinguish various text elements, a standard practice is to add at least 2 points to distinguish captions, body text, different levels of headings, and so forth.

Alignment and Hyphenation

The Alignment dialog box (shown below) defines the way in which the edges of text in a selected paragraph are lined up within a column, and includes controls for hyphenation and indented or outdented text. With the "Horizontal Alignment" option, you can set the text to line up evenly with the left or right column guide, center between column guides, line up with both column guides, called *justified*, or line up on a decimal. In typesetting terms, text that aligns evenly with the left margin only is also called *flush left* or *ragged right*, and text that aligns evenly with the right margin only is also called *flush right* or *ragged left*.

When you pick the "Horizontal Alignment: Decimal" option, the selected paragraph is automatically aligned on the decimals in each

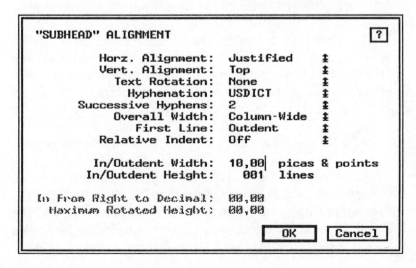

This Alignment dialog box shows the settings for a "Subhead" tag. A one-line outdent of 10 picas is specified, which means the text will be forced out from the edge of the column by 10 picas.

line of text, allowing you to format a table consisting of numbers without using tabs. Ventura places the first decimal point in each line at the distance from the right margin that you define using the "In From Right to Decimal" option (at the bottom of the dialog box), which is only available if decimal alignment is enabled. With the "Vertical Alignment" option, you can align a paragraph vertically, within a frame or box text, by using the "Top," "Middle," or "Bottom" setting. You can also use vertical alignment for text placed on the base page, which is useful for creating titles and word charts.

A unique feature in the Alignment dialog box is the ability to rotate a selected paragraph in 90-degree increments (i.e., 90, 180, and 270 degrees) around the original paragraph starting point. Rotated text is great for adding table headings, annotating charts and graphs, creating margin tabs, and embellishing a publication's typographic design. However, even though Ventura shows rotated text on any display system, only certain output devices, such as PostScript printers, can print rotated text. (Print the CAPABILI.CHP supplied on the Examples Disk to see if your printer supports rotated text.) When the "Text Rotation" option is enabled, the "Maximum Rotated Height" option (at the bottom of the dialog box) is also available, and you can set it to accommodate the height you want. For example, if rotated text doesn't fit in the area (frame or box text) where you place it, you may need to increase the "Maximum Rotated Height" setting or enlarge the area in which it is used. Working with rotated text is not as easy as using normal text, however, and you should practice applying this feature in advance if you intend to use it often.

The "Hyphenation" option lets you turn hyphenation on or off for a selected paragraph, and the "Successive Hyphens" option lets you pick the number of lines in a row that can be hyphenated. When hyphenation is on, the program uses a series of hyphenation tools each time a text file is loaded into the program and each time the file is paginated. These tools consist of files which are automatically placed in the VENTURA subdirectory during the installation process.

The first hyphenation tool is a computer algorithm, or logic program, built on certain rules of word construction that allow hyphens to be used with prefixes, suffixes, double consonants, and so forth. The default hyphenation algorithm is an American English file, called USENGLSH.HY1, but other algorithms for French, Italian, Spanish,

Text rotated by 270 degrees

Text rotated by 90 degrees

German, and U.K. English are also provided on the Ventura Publisher Loadable Filter Disk. These extra algorithms all contain an .HY2 file extension and you can install and use any two algorithms (one .HY1 and one .HY2 file) in the VENTURA subdirectory at the same time. To do so, copy the desired .HY2 file to the VENTURA directory from the Loadable Filter Disk. From then on, both algorithms are available for use in the same document, which allows you to hyphenate bilingual publications effectively. For example, to create a voter information pamphlet in which the text is written in both English and Spanish, you would create two identical sets of tags for titles, body text, subheads, and so on. The tags for paragraphs written in English would use the "Hyphenation: USENGLISH" option, and tags for paragraphs written in Spanish would use the "Hyphenation: SPANISH" option.

The program also provides a second American English algorithm, called USENGLS2.HY2, which offers more exhaustive hyphenation but isn't as fast as the default USENGLSH.HY1 algorithm. In producing justified and hyphenated documents with narrow columns, for instance, the USENGLS2.HY2 algorithm is recommended since it usually produces fewer loose lines than the default algorithm.

If the chosen algorithm's rules of logic fail to hyphenate a word, Ventura uses a second file, called HYPHEXPT.DIC, which provides a 329-word exception dictionary with the ability to override the algorithm in use. A third hyphenation file Ventura uses is a user hyphenation dictionary, called HYPHUSER.DIC, which initially contains 37 sample words, such as "bib-li-og-raphy" and "re-place-ment." By using an ASCII text editor or word processor that saves text as an ASCII file, you can add words to the HYPHUSER.DIC file to expand its usefulness and reduce the number of discretionary hyphens you may need to add manually when using Ventura. You can also add words you don't want hyhenated, such as a company name like Polaris International Publishing, by entering the words in the file *without* any hyphens. For example, adding the words "Polaris," "International," and "Publishing" will keep Ventura from hyphenating "Polaris International Publishing." (Note: If your word processor won't save text as an ASCII file, load the HYPHUSER.DIC file into Ventura after adding words to it and use the Edit menu's File Type/Rename option to save it as an ASCII text file in the VENTURA directory.)

The Ventura Publisher Loadable Filter Disk contains seven hyphenation algorithms:

❶ *USENGLSH.HY1*
❷ *USENGLS2.HY2*
❸ *UKENGLSH.HY2*
❹ *FRENCH.HY2*
❺ *ITALIAN.HY2*
❻ *SPANISH.HY2*
❼ *GERMAN.HY2*

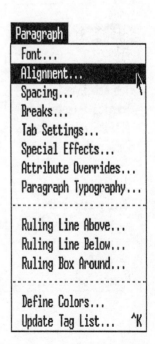

Paragraph
Font...
Alignment...
Spacing...
Breaks...
Tab Settings...
Special Effects...
Attribute Overrides...
Paragraph Typography...
Ruling Line Above...
Ruling Line Below...
Ruling Box Around...
Define Colors...
Update Tag List...   ^K

Frame-wide headings on the base page.

```
┌──────────────────────────────┐
│ Paragraph                    │
├──────────────────────────────┤
│ Font...                      │
│ Alignment...                 │
│ Spacing...                   │
│ Breaks...                    │
│ Tab Settings...              │
│ Special Effects...           │
│ Attribute Overrides...       │
│ Paragraph Typography...      │
│ ·····························│
│ Ruling Line Above...         │
│ Ruling Line Below...         │
│ Ruling Box Around...         │
│ ·····························│
│ Define Colors...             │
│ Update Tag List...      ^K   │
└──────────────────────────────┘
```

The next item in the Alignment dialog box lets you override column settings and force a paragraph to run across an entire frame or page by selecting the "Overall Width: Frame-Wide" option. Frame-wide paragraphs are useful for creating headlines on multicolumn pages (as shown on the left), especially since they temporarily interrupt any vertical rules separating the columns. Plus, if you use the Chapter Typography option and set the base page for "Column Balance: On," the body text preceding the frame-wide paragraph will automatically flow equally into all of the columns above it.

However, a frame-wide paragraph on the base page also prints over any text placed to the left of it, so using it in any column other than the first requires a bit more work. Consider, for example, a three-column newsletter in which headings extend across the second and third columns to start new articles. To keep a frame-wide heading in the second column from extending into the first, you could indent it to force it where you want, or block it by adding a thin vertical frame to its left — use the Frame menu's Sizing & Scaling option and set the thin frame for "Flow Text Around: On."

However, if the newsletter has vertical rules, neither of these techniques will keep the frame-wide heading from interrupting them, and a third technique is required as follows. Draw a frame over the second and third columns where you want the next article to begin, select the Frame menu's Margins & Columns option to format the frame for two columns — using the same column and gutter widths as for the base page — and place the text inside this frame. The frame-wide heading will then extend properly across both columns within the frame, which comprise the second and third columns on the base page.

The remaining options in the Alignment dialog box all pertain to indents and outdents, which are commonly used for the first line in a paragraph or the lead paragraph in an article. The space width and line settings you define will force the text in or out from the left edge of the column. First, indicate whether you want an indent or outdent by clicking on the corresponding "First Line" option box, then type the amount of space in the "In/Outdent Width" line, using the measurement unit of your choice. To change the measurement unit, click on the unit words in the usual manner. If you want the indent to affect more than the first line, type in the desired number of lines

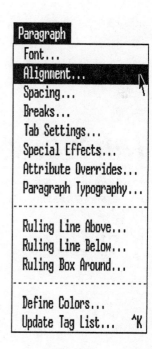

Using the Alignment dialog box, you can create an indent of several lines to make space for a colophon in the first paragraph of every chapter or section. This paragraph has an indent of 00.55 inches and an indent height of three lines. The indent for this visual embellishment could also be created by drawing a frame within the specified space. The sample colophon shown above was created with Ventura's Graphic Drawing mode.

I. Outdents are used to place one or more lines of a paragraph to the left of the frame or page margin. They are useful for many types of situations, including marginal headings, section numbering, and simulated hanging indents, which are otherwise created by indenting all lines except the first line in a paragraph.

in the "In/Outdent Height" line. Finally, use the default setting for "Relative Indent: Off," unless you want to add an additional amount of space equal to the length of the last line in the previous paragraph.

For example, to place a section-numbered paragraph on the same line as its automatically generated number, or to place a free-form caption on the same line as an automatic caption label, you would pick "Relative Indent: On" and add an "In/Outdent Width" of 1 pica for the section-numbered or caption paragraph. You would also use the Paragraph menu's Breaks option and select "Line Break: After" for both paragraphs and either "Line Break: Before" or "Line Break: No" for the automatic number (Z_SEC#) and automatic caption (Z_LABEL CAP, Z_LABEL FIG, or Z_LABEL TBL) paragraphs that precede them. (For more on this type of relative indent, see page 130 regarding automatic section numbers.)

The Spacing Controls

The Spacing menu option lets you control the vertical space between lines and paragraphs and add horizontal space to the left and right margins on a per paragraph tag basis. Although most of the features in the Spacing dialog box are fairly straightforward, Ventura uses several factors when calculating paragraph spacing, and its formulaic procedure takes time to learn.

Unlike dialog boxes that contain settings based on a single unit of measurement, the Spacing dialog box includes three separate controls for measurement units. For instance, you can use inches for the left and right margin options, picas and points for the "Above" and "Below" paragraph spacing, and fractional points for the most accurate "Inter-Line" spacing.

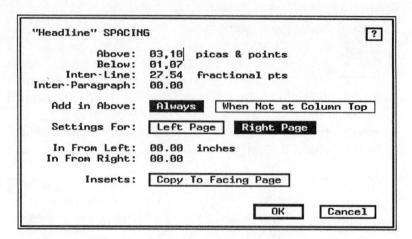

```
"Headline" SPACING                                    [?]

            Above:    03,10|  picas & points
            Below:    01,07
       Inter-Line:    27.54   fractional pts
  Inter-Paragraph:    00.00

   Add in Above:   [ Always ]  [ When Not at Column Top ]

   Settings For:   [ Left Page ]  [ Right Page ]

  In From Left:    00.00   inches
 In From Right:    00.00

      Inserts:   [ Copy To Facing Page ]

                                   [   OK   ]  [ Cancel ]
```

The one value in the Spacing dialog box (shown above) always present and used by every paragraph tag is "Inter-Line" spacing, also called *leading*, which controls the space between lines in the same paragraph. For a simple document that only uses one type size, such as a business letter, you probably won't need to use the other settings. Inter-line spacing is measured from the baseline of the characters in one line to the baseline of the characters in the next line. As a rule, inter-line spacing is set at 1 or 2 points more than the type size being used, for example, 10-point type is usually set on 11 or 12 points of inter-line spacing. For tighter line spacing, you can use inter-line spacing equal to the type size, also called *solid leading*, such as 10-point type set on 10 points inter-line spacing (as shown below).

Inter-line

Inter-line spacing is measured baseline to baseline.

spacing

Line spacing has a strong affect on the readability of a document. This line is set 10 on 10 Times.

Line spacing has a strong affect on the readability of a document. This line is set 10 on 12 Times.

Line spacing has a strong affect on the readability of a document. This line is set 10 on 11 Times.

Line spacing has a strong affect on the readability of a document. This line is set 10 on 13 Times.

By default, Ventura will adjust inter-line spacing automatically — using a value of about 20 percent — whenever you use the Paragraph menu's Font option to change a paragraph tag's type size. For instance, if you change 10-point type to 12-point type, the program increases the inter-line spacing from 12 to 14 points; if you change the size again to 8-point type, Ventura decreases the inter-line spacing to 10 points. If you don't want Ventura to control inter-line spacing automatically, do not select "Styles" or "Both" for the "Auto-Adjustments" option in the Options menu's Set Preferences dialog box. After you turn off automatic inter-line spacing, the space between lines stays at the previous setting whenever you change type sizes. Constant inter-line spacing is often used when creating tables with mixed type sizes.

If you lack experience in specifying type or simply don't want to worry about inter-line spacing, you can use Ventura's default inter-line spacing for most body text up to about 12 points. However, for larger type sizes, you may find that Ventura adds too much space to inter-line spacing. For instance, a 24-point headline will have 28 points of inter-line spacing, if automatic line spacing is applied. However, by using the Spacing dialog box for that paragraph tag, you can manually change the line spacing to a smaller value, such as 26 points. To do so, you simply use the typing cursor to enter the amount you want for the "Inter-Line" spacing value.

24-point type on 28 points

24-point type on 25 points

The measurement unit used for setting inter-line spacing in the Spacing dialog box is also used to control the "Inter-Paragraph" setting, which adds space between paragraphs using the same tag. However, Ventura does not use a default value for inter-paragraph spacing. Instead, if a text file contains two paragraph returns after each paragraph, which is a common way to prepare text with a word processor, Ventura adds an additional line space between paragraphs. For instance, with 10-point type set on 12 points, Ventura will add 12 points of spacing for each extra paragraph return.

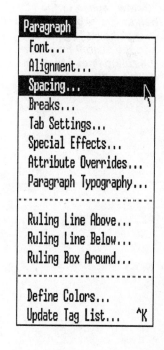

If you want to add more paragraph spacing, use the typing cursor and enter the amount in the "Inter-Paragraph" line. For text that will be placed in adjacent columns, use an integer multiple of the inter-line spacing value for the amount to ensure that the columns of text are aligned. In other words, use a whole number that is a multiple rather than a fraction of the line spacing amount — for instance, use inter-paragraph spacing of 10 or 15 points for paragraphs with inter-line spacing of 10 points; or use 12 or 18 points of paragraph spacing when using an inter-line spacing of 12 points.

When you enter a value for "Inter-Paragraph" spacing, Ventura adds that amount between paragraphs with the *same* tag, but ignores it when adding space between paragraphs with *different* tags. So far, so good, but there's an exception to this rule. If the inter-paragraph spacing used by two different tags is *identical,* that amount is also added between the paragraphs. In most cases, however, you'll use two other controls in the dialog box — the "Above" and "Below" spacing options — to add space between paragraphs with different tags, such as a heading and body text. The measurement unit for these two options is located to the right of the "Above" line. To apply either or both of these controls, set the measurement unit as desired, and use the typing cursor to enter the amounts.

Unlike the "Inter-Paragraph" spacing option, which provides a single amount to add between all paragraphs with the same tag, the

In this screen shot of a newsletter placed on the base page, the paragraph spacing between the ID (volume/date) tag and the headline tag ("What Price Really?") includes the amount for the ID's "Below" space or the headline's "Above" space — whichever is greater — and the overall height of the ruling lines below the ID line, plus the inter-line space for the ID line.

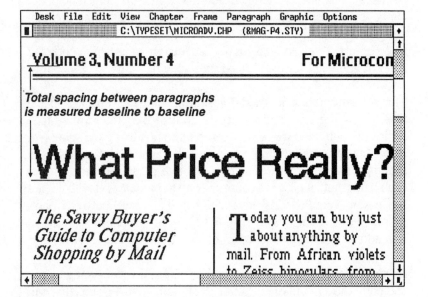

"Above" and "Below" options require Ventura to make an additional calculation. When a paragraph tagged for "Below" line spacing is followed by a paragraph tagged for "Above" line spacing, Ventura only adds the *greater* of the two amounts. For example, when a heading tagged for 20 points "Below" spacing is followed by text tagged for 15 points "Above" spacing, Ventura only adds 20 more points between the paragraphs and ignores the smaller (15 points) amount. Finally, if you don't want the "Above" space added when the paragraph appears at the top of a new page or column, select the "Add in Above: When Not at Column Top" option.

In addition to inter-line, inter-paragraph, and above/below spacing amounts, Ventura considers one more factor when it calculates how much spacing to put between paragraphs. As explained later in this section of the chapter, you can add ruling lines to a paragraph tag by using the Paragraph menu's Ruling Line Above, Ruling Line Below, or Ruling Box Around options. With any of these options, you can specify up to three ruling lines plus extra spacing above and below each rule, which results in an "Overall Height" for the rules. Ventura also includes this amount when it adds paragraph spacing.

By now it should be evident that there are several factors to consider in determining how much space Ventura adds between the various paragraphs in a document. As mentioned earlier, producing simple documents won't usually require that much work in terms of using the Spacing dialog box; but for complex documents with multiple columns and numerous tags, you may find it best to keep a pad and pencil close at hand.

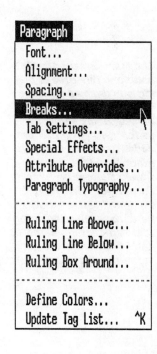

To summarize the information Ventura uses to calculate paragraph spacing, the essential factors the program adds together (when applicable) include:

- Inter-line space for Tag #1
- Inter-paragraph spacing when identical for both paragraphs
- The larger value between Tag #1's Below spacing and Tag #2's Above spacing
- The overall height for Tag #1's Ruling Line Below or Ruling Box Around options
- The overall height for Tag #2's Ruling Line Above or Ruling Box Around options

The remaining options in the Spacing dialog box are used for setting *temporary* margins on the left side, right side, or both sides of each left and right page (permanent page margins are set by using the Frame menu's Margins & Columns option). The word "temporary" is used to emphasize the fact that each tag can specify a different setting for these margins. The "In From Left" and "In From Right" controls refer to the distance from the column edges to inside the column where the text will line up. Both of these values are controlled by the measurement unit on the right side of the "In From Right" option.

The ability to add temporary margins has many applications, including indents for quotations, lists, bulleted items, and film or audiovisual scripts. In this book, the "In From Left" and "In From Right" options were used to indent all body copy on the left and right pages, respectively. As with other dialog boxes, you can either click on the opposite page in the "Settings For" option and manually reset the information to create complementary pages, or you can click on the "Inserts: Copy to Facing Page" option and Ventura will automatically copy the same settings to the opposite page.

Using Breaks
With Ventura, the term *breaks* refers to forced interruptions in the flow of text between two paragraphs. With the Breaks option, you can create three types of breaks: page, column, and line breaks. The

The "Line Break: After" setting in this Breaks dialog box enables the selected paragraph to be placed on the same line as the paragraph that precedes it — if the first paragraph is set for "Line Break: Before" or "Line Break: No." The "Next Y Position" setting shown here places the beginning of this paragraph at the end of the last character in the previous paragraph.

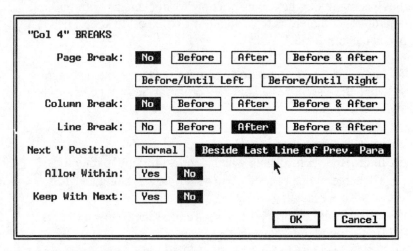

order in which the various controls appear in the Breaks dialog box (shown above) indicates their hierarchy, from top to bottom, that is, each option overrides those below it. Although the default settings in the Breaks option dialog box are usually appropriate for most paragraph tags, several special formatting effects are available if you manipulate some of the settings.

The "Page Break" option is particularly important because Ventura ignores any page break commands placed in a text file with a word processor. The choices you can pick for page breaks are fairly self-explanatory. For a title page of a book or report, for instance, select the "Page Break: After" option for the main title tag if you want the following paragraph to start on a new page or in a new frame. To make sure each chapter or section heading starts at the top of a new page, pick "Page Break: Before" or use "Page Break: Before/Until Right" or "Page Break: Before/Until Left" if you want each chapter to start on a right or left page only.

The "Column Break" options are just like the "Page Break" options except that they interrupt the column-to-column flow of paragraphs. All other options in the Breaks dialog box pertain to line breaks. For standard tags like body text, the "Line Break: Before" setting is appropriate, but by combining the "Line Break: No" and "Line Break: After" options for other tags, you can produce unique formats, such as paragraph lead-ins, hanging indents, and vertical tabs.

With Ventura, the term *paragraph lead-in* refers to the use of mixed type styles or type sizes in the first sentence of a paragraph. A common example of this is the dateline used at the beginning of a newspaper article or press release, mentioning the location and/or date. There are two ways to create this type of effect with Ventura. The first method is to use the Text Editing function, select the lead-in words with the mouse cursor, and then click on the desired text attribute, such as bold or italic, in the side-bar's assignment list. Or, a faster method is to use the Paragraph Tagging function and apply special tags to automatically format the paragraph lead-in.

To create paragraph lead-ins with the Paragraph Tagging method, first use the Breaks option to place two paragraphs with different tags on the same line. This is accomplished by selecting the Breaks dialog box for each paragraph, and setting paragraph 1 for "Line Break: Before" and paragraph 2 for "Line Break: After." These settings eliminate any line break between the paragraphs and place them on the same line — usually in the same spot at the left edge of the column. Therefore, to keep the paragraphs from overlapping, you next use the Alignment dialog box for paragraph 2, enter a small value (such as 1 pica) for the "In/Outdent Width" option, and click on the "Relative Indent: Length of Previous Line" option. These parameters will automatically indent paragraph 2 to the space where paragraph 1 ends and also add a blank space between them.

The same technique used for paragraph lead-ins can be applied to place a caption or section-numbered paragraph on the same line as

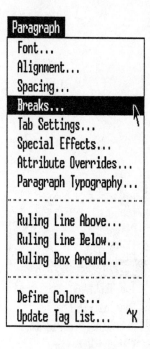

Paragraph 1 is a bold-face lead-in set for "Line Break: Before."

NEW YORK — The highly anticipated joint manned mission to Mars was announced yesterday by the United States and the Soviet Union during an unprecedented US/Soviet news conference held at the United Nations.

Paragraph 2 (The highly anticipated ...) is normal text set for "Line Break: After."

a program-generated caption label or section number, as mentioned in earlier parts of this book. With captions, you treat the "Z_LABEL CAP," "Z_LABEL FIG," or "Z_LABEL TBL" tag the same as paragraph 1 set for "Line Break: Before," and treat the "Z_CAPTION" (free-form caption) tag as paragraph 2 set for "Line Break: After." With section numbers, you likewise set each "Z_SEC#" tag for "Line Break: Before," and set each numbered paragraph for "Line Break: After."

By applying a variation of the technique just described, you can also create a *hanging indent,* in which the first line of a paragraph is flush left, but all the rest of the paragraph's lines are indented by an equal amount. Hanging indents are similar to outdents in that they clearly distinguish the occurrence of a new item, such as each section in a report or each listing in a directory. To create a hanging indent, follow the same procedure using the Breaks option to place two paragraphs on the same line. However, instead of using the Alignment option to indent the first line in paragraph 2, use the Spacing option's "Indent From Left" setting to indent the *entire paragraph* by whatever amount you desire. These parameters produce a paragraph in which the first line is flush left and the remaining lines are all indented equally due to the temporary margin you created.

A variation of the technique applied to create hanging indents can also be used to create *vertical tabs,* in which a columnar effect is produced by forcing multiple paragraphs to start on the same line but with vertical space added between them. Unlike horizontal tabs used for single-line entries, such as numeric data, vertical tabs can be used to manage whole paragraphs, including word-wrap, so the additional lines of text in each paragraph align with the first line in that particular paragraph (as shown on the following page). The trick is to use the Spacing option and force each paragraph to wrap vertically within its own set of temporary margins. To do this, you create a tag for each "column" (read paragraph) and adjust its "Indent From Left" and "Indent From Right" settings so that each paragraph assigned that tag occupies its own vertical space and does not overlap the other columnar material.

To create vertical tabs, follow the same procedure for hanging indents, but use the Spacing menu's "Indent From Right" option to keep the first paragraph from overlapping the second. The result will resemble two columns of text that are created automatically by

Paragraph

Font...
Alignment...
Spacing...
Breaks...
Tab Settings...
Special Effects...
Attribute Overrides...
Paragraph Typography...

Ruling Line Above...
Ruling Line Below...
Ruling Box Around...

Define Colors...
Update Tag List...   ^K

Common Binding Styles

Type	Description	Comments	Order#
Glued Binding	Glue or padding cement with a piece of cheesecloth or thin gauze to add durability.	Inexpensive method to bind thin books or booklets at spine or top edge. Sheets removed easily. Not for repeated use.	10-250-B1
Saddle Stitched	Wires inserted through backbone into center spread. Can be bound with a self-cover or separate, heavier cover.	Common binding method for pamphlets, booklets, catalogs, bulletins. Simple and inexpensive. Allows pages to open fully and lie flat for easy reading.	10-250-B2
Side Stitched	Wires inserted from front page to back page (1/4 inch from the edge); covers of heavy stock then glued on and trimmed. Use determined by the bulk and number of pages.	Used for books, magazines, manuals. A disadvantage is that the wires prevent pages from opening flat. Requires wide inside margin to compensate for the extra space required by wires.	10-250-B3
Plastic Binding	Pages and cover are trimmed, slotted or round holes are drilled, and plastic coils are inserted into the holes.	Book lies flat when open, ideal for textbooks, manuals. Plastic coils in many colors. Requires drilling or hole punching. Books do not usually stack or pack well.	10-250-B4
Spiral Binding	Uses metal or wire coils with single, double, or multiple rings. Cover and pages are trimmed, holes are made, wire is spiral inserted.	Designed for constant use, stronger than plastic binding. Opens easily, lies flat. Hand- or machine-inserted spiral coil requires extra time and expense.	10-250-B5
Perfect Binding	Pages held together and fixed to the cover by adhesive (plus gauze) glued over the spine. Hard or soft cover pasted to spine after pages trimmed.	Relatively inexpensive and durable, used for paperbacks, manuals. Requires certain amount of thickness to be used; does not work on thin booklets.	10-250-B6
Staple Binding	Same principle as an ordinary hand stapler using preformed strips of thin wire staples, operated by foot pedal.	Very inexpensive, simple and fast, but unattractive binding method. Restricts full opening; pages can be torn off.	10-250-B7
Velo Binding	Consists of plastic strips with molded fingers inserted in prepunched holes. Takes 1/4-inch margin.	Very strong. Good for documents which are to be kept intact; pages cannot be removed. More costly than spiral. Sheets will not lie flat when document is opened.	10-250-B8

This columnar material is created with vertical tabs using the Breaks and Spacing menu options. From left to right, column 1 uses "Line Break: Before," columns 2 and 3 use "Line Break: No," and all three columns use "Next Y Position: Normal." Column 4 uses "Line Break: After" and "Next Y Position: Beside Last Line of Previous Paragraph." Each column is formatted with a different tag and requires different settings for its temporary "In From Left" and "In From Right" margins.

applying two paragraph tags. You can also add more vertical tabs by manipulating each new paragraph tag's temporary margin settings, using the "Indent From Right" and "Indent From Left" options.

Whenever the "Line Break: No" or "Line Break: After" options are chosen for a paragraph tag, the vertical position of any text assigned that tag is also affected by the "Next Y Position" option in the Breaks dialog box. If you use the "Normal" default setting, the text begins on the first line of the previous paragraph. This is the setting used to create the formating effects for lead-ins, hanging indents, and vertical tabs. However, if you select the "Beside Last Line of Previous Paragraph" option, the text begins on the same line as the last line of the preceding paragraph. If you want to use multiple-line lead-ins, for instance, you can use this option to make paragraph 2 begin on the same line on which paragraph 1 ends. A typical application of this type of lead-in is found in interviews, when a multiple-line question is followed by an answer without a line break.

The final two options in the Breaks dialog box give you control over paragraphs that you don't want to split up on separate pages or frames. Select "Allow Within: No" if you don't want a paragraph to contain any line breaks within the paragraph itself. Use "Keep With Next: Yes" to keep the selected paragraph on the same page as the paragraph that follows it, for instance, this option is often used to keep headings from being left at the bottom of a page or column.

Setting Tabs

Tab Settings is the next Paragraph menu option. When selected, Ventura provides a dialog box that enables you to establish up to 16 horizontal tabs for any given paragraph tag. At each tab stop, you can also choose whether you want the text/numbers left, right, center, or decimal aligned. Unlike the vertical tabs you can create using the Breaks and Spacing options, horizontal tabs are designed to be used on a single line. Although the Tab Settings option is primarily used to format tables containing single-line text entries or decimally aligned numbers, it's also an effective tool for creating price lists, directories, tables of contents, indexes, and other types of documents with special alignment needs.

If you're using a word-processed text file, Ventura will recognize any actual tab characters placed in the file, but it uses the locations specified in the Tab Settings dialog box to determine each tab's position on a given line. Using Microsoft Word, WordPerfect, or WordStar, for instance, you normally prepare tabular material by setting tab stops and by pressing the Tab key whenever you want the cursor to move to the next tab stop for that line. However, unless your word processor's tab stops match those in Ventura's Tab Settings dialog box, the text will not align properly. Therefore, to avoid misalignment errors, use tab settings in your word processor that match the tab settings in the Ventura style sheet you're using, or prepare text without any tabs and add them later inside Ventura, using the Text Editing mode.

If you follow the first approach and add tabs in text files using a word processor, make certain that a true tab character is inserted when you press the Tab key. With some word processors, such as

Paragraph

Font...
Alignment...
Spacing...
Breaks...
Tab Settings...
Special Effects...
Attribute Overrides...
Paragraph Typography...

Ruling Line Above...
Ruling Line Below...
Ruling Box Around...

Define Colors...
Update Tag List...   ^K

Microsoft Word, the tab character is represented by the same symbol (→) that Ventura displays; with others, each tab is depicted as ^I (Ctrl-I). With a few programs, such as WordStar, the tab character may not be represented on screen at all, which makes it more difficult to know if actual tabs are being inserted instead of a series of spaces. It's also important to insert only *one tab character* between each set of numbers or string of text that you want Ventura to place in columns. Although this usually results in text or numbers that appear misaligned on screen when using a word processor, it will be much easier to format the file when using Ventura.

Inserting tabs in a text file placed on a page inside Ventura is relatively easy, although it can be a time-consuming process. Select the Text Editing mode and use the typing cursor in the usual way, pressing the Tab key whenever you want to enter an actual tab character. If you select the Show Tabs & Returns command in the Options menu, which is highly recommended when using the Text Editing mode, you'll see the tab character symbol displayed on screen. If your file requires lots of tabs, you can speed things up by using the mouse cursor and keyboard together. With one hand, move the mouse and press the button to insert the typing cursor at each space you want a tab, then press the tab key with the other hand. It should also be noted that justification overrides tab settings; therefore, you must select "Alignment: Left" (using the Alignment menu option) for each paragraph tag that requires tabs. Ventura won't stop you from adding tabs to a paragraph that is justified, but it will display a pop-up message reminding you to choose left-aligned text in order for the tab settings to take effect.

To use the Tab Settings dialog box (shown on the following page), the basic steps are to pick the "Tab Number" you want to set and the "Tab Type," then use the typing cursor to enter the "Tab Location," which is measured from the *left edge of the column*. After setting the first tab, select "Tab Number: 2" and repeat the other steps, select "Tab Number: 3," and so on, for as many of the 16 tabs as needed. When finished, each time Ventura encounters a tab character in a line, it will automatically place the next character at the horizontal location specified for that tab number. If you use the "Open Space" default for the "Tab Shown As" setting, the space between tabs that isn't occupied by text or numbers is open. If you select "Leader Char" instead, this area is filled with characters, such as periods or

Paragraph
Font...
Alignment...
Spacing...
Breaks...
Tab Settings...
Special Effects...
Attribute Overrides...
Paragraph Typography...

Ruling Line Above...
Ruling Line Below...
Ruling Box Around...

Define Colors...
Update Tag List...   ^K

In this Tab Settings dialog box, the third tab stop is set for right alignment, leader characters turned on, and at 3 inches from the left margin. The "Leader Char" setting is for leader dots (ASCII character 46) with three spaces between each dot. You can also pick other "Leader Char" options or use the typing cursor to enter a different ASCII decimal code.

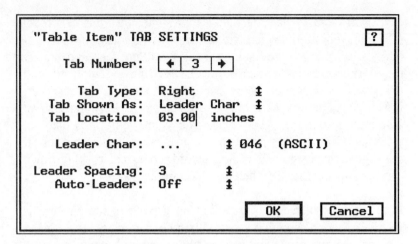

leader dots, underlines, spaces, or any other ASCII character. For instance, leader dots are commonly used in tables of contents, as in the following example:

Chapter Title **10**
Subhead **15**
Subhead **20**

If the "Auto-Leader: On" setting is selected, Ventura inserts leader characters from the end of the paragraph to the right margin, without requiring any additional tab settings. This feature is often used in preparing tables and forms, for instance, when you want to indicate that an otherwise blank area in a given line or row is intentional.

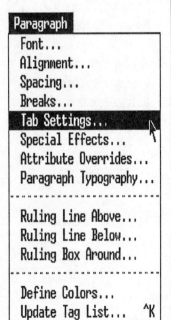

To disable any tab from being used, just select the "Tab Type: Off" option; to edit any tab's settings, select the appropriate tab number first, then make the changes. Note that each time you select the Tab Settings dialog box, the "Tab Number: 1" setting is displayed first; therefore, make sure you click on the left or right arrow to select the tab number you want to edit before changing any of the settings.

To help measure the exact location for each tab stop, use the program's on-screen rulers. First, reset the zero point on the horizontal ruler so it is equal to the left margin of the base page or whatever frame the text has been placed in. To do this, select the Show Column Guides option in the Options menu and use the scroll tools to move the page as necessary until the left edge of the column is displayed on the screen. Then click on the zero point box and hold, drag the cursor to the edge of the left column guide, and release the mouse button. The numbers on the horizontal ruler will now show the distance from the edge of the left column instead of the page.

As a formatting aid or to help learn how to control tabs, try setting tabs with a sample paragraph of text that contains as many horizontal tabs as needed, followed by text that clearly indicates each tab number. For example, if you need to use five tabs, your sample unformatted paragraph could be as follows (tab characters are represented by arrows):

No tab→Tab 1→Tab 2→Tab 3→Tab 4→Tab 5

The words "No tab" represent the text that will align with the left margin before the first tab is used. If your tabular text is longer or shorter than the text used in this sample, use more or less characters between the horizontal tabs in your own sample paragraph, or you may want to use a sample that contains numbers and decimal points. To proceed, select the Paragraph Tagging mode, click on your sample paragraph, and assign it the tag name (such as "Table Item") to be used for the actual tabular material. Next, select the Font option to specify the type size you want to use, then select the Tab Settings option and try out various tab locations until the text aligns the way you want it. After you're satisfied with the tab settings, delete the sample paragraph and proceed to tag the actual tabular text.

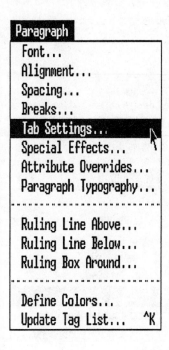

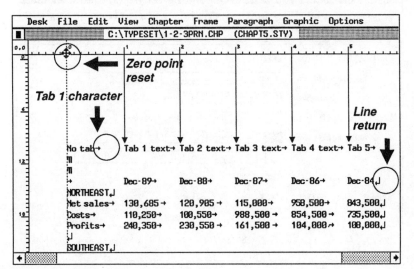

In this screen shot, the zero point is reset so tab settings are more easily measured from the left edge of the column. The tabs are set 1 inch apart and aligned left: Tab 1 at 1 inch, Tab 2 at 2 inches, Tab 3 at 3 inches, and so on. Line returns, rather than paragraph returns, have been used to terminate each line.

Finally, when using the Text Editing function to edit the text in a table, use line breaks rather than paragraph returns to terminate the end of a line whenever possible. To create a line break, hold down the Control key and press the Enter key. This places the text on the next line where you want it, but it remains part of the same paragraph. The advantages of using line breaks rather than returns are: there are less paragraphs to tag, less memory is consumed, and it's easier to add ruling lines to tables. For example, if you apply the Ruling Line Below option to the tag used for each basic line in a table, the program adds the specified ruling line after every line that ends with a paragraph return. However, if you use line breaks to separate a series of lines, for instance, all lines under a major heading, such as "Sales," the ruling line below will only appear after the last line in the series, when a paragraph return is used.

Special Effects

The next Paragraph menu option, Special Effects, includes features that are not required for standard formatting purposes, but nevertheless provide you with additional levels of control over the automatic preparation of your documents. When you select the Special Effects option, the dialog box provided (shown below) enables you to add one of two special characters to the beginning of a paragraph. "Big First Char" creates a large capital letter, also called a *drop cap,* in which the character's baseline drops below the first line of text in the paragraph. "Bullet" adds a standard bullet symbol (•) or any other ASCII character you select. Depending on which character effect you select, other lines in the dialog box will also become available.

Paragraph

Font...
Alignment...
Spacing...
Breaks...
Tab Settings...
Special Effects...
Attribute Overrides...
Paragraph Typography...

Ruling Line Above...
Ruling Line Below...
Ruling Box Around...

Define Colors...
Update Tag List...   ^K

The options selected in this Special Effects dialog box will add a "Bullet" (ASCII character 195), followed by a 1-pica indent, at the beginning of each paragraph assigned the tag called "Bullet Body." Note that when the bullet option is selected, the "Space for Big First" line is not available.

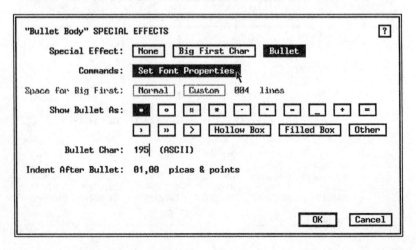

This paragraph begins with a 48-point capital letter that is created by using the Special Effects option. "Big First Char" is used for the "Special Effect" setting, and the "Set Front Properties" command for picking the typeface, type size, style, and color. A 3-line indent for the first big character is created by using the "Space for Big First: Custom" setting.

● A bullet can also be used to automatically start a paragraph by applying the Special Effects menu option.

✳ Or, instead of using a bullet, you can use any other ASCII character at the beginning of a paragraph.

If you later decide you don't want to use this character effect, just select "Special Effect: None."

After selecting either of these effects, you click on the "Set Font Properties" command to access the Font Setting For Big First Character dialog box for specifying the type attributes for the drop cap or bullet character (i.e., typeface, type size, style, and color options). The dialog box the program provides for this purpose is the same dialog box you use when you pick the Font option in the Paragraph menu or when you click on the side-bar's "Set Font" button using the Text Editing cursor. If you want to change the character's vertical placement, the "Shift" option can also be applied. To review how to use the various features in this dialog box, consult the "Text Editing" section in Chapter 4. When you finish specifying the font information, select "OK" and Ventura returns you to the Special Effects dialog box.

With the "Space for Big First" option, you select "Normal" if you want Ventura to automatically adjust the number of indented lines required to accommodate the drop cap, or click on the "Custom" option and use the typing cursor to enter the exact number of indented lines you want. All of the remaining options in this dialog box are used for formatting a bullet character. You can either click on one of the common symbols conveniently displayed after the "Show Bullet As" option, or you can click on "Other" and use the typing cursor to enter the ASCII character you want on the "Bullet Char" line. The "Indent After Bullet" option is used to add space between the bullet character and the first character in the paragraph.

Paragraph

Font...
Alignment...
Spacing...
Breaks...
Tab Settings...
Special Effects...
Attribute Overrides...
Paragraph Typography...

Ruling Line Above...
Ruling Line Below...
Ruling Box Around...

Define Colors...
Update Tag List...   ^K

With the Attribute Overrides dialog box, you can also customize the line features used for the overscore, strike-thru, underline, and double underline text attributes, as well as superscript, subscript, and small cap size.

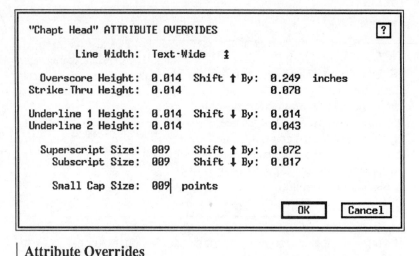

```
 ┌──────────────────────────────────────────────────────────────┐
 │ "Chapt Head" ATTRIBUTE OVERRIDES                          [?]  │
 │                                                                │
 │            Line Width:   Text-Wide    ↕                        │
 │                                                                │
 │   Overscore Height:   0.014   Shift ↑ By:   0.249   inches     │
 │ Strike-Thru Height:   0.014                 0.078              │
 │                                                                │
 │ Underline 1 Height:   0.014   Shift ↓ By:   0.014             │
 │ Underline 2 Height:   0.014                 0.043             │
 │                                                                │
 │   Superscript Size:   009     Shift ↑ By:   0.072            │
 │     Subscript Size:   009     Shift ↓ By:   0.017            │
 │                                                                │
 │     Small Cap Size:   009│    points                          │
 │                                                                │
 │                                          [ OK ]   [ Cancel ]   │
 └──────────────────────────────────────────────────────────────┘
```

Paragraph

Font...
Alignment...
Spacing...
Breaks...
Tab Settings...
Special Effects...
Attribute Overrides...
Paragraph Typography...

Ruling Line Above...
Ruling Line Below...
Ruling Box Around...

Define Colors...
Update Tag List...   ^K

Unlike the default, the underline in line 2 is shifted down 5 points to keep it from running into the descending parts of certain letters.

Attribute Overrides

The dialog box Ventura provides for the Attribute Overrides option gives you considerable typographic precision over several of the text attribute features that appear in certain font-related dialog boxes and in the side-bar assignment list when the Text Editing mode is active. First is the "Line Width" option, which determines whether a text attribute will apply to the selected text only or all the way to the right margin. Although you'll probably use the default "Text-Wide" setting for most cases, selecting "Margin-Wide" lets you extend the attribute across the entire line, from the left to the right margin.

The next two groups of options in the Attribute Overrides dialog box let you modify the ruling lines Ventura adds when you select the text attributes for overscore, strike-thru, underline, and double underline. On the left are "Height" (thickness) controls and on the right are the respective "Shift" (vertical placement) controls for each of these attributes. To change any of the default settings, you use the typing cursor to enter the amount in the usual fashion. The measurement unit for all of these settings is located to the right of the first "Shift" option. As you might expect, you can shift the overscore and strike-thru lines upward, and shift the underlines downward. The

abcdefghijklmnopqrstuvwxyz

abcdefghijklmnopqrstuvwxyz

two controls for "Underline 1" serve double duty: they define the height and vertical shift for both the single underline and the top line in the double underline. The "Underline 2" controls affect only the bottom line in the double underline.

The last three options in the Attribute Overrides dialog box control the type size and vertical placement for superscript, subscript, and small caps. The measurement unit for the type size is permanently set in points, while the "Shift By" control is governed by the same unit set for the other shift controls at the top right of the dialog box. A trick with the "Small Cap Size" option is that you can not only set it for a type size that is smaller than a paragraph type size, but *larger* as well. For instance, you could set this control for 18 point type and use it to create a drop cap for any selected character(s) in a paragraph set for 12-point text. Whenever you want a character to jump to 18 points, you just use the Text Editing cursor to select the text and then assign it the "Small" attribute from the side-bar assignment list.

Typographic Control by Paragraph

For the Paragraph Typography option, Ventura provides a complex dialog box (shown below) that requires some effort to master, particularly for those with little or no background in typesetting. Fortunately, however, you can safely use the default settings for most of your documents — at least, until you're ready to spend some time experimenting with the Paragraph Typography dialog box. Even those experienced in managing typographic aesthetics should test Ventura's implementation of these sophisticated features to learn how various settings affect the typeset output on a given system.

Paragraph

Font...
Alignment...
Spacing...
Breaks...
Tab Settings...
Special Effects...
Attribute Overrides...
Paragraph Typography...

Ruling Line Above...
Ruling Line Below...
Ruling Box Around...

Define Colors...
Update Tag List...   ^K

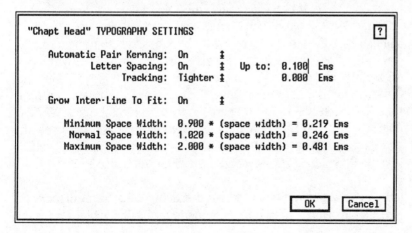

```
"Chapt Head" TYPOGRAPHY SETTINGS                        [?]

    Automatic Pair Kerning:  On        ‡
           Letter Spacing:  On        ‡  Up to:  0.100  Ems
                Tracking:  Tighter ‡           0.000  Ems

    Grow Inter-Line To Fit:  On        ‡

        Minimum Space Width:  0.900 * (space width) = 0.219 Ems
         Normal Space Width:  1.020 * (space width) = 0.246 Ems
        Maximum Space Width:  2.000 * (space width) = 0.481 Ems




                                        [ OK ]  [ Cancel ]
```

The Typography Settings dialog box enables you to use several sophisticated typesetting features, which include kerning, tracking, letter spacing, and word spacing.

In general, most of the features in the Paragraph Typography dialog box let you control the horizontal placement of text on a given line in very precise increments. First is the "Automatic Pair Kerning" option, which enables you to turn kerning on or off for any given paragraph tag. In most cases, you'll use automatic kerning for headline, title, and subhead tags, but not as often for body text and smaller text tags, such as captions and diagram words. As discussed earlier in other parts of this book, this control has no affect on your document if the "Pair Kerning: Off" option is selected in the Chapter menu's Chapter Typography dialog box. (To review the effect of kerning in general, consult the "Text Editing" section in Chapter 4.)

The "Letter Spacing" and "Space Width" options are related controls that affect the amount of space between letters and words, respectively. "Tracking" is an additional control used to increase or decrease letter spacing. All three of these options are calculated in units based on the width of an em space, which equals the width of the @ character in the current point size. To change any of these settings, use the typing cursor in the usual manner. Each amount entered for the three "Space Width" options is expressed as a percentage of a normal space width; to alter any of these, you enter the percentage value and Ventura calculates and displays the actual unit value in ems at the end of the line, which varies according to the font in use.

The "Normal Space Width" option lets you define the amount of space you want Ventura to use between each word in the selected paragraph. The standard setting is 1.000; a setting of 2.000 doubles the space and 3.000 triples it. Whenever Ventura justifies and places text on a page, it proceeds to use the "Normal Space Width" value as often as possible. When Ventura cannot make the words fit on the line, it uses the other "Space Width" settings to determine a smaller or larger amount of space to use between the words. The "Minimum Space Width" allows Ventura to reduce the spacing by a value that is less than the normal amount, for example, a standard setting is 0.600, which is equal to 60 percent of the "Normal Space Width." The "Maximum Space Width" lets Ventura increase word spacing by using a value greater than the normal amount — a typical setting is 2.000, which is 200 percent of the "Normal Space Width."

But even with these powerful word-spacing tools, Ventura may still be unable to make the words fit properly on the line, which will result

---

Paragraph

Font...
Alignment...
Spacing...
Breaks...
Tab Settings...
Special Effects...
Attribute Overrides...
Paragraph Typography...

Ruling Line Above...
Ruling Line Below...
Ruling Box Around...

Define Colors...
Update Tag List...   ^K

TRACKING
EFFECTS

TRACKING
EFFECTS

*To create matching word
lengths, the example on
the right uses "Looser"
tracking set at 0.070 ems
for the word "EFFECTS."*

in a loose line. If you have selected the Show Loose Lines option in the Options menu, Ventura will highlight all lines that fit into this category. The easiest way to fix a loose line is to use the Text Editing function and edit the text as necessary until it fits properly. In some cases, you may only need to add a discretionary hyphen (Control key plus hyphen key) to the first word in the line below the loose line. If you still can't fix a loose line, however, you can try implementing the "Letter Spacing: On" option, which permits Ventura to increase the space between letters *on loose lines* until the space between words is less than the amount specified for the "Maximum Space Width." To control how much latitude Ventura has in adding this selective letter spacing, you enter a maximum amount in the "Up to:" option line based on the width of the current em space. Finally, you can also increase or decrease the space between letters *on all lines* by using the "Tracking" option, which allows you to choose between "Looser" or "Tighter" and set a value again based on the width of an em space.

To summarize the difference between tracking and letter spacing: tracking affects spacing between all letters in a paragraph and is commonly used for headlines and display type (as shown above); letter spacing, however, affects spacing between the letters in loose lines and is generally applied to body text.

The "Grow Inter-Line to Fit" option is intended for cases in which you want to use the Text Editing function's Set Font button to increase the size of selected text within a paragraph but don't want the enlarged text to overlap the previous line. By activating this option, the line spacing between lines A and B, for example, is automatically increased if line B contains any text larger than the size specified by the paragraph tag. This feature is also useful for documents that contain formulas or equations, or whenever you use the Insert Fraction option to place one value over another value, such as $\frac{78.6}{144} = 0.547$ ft^2 or *Wave length* $= \frac{velocity}{frequency}$ within a paragraph.

Paragraph

Font...
Alignment...
Spacing...
Breaks...
Tab Settings...
Special Effects...
Attribute Overrides...
Paragraph Typography...

Ruling Line Above...
Ruling Line Below...
Ruling Box Around...

Define Colors...
Update Tag List...   ^K

This Ruling Line Below dialog box contains the settings used to create the ruling lines below the chapter number heading at the beginning of every chapter in this book. The results of these settings are also shown below.

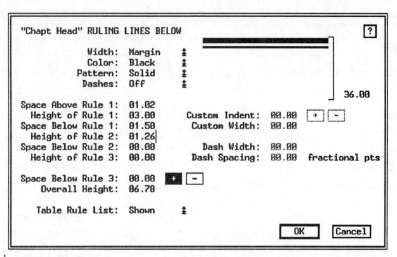

```
"Chapt Head" RULING LINES BELOW                          [?]

              Width:  Margin     ‡
              Color:  Black      ‡
            Pattern:  Solid      ‡
             Dashes:  Off        ‡
                                                          ┐
 Space Above Rule 1:  01.02                               │  36.00
 Height of Rule 1:    03.00       Custom Indent:   00.00  [→] [–]
 Space Below Rule 1:  01.50       Custom Width:    00.00
 Height of Rule 2:    01.26│
 Space Below Rule 2:  00.00       Dash Width:      00.00
 Height of Rule 3:    00.00       Dash Spacing:    00.00  fractional pts

 Space Below Rule 3:  00.00       [+] [–]
 Overall Height:      06.78

 Table Rule List:     Shown     ‡

                                              [  OK  ]  [Cancel]
```

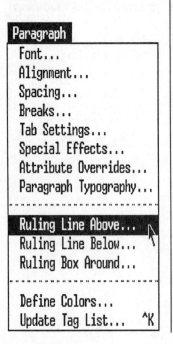

```
Paragraph
 Font...
 Alignment...
 Spacing...
 Breaks...
 Tab Settings...
 Special Effects...
 Attribute Overrides...
 Paragraph Typography...
 ...........................
 Ruling Line Above...
 Ruling Line Below...
 Ruling Box Around...
 ...........................
 Define Colors...
 Update Tag List...    ^K
```

Adding Rules

The next three Paragraph menu options — Ruling Line Above, Ruling Line Below, and Ruling Box Around — allow you to automatically add ruling lines to any selected paragraph. When chosen, each option provides you with the same basic dialog box (shown above), referred to here as the Ruling Lines dialog box. With any one of these options, you can create one, two, or three ruling lines of any thickness up to a total of 0.5 inch, including the space above and below the rules, which you also control. The Ruling Line Above and Ruling Line Below options can be applied to any paragraph, but the Ruling Box Around option overrides the other two. As mentioned earlier in this chapter, Ventura also uses the same dialog box when you select the Frame menu's Ruling Line Above, Ruling Line Below, and Ruling Box Around options.

To use the Ruling Lines dialog box, you follow the same essential steps described for adding rules to frames, with one main difference. Instead of being limited to frame-wide ruling lines only, you can create rules that match the text, margin, or column length, or you can specify a custom width. An example of a ruling box around text is shown in the "Paragraph Tagging" section in Chapter 4. If you pick "Width: Margin," Ventura automatically subtracts any temporary margins you've added (by using the Spacing menu option) from the length of the ruling line. However, any space you've allocated for indents (using the Alignment menu option) will not be subtracted from the rule's length unless you pick the "Width: Text" option or use the custom width option.

When "Width: Custom" is selected, two other options in the Ruling Lines dialog box are available: the "Custom Width" line, which controls the length of the ruling line; and the "Custom Indent" line, which controls the space between the left margin and the left end of the ruling line. The plus (+) option box is the normal setting for a custom indent, but if you select the minus (-) box, the ruling line will be shifted to the left — outside the left margin, if necessary — by whatever amount you enter. The easiest way to determine the custom indent and width amounts is to select the Show Rulers option in the Options menu and use the on-screen rulers as an aid. Also, before using the typing cursor to enter any amounts in the dialog box, select the desired measurement unit located above the "OK" box.

The remaining controls are applied in the same way that you use the Ruling Lines dialog box with various Frame menu options. To summarize these steps, you next pick the "Color" and "Pattern" for the ruling lines. Only one color and pattern can be used for all three ruling lines applied to a selected paragraph. If the text is placed in a frame that has a black background, Ventura will automatically change any ruling lines inside the frame to white. If you use dashes rather than a solid line or number pattern, two more options will become available: "Dash Width" represents the size of all dashes, and "Dash Spacing" defines the space between them.

To proceed, enter a value for the height of each ruling line you want to add, plus the amount of spacing you want above and below each rule. As you enter the various amounts, Ventura displays the resulting rules in the center of the dialog box and you can make adjustments until you're satisfied with the results. To remove any ruling lines added to a paragraph, select the "Width: None" option and the rules will no longer be applied, even if they are still displayed within the Ruling Lines dialog box.

After using the Ruling Line Above, Ruling Line Below, and Ruling Box Around options to add conventional rules to a paragraph, you may want to try creating some special effects. For example, by selecting "Width: Custom" in the Ruling Box Around dialog box and applying the "Custom Indent" and "Custom Width" options, you can create a *change bar*, which is a vertical rule on the left side of a paragraph. Some documents require change bars to alert readers that a section has been added or that its contents have been changed. To

Paragraph
- Font...
- Alignment...
- Spacing...
- Breaks...
- Tab Settings...
- Special Effects...
- Attribute Overrides...
- Paragraph Typography...
- **Ruling Line Above...**
- Ruling Line Below...
- Ruling Box Around...
- Define Colors...
- Update Tag List...   ^K

create this type of rule, enter the amount of space you want between the rule and the left edge of the text in the "Custom Indent" line and click on the minus (-) option box beside it. If you enter 1 pica, for instance, this step places the vertical rule outside the left margin by that amount. Next, enter the amount you want for the rule's length in the "Custom Width" option. Make this a small amount to create a thin rule or slightly larger for a thicker rule. The final step is to enter a nominal amount for "Height of Rule 1" line, such as 2 points. (Note: You may need to adjust the figures used in this and the following examples to obtain the effect you want.)

By using a variation of this same technique with the Ruling Line Above and Alignment options, you can add a square bullet to the beginning of a paragraph. This effect also demonstrates a special application of the "Space Below Rule 3" option, which is found at the bottom of the Ruling Line dialog box. Although the name of this feature specifies "Rule 3," it is somewhat misleading since this option can also be used to manipulate the placement of the first rule if only that rule is used, or the first two rules if only those rules are used. For instance, if you enter an amount for the "Space Below Rule 3" line and click on the minus (-) option box, Ventura will *subtract* space and move the first ruling line down if it's the only ruling line applied. Therefore, you should regard this feature as the "Space Below *Last* Rule" option, rather than just Rule 3.

To create a square bullet, use the Alignment option's "In/Outdent Width" line to enter the amount of space you want between the bullet and text, and "In/Outdent Height" line to enter the number of lines you want indented to create space for the bullet. If you want the whole paragraph indented so the bullet stands apart from the text, choose the maximum number of lines. In the Ruling Line dialog box, pick "Width: Custom," leave the "Custom Indent" line blank, and enter an amount for the "Custom Width" that equals at least half the point size of the text used for that paragraph. For instance, enter 6 points if the text is 12-point type. Next, set the spacing and height for the bullet to properly align with the first line in the paragraph. To create a square bullet, the "Height of Rule 1" line should match the "Custom Width" amount. To create suitable spacing, enter about half the type size for the "Space Above Rule 1" and use the rule's height for the "Space Below Rule 3" line. The final step is to select the minus option box for the "Space Below Rule 3."

Paragraph

Font...
Alignment...
Spacing...
Breaks...
Tab Settings...
Special Effects...
Attribute Overrides...
Paragraph Typography...

Ruling Line Above...
Ruling Line Below...
Ruling Box Around...

Define Colors...
Update Tag List...   ^K

1 These reverse numbers are created by applying three of the Paragraph menu options to a paragraph that contains nothing more than the number itself. The text paragraphs that follow each reverse number are created by applying a different tag.

2 The Ruling Line Above option is used to create the square bullet, which has a height and custom width of 20 points. The space above Rule 1 is 3 points, and the space below Rule 3 is minus (-) 23 points. A custom indent of minus 3 points is also applied.

3 The Special Effects option is used to set the font properties for the large number, which is white 18-point Helvetica bold italic. The vertical shift option is used to lower the character by 2 points.

4 Using the Breaks option, the number paragraph is set for "Line Break:Before," and the text paragraph is set for "Line Break: After" and "Next Y Position: Beside Last Line of Prev. Para." The text paragraph also has a 2-line, 9-point indent, using the Alignment option.

Another technique using the Rule 3 minus option box is to create *reverse type,* or white letters on a black background, if your printer supports this type of printing. Producing this effect requires both the Font and Ruling Line Above menu options. With the Font dialog box, you simply select white text for the paragraph tag; with the Ruling Line Above dialog box, you need to make some calculations. The basic trick is to enter an amount for the "Height of Rule 1" that is larger than the type size for the selected paragraph. The exact amount depends on the height you want to use for the black background surrounding the type.

For example, if you select a 24-point rule for 16-point type, it'll leave 4 points of black background above and below the type when the effect is complete (as shown on the right). Next, calculate the space Rule 1 should be shifted down in order to center the text within the ruling line. The basic formula is to add the type size and Rule 1's height together, divide the total in half, and enter this amount in the "Space Below Rule 3" line. With the previous figures, for instance, the total of the type size (16 points) and the ruling line height (24 points) equals 40, and half of that amount is 20. Therefore, start with 20 for the value in the "Space Below Rule 3" option and select the minus option box. You can expect to make some adjustments and print a few tests before you're satisified. Also, use a custom width if you want to make the rule extend beyond the type on either side.

Reverse Type

Adding Colors

Color has always been an effective channel for communication and it is one of the most important tools you can use in publications. Color can help to highlight a document's text and graphics and enhance the overall design. If you plan to use color in a document, Ventura's Define Colors option can help you preview and prepare the various colors you want to use.

The three ways you can use Ventura to produce color documents are:

1. You can print a document in a large range of colors on a PostScript color printer, such as the QMS ColorScript 100, or in a small range of colors on a Xerox 4020 Color Ink Jet Printer.

2. You can print a document on a black-and-white laser printer or typesetter and the colors will be converted into shades of gray.

3. You can print separate pages, called "spot-color overlays," for each color (including black) you use in a document. Each spot-color overlay is printed in black and contains only the elements you want printed in that particular color.

Before proceeding, however, you should understand the difference between *spot-color printing* and *four-color process printing*. In the printing industry, spot-color printing is simply the addition of a second ink, or more, to a page. For example, a two-color newsletter might use black ink for all of the body text and blue ink for the logo, headlines, and ruling boxes around frames that contain tables, charts, and pictures. You can also screen these colors to achieve different shades of each color. When you take the camera-ready copy to a commercial printer, you specify the colors you want to use by picking numbered colors from a color matching system, such as the widely used Pantone Matching System, commonly referred to as PMS colors. Each additional color you add to a page means another run through the printing press, as well as additional charges.

Four-color process printing uses the three primary colors — cyan (process blue), magenta (process red), and yellow — and black, collectively known as the "CMYK" process colors, to reproduce full-color illustrations that contain continuous tone, such as color photographs, transparencies, and paintings. This costly procedure,

---

Paragraph

Font...
Alignment...
Spacing...
Breaks...
Tab Settings...
Special Effects...
Attribute Overrides...
Paragraph Typography...

Ruling Line Above...
Ruling Line Below...
Ruling Box Around...

Define Colors...
Update Tag List...   ^K

commonly used in magazine publishing, requires color separations (negative overlays that break down the original full-color image into the four process colors) and the precise registration of four printing plates, as well as running each full-color page through the printing press four times. When printed on top of one another, the four process colors duplicate the full range of colors in the original image.

If you want to publish a document using spot-color printing, you can use Ventura to print the camera-ready pages to take to an outside printing facility. If you want to use four-color process printing, however, the current version of Ventura is unable to produce the color separations needed. The reason this can become confusing is because Ventura's Define Colors option lets you replace the program's default colors (red, blue, green, cyan, yellow, and magenta) with other colors by mixing percentages of the same CMYK process colors used in four-color printing. More specifically, you can use the Define Colors dialog box (shown below) to define colors or shades of gray (up to six per style sheet), assign a color name to each color you define, and then apply these colors to text, ruling lines, frames, and any graphic objects you create with Ventura's drawing tools.

The first control in the Define Colors dialog box, "Screen Display," lets you choose colors or shades of gray for what you'll see on screen. If you choose "Colors," the colors you'll see on an EGA display are limited to Ventura's default colors; on a VGA color

Paragraph
Font...
Alignment...
Spacing...
Breaks...
Tab Settings...
Special Effects...
Attribute Overrides...
Paragraph Typography...
- - - - - - - - - -
Ruling Line Above...
Ruling Line Below...
Ruling Box Around...
- - - - - - - - - -
Define Colors...
Update Tag List... ↑ ^K

DEFINE COLORS [?]

Screen Display: ✓ Colors | Shades of Gray

Color Number: ← 2 →

Color Setting: Enabled ↕

Color Name: Tan (PMS-166C)

Cyan: ← [▒▒▒▒▒▒▒▒▒▒] → 000.0 %

Magenta: ← [▒▒▒▒▒▒ ▒▒▒] → 049.2

Yellow: ← [▒▒▒▒▒▒ ▒▒▒] → 049.2

Black: ← [▒ ▒▒▒▒▒▒▒▒] → 001.6

[OK] [Cancel]

Using the Define Colors dialog box, the "Color Number 2" has been renamed using a Pantone Color Matching System number (PMS-166C), and the appropriate color percentages have been mixed so that the actual color can be approximated on a VGA color display. Without VGA color, however, colors will only appear as shades of gray, as shown here.

display, however, you can actually see an approximation of all the new colors you define (e.g., tan, orange, and turquoise). You can also use the Define Colors option on a monochrome display and output color pages or color overlays as usual, however, the colors can only be displayed as shades of gray on screen. The "Shades of Gray" setting lets you view the actual shades of gray in a gray-scale TIFF image on a VGA display. In other words, it's like looking at the actual photograph as it will appear on the page.

Use the scroll arrows on the "Color Number" line to find the default color, numbers 2 through 7, you want to change. Because the colors black and white cannot be altered, numbers 0 and 1 are unaccessible. The "Color Setting" option is only used when printing color overlays: "Enable" tells Ventura to print a color overlay for that particular color number; "Disable" tells it to suppress printing a color overlay. On the "Color Name" line, you can replace the default name with one of your own choosing, such as the number for a PMS color.

The remainder of the dialog box contains scroll bars for mixing the process colors. Use the sliders for broad changes and the scroll arrows for precise increments of 0.2 percent. For example, to create PMS-166C, which is a tan color consisting of red (49.2 percent), yellow (49.2 percent), and black (1.6 percent), you would adjust the settings in the magenta, yellow, and black colors until the proper percentages appeared. You can also create 500 shades of gray by specifying percentages of black only. On a 300-dpi laser printer, you won't be able to produce anything close to that many different grays; however, if you output your document on a high-resolution typesetter, you can take fuller advantage of this extensive range of grays.

After you finish using the Define Colors option and assigning colors to various text and graphics elements, use the "Spot Color Overlays: On" option in the To Print dialog box to produce separate color overlays on a standard laser printer. If the document page size is smaller than the printer's paper, Ventura will print the color name and camera registration marks on each overlay. You can also use the "Crop Marks: On" option to print crop marks on each page. Click "OK" and Ventura prompts you with a final pop-up message that lets you confirm the number of color overlays you want to print. If the number of overlays is more than you need, return to the Define Colors option and disable all of the colors you don't want to use.

Paragraph
Font...
Alignment...
Spacing...
Breaks...
Tab Settings...
Special Effects...
Attribute Overrides...
Paragraph Typography...

Ruling Line Above...
Ruling Line Below...
Ruling Box Around...

Define Colors...
Update Tag List... ^K

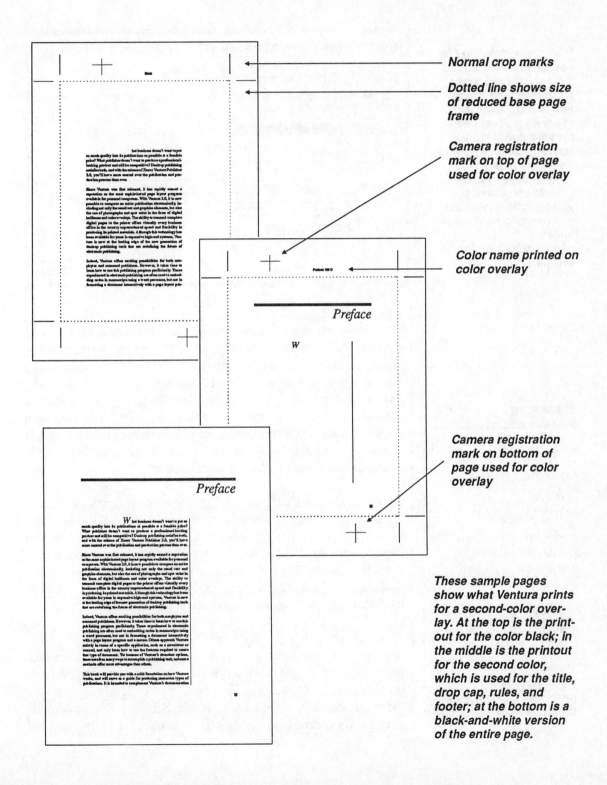

Normal crop marks

Dotted line shows size of reduced base page frame

Camera registration mark on top of page used for color overlay

Color name printed on color overlay

Camera registration mark on bottom of page used for color overlay

These sample pages show what Ventura prints for a second-color overlay. At the top is the printout for the color black; in the middle is the printout for the second color, which is used for the title, drop cap, rules, and footer; at the bottom is a black-and-white version of the entire page.

With the Update Tag List option, you can perform a number of important tasks designed to help you manage each and every style sheet used for your publications. Not only can you remove unwanted tags and rename others for the sake of consistency within a style sheet, but you can also print a style sheet to disk and view all of the various settings at one time.

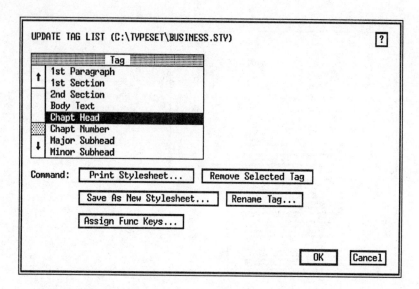

UPDATE TAG LIST (C:\TYPESET\BUSINESS.STY)   [?]

Tag
1st Paragraph
1st Section
2nd Section
Body Text
Chapt Head
Chapt Number
Major Subhead
Minor Subhead

Command: [Print Stylesheet...]   [Remove Selected Tag]
            [Save As New Stylesheet...]   [Rename Tag...]
            [Assign Func Keys...]

                                        [OK] [Cancel]

Paragraph
Font...
Alignment...
Spacing...
Breaks...
Tab Settings...
Special Effects...
Attribute Overrides...
Paragraph Typography...

Ruling Line Above...
Ruling Line Below...
Ruling Box Around...

Define Colors...
Update Tag List...   ^K

Updating Tag Lists

The Paragraph menu's Update Tag List option provides several valuable tools to help you manage all of the tags incorporated in the various style sheets you use. With this feature, you can remove tags you no longer use, rename tags to make them easier to find, and produce a printed copy of all the settings in the style sheet. Before you use this feature, however, the style sheet you want to work with must be the current style sheet, which is displayed in the title bar. If another style sheet is listed, use the File menu's Load Different Style option to load the .STY file you want to update.

To proceed, select the Paragraph Tagging mode and pick the Update Tag List option from the Paragraph menu (or use Ctrl-K). If a chapter is already loaded, Ventura will prompt you with a dialog box that lets you save or abandon any changes you've made before it provides the Update Tag List dialog box (shown above). This dialog box displays the current style sheet and includes a "Tag" directory list (with vertical scroll tools) and several "Command" options.

If you choose the "Print Stylesheet" command, Ventura will automatically generate a text file that contains all of the settings for each tag in the current style sheet. After you pick this command, Ventura provides an item selector that lets you name the file it will print, with the extension .GEN automatically added. Select "OK" and Ventura goes to work, extracting the information from the style sheet and generating the file in a matter of seconds or minutes, depending on the number of tags in the style sheet. As soon as Ventura finishes this job, you can exit the Update Tag List dialog box and load the file by using the "Text Format: Generated" setting in the Load Text/Picture option. Ventura also provides a special style sheet, STYLOG.STY, which you can use to format the generated text file into a well organized and highly readable format.

Before you can remove or rename a tag in the current style sheet, you must click on a tag name in the directory list (use the scroll tools to first locate the tag if necessary). If you pick the "Remove Selected Tag" command, Ventura provides the Remove Tag dialog box (shown below). In this dialog box, the tag name you selected is placed on the "Tag Name to Remove" line, and the tag name that each paragraph assigned the selected tag will be changed to is placed on the "Tag Name to Convert to" line. Although Ventura automatically uses the Body Text tag name as the default for the converted tag name, you can use the Backspace key to delete the default and enter any other tag name. For example, if you had inadvertently created two tags called "First para" and "First Para" with otherwise identical paragraph settings, you would place one of these tag names on the "Tag Name to Remove" line and enter the other name on the second line. This procedure would have the effect of merging a group of paragraphs under one tag name while eliminating a duplicate and unnecessary tag name.

If you pick the "Rename Tag" command, Ventura provides the Rename Tag dialog box (shown below). In this dialog box, the tag name you selected is placed on the "Old Tag Name" line and the replacement tag name is placed on the "New Tag Name" line. This option is particularly valuable as you become more experienced in

```
┌─────────────────────┐
│ Paragraph           │
├─────────────────────┴──┐
│ Font...                │
│ Alignment...           │
│ Spacing...             │
│ Breaks...              │
│ Tab Settings...        │
│ Special Effects...     │
│ Attribute Overrides... │
│ Paragraph Typography...│
│ - - - - - - - - - - -  │
│ Ruling Line Above...   │
│ Ruling Line Below...   │
│ Ruling Box Around...   │
│ - - - - - - - - - - -  │
│ Define Colors...       │
│ Update Tag List...  ^K │
└────────────────────────┘
```

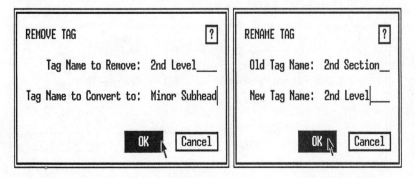

REMOVE TAG	?
Tag Name to Remove: 2nd Level	
Tag Name to Convert to: Minor Subhead	
	OK Cancel

RENAME TAG	?
Old Tag Name: 2nd Section	
New Tag Name: 2nd Level	
	OK Cancel

On the left is the Remove Tag dialog box and on the right is the Rename Tag dialog box. With these tools, you can effectively control the names and the amount of tag names used in a style sheet.

Paragraph

Font...
Alignment...
Spacing...
Breaks...
Tab Settings...
Special Effects...
Attribute Overrides...
Paragraph Typography...

Ruling Line Above...
Ruling Line Below...
Ruling Box Around...

Define Colors...
Update Tag List...   ^K

using Ventura and at creating mnemonic tag names — especially if a style sheet is to be shared by multiple users. For example, since tag names are listed alphabetically in the assignment list, it's easier to find related tags if you use names like "Head 1" and "Head 2" rather than "First Head" and "Second Head." With the Rename Tag option, you can change the names of the existing tags as needed to create the most logically ordered list possible.

It is important to note that removing or renaming a tag affects every assignment of the tag throughout the document as well as in all other documents that use the same style sheet. Therefore, after using the "Remove Tag" or "Rename Tag" commands, you may want to use the "Save as New Stylesheet" command and save the current style sheet under a new name to ensure that the old style sheet is still available. This command works the same way as the File menu's Save as New Style option; Ventura provides an item selector with the .STY extension and allows you to create a new name.

Assign Function Keys is the final command in the Update Tag List menu option. Although it isn't necessary to use this feature to format a document, it can accelerate the process of assembly-line page processing and formatting when it's necessary to assign several different tag names to a large document. Unlike the other options in the Paragraph menu, it's also possible to access this option when the Text Editing mode is selected, as explained in the "Paragraph Tagging" section in Chapter 4.

With the Assign Function Keys dialog box (shown below), you can assign tag names to as many as 10 keyboard function keys; if your

After you use the Assign Function Keys dialog box to assign tags to the function keys, you can format a document much faster when using the Paragraph Tagging mode. Better still, you can also apply the function keys to assign tags when using the Text Editing mode.

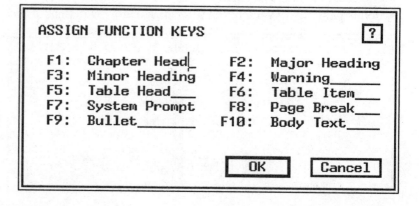

```
ASSIGN FUNCTION KEYS                              [?]

  F1:  Chapter Head|        F2:  Major Heading
  F3:  Minor Heading        F4:  Warning_____
  F5:  Table Head___        F6:  Table Item___
  F7:  System Prompt        F8:  Page Break___
  F9:  Bullet_____       F10:  Body Text____


                     [  OK  ]      [ Cancel ]
```

computer has more than 10 function keys, however, Ventura will only recognize F1 through F10. Since you can't assign more than 10 tags, try to apply the tag names that you'll use most frequently. Also, try to use the same logic that you applied in creating the tags. For example, you may find it best to assign function keys in the same alphabetical order in which the tags appear in the assignment list. Or, you may want to list the tags in hierarchical order and assign the first heading level (such as the chapter title) to F1 and the smallest level (which might be captions or footnotes) to F10.

Any of the tags assigned function keys can be applied in either the Paragraph Tagging or Text Editing mode, simply by pressing the appropriate function key. You can also use the function keys to tag a selection of multiple paragraphs (using the Paragraph Tagging cursor), or tag a block of text highlighted over several paragraphs (using the Text Editing cursor). Finally, if you want to access the Assign Function Keys dialog box directly from the Text Editing mode, you can do so by using the Ctrl-K shortcut.

Graphic Menu

When producing different types of documents, you can use Ventura's built-in drawing function for both practical and creative purposes. In this book, for example, Ventura's drawing tools are used to enhance certain illustrations by adding arrows, circles, borders, and box text for diagram words. The basics involved in generating graphic objects with Ventura's Graphic Drawing function are covered in the "Graphic Drawing" section of Chapter 4, so the focus in this section is on using the Graphic menu options.

The Placement Controls

The Show On All Pages option lets you print any selected graphic object (or objects) at the exact same location on every base page (left and right) in a document. The most obvious use for this command is to repeat camera crop marks in identical positions near the edge of each page, a technique used to produce the camera-ready pages for this book. Other graphic objects that you might want to repeat on all pages include horizontal lines used at the top or bottom of a page, vertical lines used as custom column guides that are not centered between columns, and box text used to create custom headers and footers or margin tabs. To disable this feature, select the graphic object(s) you don't want to show on all pages and pick the

```
Graphic
Show On All Pages
Send to Back        ^Z
Bring to Front      ^A
------------------------
Line Attributes... ^L
Fill Attributes... ^F
------------------------
Select All          ^Q
Grid Settings...
```

Show On This Page option, which appears as the first option in the Graphic menu whenever you select an object previously set to repeat on all pages. To place different graphic objects on left and right pages, use the Repeating Frame option (Frame menu) to create separate repeating frames for the left and right page; then attach all objects for left pages to the left-page repeating frame, and attach all objects for right pages to the right-page repeating frame.

The Send to Back and Bring to Front options are both single-action commands designed to help you arrange the order of overlapping graphic objects tied to a selected frame. Normally, the best way to create a series of stacked graphic objects is to draw the bottom object first and then draw each object on top of the next. However, if you need to rearrange the order, you can easily do so by applying either of these commands. For example, after selecting the object you want on the bottom, just use the Send to Back command; or to move the bottom object on top, select it and use the Bring to Front command. You can also apply these commands by using the Ctrl-Z (^Z) and Ctrl-A (^A) keyboard shortcuts.

A common application that often requires the Bring to Front and Send to Back commands is when you create diagram words and arrows by using the drawing tools for box text and lines. In some cases, the end of the line connected to the box text may be cut off when printed, even though the end of the line is visible on the screen. Typically, the reason is because the perimeter of the box text, while appearing transparent, is actually overlapping the end of the line. To correct this, select the line and use the Bring to Front command.

The Select All option is another single-action command you can use to control the placement of graphic objects, among other tasks. When you use this option, all graphic objects tied to the selected frame are automatically selected, that is, each graphic linked to the frame is surrounded by black boxes or line markers. If you next move the cursor inside any one of the selected graphic objects, hold down the mouse button, and drag the mouse in any direction, *all* of the selected graphic objects will move in the same direction.

The Select All feature is particularly useful if you need to move a series of stacked graphic objects without disturbing their order or alignment. You can also apply the Select All command by using the

Ctrl-Q (^Q) keyboard shortcut. Unlike the other Graphic menu options, this shortcut also works when the Frame Setting mode is active, which makes it possible to see which graphic objects are tied to which frames *without* changing to the Graphic Drawing mode. For example, if a page contains several frames and each frame has its own graphic objects scattered about the page, you can use the Ctrl-Q shortcut to quickly identify which frame is the one you should select to access a particular graphic object or group of objects.

The Grid Settings option provides a simple dialog box (shown below) that allows you to define an invisible grid to ensure perfect vertical and horizontal alignment of the graphics objects you draw. In addition, each frame that different graphic objects are linked to can have different grid specifications. The Grid Settings option is

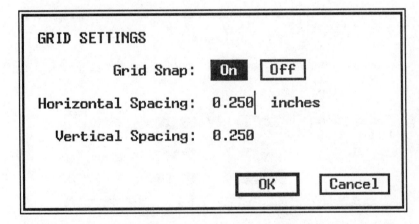

With the Grid Settings dialog box, you can create an invisible grid within the base page frame or an added frame. As a result, all of the graphic objects you draw will "snap" to the nearest horizontal or vertical point.

usually active by default, but if it isn't, select the "Grid Snap: On" option inside the dialog box to use it. Then, choose the measurement unit you prefer to work with and use the typing cursor to enter the amount of horizontal and vertical spacing desired. If you want just a horizontal or vertical grid only (but not both), leave the other setting blank (filled with zeros).

For maximum flexibility in drawing and placing graphic objects on a page, you may want to select the "Grid Settings: Off" option to prevent the objects from snapping to the nearest grid points. However, if you have trouble drawing a straight line when the grid is turned off, turn it back on and draw the line, then turn it off again and move it to its final location.

```
┌─────────────────────────┐
│ Graphic │               │
├─────────────────────────┤
│ Show On All Pages        │
│ Send to Back         ^Z  │
│ Bring to Front       ^A  │
│ ·······················  │
│ Line Attributes... ^L    │
│◥Fill Attributes... ^F    │
│ ·······················  │
│ Select All          ^Q   │
│ Grid Settings...         │
└─────────────────────────┘
```

The Attributes Options

The Graphic menu's Line Attributes and Fill Attributes options provide dialog boxes that let you assign various characteristics to graphic objects. Because you can create five different types of objects (lines, circles, rectangles, rounded rectangles, and box text), the program actually provides a separate dialog box for each type of object, as indicated in the dialog box's title. As with a few other program features, the availability of some options included in these dialog boxes — namely, the color and transparent fill options — depends on the hardware system's capabilities and the display mode (color or monochrome) in which the program is installed.

To use the Line Attributes dialog box (shown below), first pick the line "Thickness" option by selecting one of the preset choices or by

The Line Attributes dialog box shown here is set to create a 0.003-inch rule around the selected graphic object, which is box text. By clicking on the "Defaults: Save To" command, you can save all of the current settings in the dialog box and they will be applied to each additional graphic object of the same type (in this case, box text) you draw.

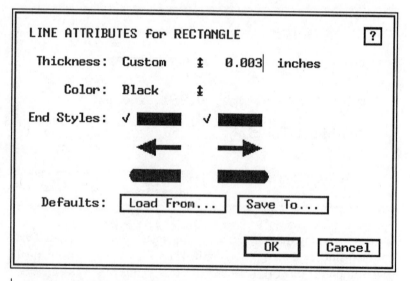

choosing the "Custom Width" option and using the typing cursor to enter the exact thickness in the measurement unit of choice. Or, if you don't want to print the outline of a graphic object, use the "Thickness: None" option. For example, when you first use the program, the default settings for box text include a thin line around the box, but you can eliminate it by picking "Thickness: None." With the "End Styles" controls, you can choose square ends, round ends, and arrows for each end of a graphic line by clicking on top of the style desired. The three styles on the left represent the end of the line where you first start drawing and those on the right are for the end where you stop. If you've installed Ventura to run in color, you can select one of eight colors for the graphic lines used to create each type of object; otherwise, you're limited to black and white.

With the Fill Attributes dialog box, you can pick one of eight colors and nine patterns for filling circles, rectangles, and box text. Printed examples of these patterns output on a 1,270-dpi Linotronic type-setter are displayed in the "Graphic Drawing" section in Chapter 4. Like the Ruling Lines dialog boxes, the selected color and pattern are also previewed in the Fill Attributes dialog box. By selecting the "Result: Opaque" option, you can make the graphic on top of a series of graphic objects block out any objects directly below it; or you can make the graphic objects below show through the graphic on top by selecting "Result: Transparent." To determine your printer's ability

```
┌─────────────────┐
│ Graphic         │
├─────────────────┤
│ Show On All Pages │
│ Send to Back    ^Z │
│ Bring to Front  ^A │
│ · · · · · · · · · │
│ Line Attributes... ^L │
│ Fill Attributes... ^F │
│ · · · · · · · · · │
│ Select All      ^Q │
│ Grid Settings...  │
└─────────────────┘
```

```
┌──────────────────────────────────────────────┐
│  FILL  ATTRIBUTES  for  RECTANGLE       [?]    │
│                                                │
│      Color:   Black        ↕                   │
│    Pattern:   1            ↕                   │
│                                                │
│    Result:   ┌──────────┐   ┌─────────┐       │
│              │░░░░░░░░░░│   │ Opaque  │       │
│              │░░░░░░░░░░│   └─────────┘       │
│              │░░░░░░░░░░│   ┌────────────┐     │
│              └──────────┘   │ Transparent │     │
│                             └────────────┘     │
│   Defaults:  ┌───────────┐  ┌──────────┐       │
│              │ Load From..│  │ Save To..│       │
│              └───────────┘  └──────────┘       │
│                                                │
│                      ┌──────┐  ┌────────┐      │
│                      │  OK  │  │ Cancel │      │
│                      └──────┘  └────────┘      │
└──────────────────────────────────────────────┘
```

The settings for this Fill Attributes dialog box will create a box text graphic object with a shaded background. The availability of two fill options, "Color" and "Transparent," will depend on the hardware system on which Ventura is installed and the printer in use.

to handle the opaque and transparent options, print the CAPABILI.CHP file provided with the other example files in the TYPESET directory.

At the bottom of the Line Attributes and Fill Attributes dialog boxes is a "Defaults" command designed to save you time when assigning attributes to the same type of graphic object. When you click on the "Defaults: Save To" command, Ventura saves all current settings in the dialog box as the defaults for each additional graphic object of that type that you draw, each time you use the program. To apply the default settings to an existing graphic object or to graphic objects in another chapter, click on the object you want to change, select the

To create this calendar for a newsletter, the vertical grid setting is determined by dividing the frame's width by the number of columns (7). To ensure that each box is square, the same amount is then used for the horizontal grid spacing. Box text is used to create the text for each event; the month, days, and dates are all part of the same text file, which changes from month to month. The grid spacing is again applied when determining the tab spacing between the dates. The camera logo is also created by using Ventura's drawing tools.

FEBRUARY

SUNDAY	MONDAY	TUESDAY	WEDNESDAY	THURSDAY	FRIDAY	SATURDAY
	1	2	3	4	5	6 BAC Filmmakers Banquet, 8 PM La Pergola, San Francisco
	2nd Annual BAC Film Festival Expo Center 7 – 9 PM					
7	8	9	10 BAC meeting, Hays Hall, U/C Berkeley 7 – 9 PM	11	12 Lincoln's Birthday	13
14 Valentine's Day	15	16 Washington's Birthday Obs.	17	18	19	20 Special Screening Modern Art Museum, 3:00 (details below)
21	22	23	24	25	26	27
28	29	Special Screening Feb 20th: Alfred Hitchcock's *The Lodger* (1926) Lecture by Sir Reginald Cox, President, Brighton Cinema Society				

Graphic

Show On All Pages
Send to Back   ^Z
Bring to Front   ^A
- - - - - - - - - - - - - - - -
Line Attributes... ^L
Fill Attributes... ^F
- - - - - - - - - - - - - - - -
Select All   ^Q
Grid Settings...

Line Attributes or Fill Attributes option, and click on the "Defaults: Load From" command.

Finally, you can change the attributes assigned to *all* of the graphics tied to a frame by using the Select All command. For example, to increase the line thickness for a series of boxes and lines used to create an organizational chart, pick the Select All command first, and then use the Line Attributes option to change the "Thickness" amount. As a result, all of the graphic objects tied to the selected frame will end up with the same line thickness. Or, if you decide to place a series of graphic objects on top of a solid black frame instead of a hollow white frame, you could use the Select All command, then pick the "Color: White" option in the Fill Attributes dialog box to reverse the color for all of the graphic objects at once.

Even if you use a separate drawing program to create most of the graphic objects you use in your Ventura documents, the Graphic Drawing function often comes in handy for simple jobs and, in some cases, more complex drawings, such as the camera in the example shown above and the clipboard used at the beginning of this chapter.

Chapter 7

Tips and Techniques

*T*he primary emphasis in this book has been to explain how to produce documents inside Ventura. Yet one of the best ways to harness the power of the program's global formatting and instant pagination capabilities involves the pre-production process — the organizing and planning steps you take before using Ventura. At the very least, you should know what type of document you want to produce and what text and graphics files you'll need to prepare in advance. Beyond that streamlined scenario, however, are many other steps to consider.

In terms of a document's design, you can plan in advance what type of page layout you want to use, draw preliminary sketches, and create an organized list of the tag names required to format the text. This list can include the type specifications you intend to use, including font, alignment, spacing, tab settings, and so forth. You can also research other publications and keep a file of exemplary designs and formatting techniques that you want to incorporate in your own publications.

To expedite the formatting of text inside Ventura, you can preformat it using your word processing program. This procedure involves inserting Ventura tags and codes in a text file before importing it into the program. In short, you first create a style sheet, or use one of the sample style sheets provided with the program, and then add the style sheet's tag names throughout a text file, labeling separate paragraphs as chapter heads, subheads, tabular text, and so on. Of course, the task of preparing a text file full of tags and codes won't appeal to everyone; some people will still prefer to use the mouse, pull-down menus, and other program functions to format text inside Ventura even if it takes longer.

In terms of a document's graphics, you can prepare graphics files from a wide variety of other software programs, some of which may be more appropriate than others for the type of documents you want to publish. For many businesses, the best way to pull all of these different elements together is to divide jobs within a work group so that artists create graphics, editors manage text, designers prepare style sheets and layouts, and others assemble and print the final documents.

This chapter provides a number of tips and techniques for producing documents with Ventura, with a principal focus on the preproduction process. It includes information on style sheet management and working with text and graphics files.

Style Sheet Management

Every approach used to produce documents in Ventura ultimately involves the application of a style sheet. In previous chapters, the use of each style sheet component has usually been explained in the context of working with a specific program mode or menu option. This section pulls these components together to show you everything you control in a style sheet, and it explains how to change an existing style sheet to meet your own publication needs.

Anatomy of a Style Sheet
As the chart on the opposite page shows, a style sheet encompasses three essential areas: chapter settings, frame settings, and paragraph tags. It also includes the name of the width table (.WID) file listed in the Set Printer Info menu option. The width table determines the typefaces, sizes, and styles that will appear in each of the font-related dialog boxes provided when you select the following features:

- Font option (Paragraph menu)
- Special Effects option's "Set Font Properties" command (Paragraph menu)
- Text Editing mode's "Set Font" add button (side-bar)
- Add/Remove Fonts option (Options menu)

Style Sheet Components

Style Sheet Option	Menu	What It Affects
Page Size & Layout	Chapter	All pages
Chapter Typography	Chapter	All text
Auto-Numbering	Chapter	All text
Footnote Settings	Chapter	Text on page frame only
Margins & Columns	Frame	Page frame
Sizing & Scaling	Frame	Page frame
Frame Typography	Frame	Page frame
Vertical Rules	Frame	Page frame
Ruling Line Above or Below Ruling Box Around	Frame	Page frame
Frame Background	Frame	Page frame
Font	Paragraph	Settings for different tags
Alignment	Paragraph	Settings for different tags
Spacing	Paragraph	Settings for different tags
Breaks	Paragraph	Settings for different tags
Tab Settings	Paragraph	Settings for different tags
Special Effects	Paragraph	Settings for different tags
Attribute Overrides	Paragraph	Settings for different tags
Paragraphy Typography	Paragraph	Settings for different tags
Ruling Line Above or Below Ruling Box Around	Paragraph	Settings for different tags
Define Colors	Paragraph	Settings for different colors
Set Printer Info (width table)	Options	Printer fonts available

Chapter settings — (Page Size & Layout through Footnote Settings)
Frame settings — (Margins & Columns through Frame Background)
Paragraph tags — (Font through Define Colors)
Font width table — (Set Printer Info)

If you use the "Print Stylesheet" command in the Update Tag List option (Paragraph menu), Ventura will print (to a file) all of the settings for each tag in the current style sheet. To be most useful, augment this comprehensive list with sample printed pages that demonstrate the major characteristics of various tags.

Creating Style Sheets

There are two basic ways to create a style sheet. The first method is to modify one of the sample style sheet .STY files provided on the Ventura Publisher Examples Disk, which you usually copy onto your hard disk (in the TYPESET subdirectory) when installing the program. The advantage in using this approach is that most of the work is already done for you if the sample style sheet is similar to the one you want to create. For example, you might only need to select a different typeface or size, change the alignment, modify the margins, and add a few ruling lines to obtain the results you want.

The second method is similar to the first, except that you load and modify an empty style sheet, called DEFAULT.STY, which only contains one tag for Body Text and minimal settings for the page layout and page frame. If you want to build a style sheet from the ground up, use this approach. Regardless of which method you use, however, remember to rename a modified style sheet *before* saving the chapter if you want the original style sheet to remain intact. This step is particularly important for those who share Ventura on the same system, as it prevents someone from accidentally altering a style sheet used by others for their chapter files.

As an example of modifying a style sheet, here are some steps involved in customizing one of Ventura's sample style sheets to create the format used for this book. The &BOOK-P1.STY file is used since it's double-sided, letter-sized, portrait-oriented page format (shown on the left) is also required to produce the pages for this book. First, open the &BOOK-P1.CHP file so that text is already on the page to facilitate the process of changing the paragraph tags. When this chapter is opened, the &BOOK- P1.STY file is automatically loaded. Next, make the following changes to set up the page layout.

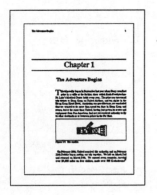

- Select the page frame and use the Margins & Columns option to set these margins *in inches*: Top margin, 01.65; all others, 01.25.

- Use the Vertical Rules option to set these rules *in inches*: Right page Rule 1 position, 05.50; Rule 1 Width, 0.001. Left page Rule 1 position, 3.00; Rule 1 Width, 0.001.

- Use the Ruling Box Around option to click on "Width: None" which removes the box around the page frame.

Because the pages for this book are smaller than the letter-sized format on which each page is prepared, the Graphic Drawing mode is used to add crop marks to the page frame (as shown on the right) to guide the commercial printer in preparing the actual printing plates. Another way to add crop marks is to reduce the size of the page frame with the Sizing & Scaling option and select "Crop Marks: On" in the File menu's To Print dialog box.

Next, delete the frame containing NOZZLE.GEM so it doesn't get in the way. To begin changing the existing tags, first select the corresponding text on the page, that is, click on the chapter number paragraph to select the "Chapter #" tag, the chapter title to select the "Chapter Title" tag, and so forth, and continue as follows:

- Use the Font option to select 11-point Times normal for the Firstpar and Body Text tags, 36-point Times italic for the Chapter Title tag, and 18-point Helvetica bold for the Chapter # tag. (Or, choose your own available fonts.)

- Use the Alignment option to select flush "Left" for the Chapter # tag, flush "Right" for the Chapter Title tag, and "Overall Width: Frame-Wide" for both. Pick "Justified" and change "In/Outdent Width" to 00,00 *picas and points* for the Firstpar and Body Text tags.

- Use the Spacing option for the Firstpar and Body Text tags, set in *picas and points*: Right page "In From Left: 00,00" and "In From Right: 10,11"; Left page "In From Left: 10,11" and "In From Right: 00,00." Set spacing for Chapter Title "Below: 14,00" and Chapter # "Above: 00,00." Set this spacing in *fractional points*: Firstpar "Below: 12,84" and Body Text "Inter-Paragraph: 12,84."

TIP: When changing the same settings for several tags, use the Ctrl-X (^X) keyboard shortcut to immediately recall the same last-used dialog box after clicking on each different tag.

- To add rules below the Chapter # tag, use the Ruling Line Above option and pick "None" to eliminate the existing rule. Then use the Ruling Line Below option to set the following in *fractional points*: "Space Above Rule 1: 01.02," "Height of Rule 1: 03.00," "Space Below Rule 1: 01.50," and "Height of Rule 2: 01.26."

Additional steps are required to create the indent for the first paragraph, headers and footers, and so on, but these initial steps will give you a basic idea of the process involved in changing a style sheet.

Working
with Text

@FIRSTPAR = This is
what a tagged paragraph
looks like. A tag can be
typed in upper case,
lower case, or capital
letters. Ventura formats
a paragraph according
to the specifications
assigned to the tag.

Style sheets are one of the big reasons for Ventura's strong appeal to corporate publishing groups or any business that requires a time-effective solution for its publishing needs. Although it often takes ample time and effort to learn how the program works when first starting to use it, you can reduce the time required to format a document by using some or all of the following "preformatting" procedures.

Preformatting Text Files

Once a style sheet is set up, you can assign the style sheet tags to your text in advance by using a word processor rather than Ventura's Paragraph Tagging mode. Although you still need to scroll through a chapter inside Ventura to see that the document is formatted correctly (as well as fix loose lines, place pictures in frames, and so on), this preformatting technique is highly recommended for maximum efficiency. All you need to add tags to a text file using a word processor are a list of the tag names and sample pages that show the formatting effects produced by various tags. Some companies have a style sheet designer or editor specify which tags to use by marking up a copy of a text file, which is then passed on to a word processing group.

The three basic rules to follow when inserting paragraph tags are:

- Insert each tag starting at the *left margin*.
- Add the @ character *before* each tag.
- Add a space, equal sign, and second space *after* each tag.

Each tag inserted at the start of a paragraph tells Ventura how to format that paragraph only. As soon as the program encounters a paragraph return, it reverts back to the default "Body Text" tag unless a different tag is inserted. Because Ventura automatically assigns all untagged paragraphs the "Body Text" tag when it first loads a text file, you don't need to insert the "Body Text" tag in a file. However, if you do insert "Body Text" along with the other tags, Ventura will recognize it accordingly and assign the paragraph the proper format.

There are several shortcuts you can use to expedite the process of inserting style sheet tags in text files. If you use a keyboard macro feature, you can assign tag names to a single key or combination of keys. Keyboard macros also help you control errors by providing the same spelling of each tag when you insert it. If your word processor lacks a macro feature, use a keyboard utility program such as Keyworks, ProKey, SmartKey, or SuperKey.

Other shortcuts include using a word processor's block copy or search-and-replace functions. With a block copy command, you can quickly insert the same tag over and over again. If a whole paragraph or part of a paragraph needs to be repeated along with the tag, you can include that text in the block copy. With a search-and-replace function, you can globally replace any *generic tags* in a text file with the actual style sheet tags required. Generic tags are simple and self-explanatory labels (e.g., "Subhead," "Bullet," and "Table Item") that are easy for an author to remember and to insert in a text file when creating it. You can also apply different style sheets tags to multiple copies of a generically tagged file.

When preparing text files with a word processor, many people add two paragraph returns between paragraphs, since this makes it easier to read. When you import the text file into Ventura, however, the extra paragraph returns add extra line spaces between paragraphs, which you may not want. This is particularly true if you intend to use the Paragraph menu's Spacing option to enter different amounts of inter-paragraph space than that produced by paragraph returns. Fortunately, a special tag tells Ventura to remove all extra paragraph returns; just insert **@PARAFILTR ON** = on the first line of the text file and the program will automatically disregard the extra paragraph returns.

Adding Text Codes

A second type of preformatting involves using a word processor to add text codes that Ventura recognizes for text attributes, non-keyboard characters, spaces and breaks, and special text references, such as footnotes, index references, and frame anchors. In Chapter 5, for example, you learned how to insert angle-bracketed codes using the Auto-Numbering and Headers & Footers options. All of these codes can also be added to a text file using a word processor, which speeds up the process of composing the text inside Ventura. The chart on the following page lists all of the text codes you can insert in your files, except for the nonkeyboard codes (i.e., Ventura's character sets and decimal codes) which are listed in the "Text Editing" section in Chapter 4.

Ventura Publisher Text Codes

Text Attributes

Lightweight type	<L>	Strike-thru	<X>
Medium-weight type	<M>	Overscore	<O>
Bold-weight type	<B>	Resume normal	<D>
Italic	<I>	Typeface	<F*n*>
Small	<S>	Point size	<P*n*>
Superscript	<^>	Color index	<C*n*>
Subscript	<v>	Base line jump	<J*n*>
Underline	<U>	Kern	<B%*n*>
Double underline	<=>		

Spaces and Breaks

Em space	<_>	Nonbreaking space	<N>
En space	<~>	Discretionary hyphen	<->
Figure space	<+>	Line break	<R>
Thin space	<l>		

Text References

Chapter number	<$R[C#]>
Page number	<$R[P#]>
Footnote	<$F*footnote text*>
Frame anchor same page	<$&*anchor name*>
Frame anchor below	<$&*anchor name*[v]>
Frame anchor above	<$&*anchor name*[^]>
Frame anchor at anchor	<$&*anchorname*[-]>
Index (primary reference)	<$I*primary*>
Index (primary and secondary reference)	<$I*primary;secondary*>
Index (*See* references)	<$S*primary;secondary*>
Index (*See Also* references)	<$A*primary;secondary*>
Hidden text	<$!*hidden text*>

Boxes and Fractions

Hollow box	<$B0>
Filled box	<$B1>
Fraction	<$E*numerator/denominator*>
Fraction	<$E*numerator over denominator*>

If you use one of the word processors supported by Ventura, you may prefer to use that program's native codes for bold, underline, superscript, subscript, strike-thru, and discretionary hyphens, and use Ventura's text codes for other features. The rules to follow when inserting Ventura text codes are:

- Text codes must include an open and close angle bracket (< and >) and can be inserted anywhere in a file
- No extra spaces should be added before or after a text code
- Several attributes can be grouped together within one set of brackets — for instance, type **<BIS>** for bold, italic, small
- If you need to use angle brackets as actual text, type double brackets to produce a single bracket, for instance, type **<<bracketed text>>** to produce: <bracketed text>
- After a text code changes an attribute, use a *resume normal* code to restore the original attribute, except at the end of a paragraph (attribute changes are terminated automatically after each paragraph return)

The last rule is particularly important since different codes are used to reset different formats. The most common of these is the **<D>** code, the same code used in various dialog boxes when you click on the "Text Attribute" option box. In effect, **<D>** is a toggle command that tells Ventura to stop formatting text with any attributes other than those specified by the paragraph tag. For typeface, color, and point size, the resume normal code uses the number 255 (as in: **<F255>, <C255>,** and **<P255>**); with base line jump, the resume normal code is **<J0>**; and with kerning, the normal code is **<D%0>**.

In the Ventura Publisher Text Codes chart, codes with italic text indicate that you must insert a numeric value or text. The proper inserts for text attribute codes is as follows:

- Typeface **<F*n*>**: Replace *n* with a font ID number
- Color **<C*n*>**: Replace *n* with a color ID number
- Point size **<P*n*>**: Replace *n* with the type size, in points
- Base line jump **<J*n*>**: Replace *n* with the amount of the vertical placement shift, in $\frac{1}{300}$ of an inch
- Kerning **<B%*n*>**: Replace *n* with a + or - symbol and the number of ems to add or subtract between each character in the selected text

The identification (ID) numbers for the colors and most common typefaces supported by Ventura are listed on the right. For additional font IDs, consult the font appendix in the *Ventura Publisher Edition Reference Guide*. To determine the proper measurements for the base

Text Color ID Numbers

White	0
Black	1
Red	2
Green	3
Blue	4
Cyan	5
Yellow	6
Magenta	7
Reset to tag color	255

Font ID Numbers

Courier	1
Helvetica (Swiss)	2
Times (Dutch)	14
New Century Schoolbook	20
Palatino	21
Bookman	23
Zapf Chancery	29
Helvetica Narrow	50
Avant Garde	51
Letter Gothic	105
Symbol	128
Zapf Dingbats	129
Reset to tag font	255

line jump and kern/track codes, use the following procedure. Inside Ventura, load a sample text file, select the Text Editing mode, and use the dialog box provided by the "Set Font" add button to produce the range of various "Shift" and "Kern" adjustments you'll need for your document. For example, if your work calls for scientific formulas, experiment with several different measurements for shifting the text, until you're satisfied with the printed results. Next, save the chapter so the adjustments you create are saved along with the text file. Then, all you have to do is look through the text file and identify which angle-bracketed codes produced the desired effects and insert those codes in the actual text file. For this book, this time-saving technique is used to insert text codes for kerning various characters in chapter titles.

If your document calls for footnotes, index entries, and frame anchors, you can also use a word processor to add the text codes that Ventura uses to create these references. However, you should first use these features inside the program and learn how to fill in the dialog boxes provided. After using these options, you can save the chapter and open up the text file in your word processor to see the reference codes Ventura has inserted in your file, which makes it easier to understand how they work.

<$Ffootnote text>

For footnote codes, type the contents of the footnote inside the angle brackets, after the characters **$F**, and insert the entire code wherever you want the footnote symbol to appear in the text file. For frame anchor codes, type the anchor name inside the angle brackets, after the characters **$&**, and insert the code before or after the text to which you want the frame referenced. To anchor the frame above the text, add the straight-bracketed command [**^**] before the close angle bracket, as in **<$&Chart above[^]>**; to anchor the frame below the text, add the straight-bracketed command [**v**], as in **<$&Chart below[v]>**; and to anchor the frame next to the anchor itself, add the straight-bracketed command [**-**], as in **<$&Chart above[-]>.**

<$&anchor name>

<$&anchor name[^]>

<$&anchor name[v]>

<$&anchor name[-]>

<$Iprimary>

Index codes can also be inserted, but they are more complex. If you only use a primary index entry, type the entry word(s) inside the angle brackets, after the characters **$I**, and insert the code before or after the reference in the text. If a secondary index entry is used, add a semicolon, *but no space,* between the two entries, as in: **<$I7 Seas Shellfish;10 Great Appetizers>.** To add sort keys, enclose the sort

<$Iprimary;secondary>

key entry in straight brackets after the primary or secondary entry, as in: **<$I7 Seas Shellfish[seven];10 Great Appetizers[ten]>**. If the index code is a "See" reference, replace **$I** with **$S**; for a "See Also" reference, use **$A**. For example, **<$AShellfish;Fish>** could be used to produce the reference "*See also* Fish" under the entry for Shellfish.

<$Sprimary;secondary>

<$Aprimary;secondary>

As an added convenience, Ventura also provides a hidden text code which you can use to include text, such as editorial notes or special instructions, that can be seen whenever the file is opened in your word processor, but not in a Ventura chapter. To insert hidden text anywhere in a text file, type the contents inside the angle brackets, after the characters **$!**. An example of a hidden text code used in a private memorandum might be as follows:

<$!hidden text>

<$!The contents of this section are confidential and should only be included in documents released to current investors.>

Anyone with experience in publishing knows that good graphics are as important as the text in attracting readers and communicating information. Desktop publishing is no exception. Charts, drawings, diagrams, photographs, and other artwork are often vital to the success of a publication, whether it's a glossy magazine or an annual report. Because Ventura supports such a wide range of graphics software applications — including drawing, painting, charting, and scanning programs — this section provides more information about the different types of graphics files you can import and use in your documents.

Working with Graphics

Line-Art Files

`Line-Art`

Using the "Type of File: Line-Art" option in the File menu's Load Text/Picture dialog box, you can import files from the following 10 programs or formats:

- GEM
- AutoCAD .SLD
- Lotus .PIC
- Mentor Graphics
- VideoShow
- Macintosh PICT
- PostScript
- CGM (Computer Graphics Metafile)
- Microsoft Windows Metafile
- HPGL (Hewlett-Packard Graphics Language)

GEM

*PostScript
Special Effects*

The GEM line-art file format is used when you want to load files from GEM Artline, GEM Draw Plus, and GEM Graph. Since the files produced by these programs are automatically encoded in the GEM graphics format, Ventura can load them directly into the program without converting them. Therefore, a big advantage in using picture files from other GEM programs in your documents is that they don't require extra storage space on your hard or floppy disk for copies of converted picture files.

The other line-art format that can be loaded directly into Ventura without usually requiring a conversion is the encapsulated Post-Script (EPS) format. An EPS file contains the page description language commands that tell a PostScript printer or typesetter how to print the text and graphics on a page. By loading an EPS file and placing it in your document, you can take advantage of PostScript's unique capabilities to produce special effects, such as text spirals, fountains or graded tints, titling and rotation of text or an object, and more. You can create EPS files with programs such as Adobe Illustrator, Corel Draw, Designer, and GEM Artline, or by typing the commands as an ASCII text file that adheres to the EPS file format.

An EPS file can be scaled and printed like any other graphic, but the picture itself cannot be displayed on screen unless it contains an "embedded" image (i.e., a low-resolution image header, TIFF image, or Windows metafile description of the image). If the file contains an embedded image, Ventura will use it to display a representation of the picture on screen; otherwise, it will place a large "X" in the middle of the frame to indicate that it contains an EPS file, and simply display the filename in the current selection box.

If you install Ventura to output to a PostScript printer, you can use the program itself to create a PostScript file that can be loaded back into the program and placed anywhere on a page. To do this, first, select "Output To: Filename" in the Set Printer Info dialog box (Options menu) to print to a disk file rather than directly to a printer. Next, use the File menu's To Print option to print a selected page, and the program will prompt you with an item selector to name the disk file, which is automatically given the extension .C00. After the page has been output to a file, you can load the .C00 file as a PostScript file by changing the file filter from *.EPS to *.C00 (or *.*) and place it in any frame in your document.

Except for GEM and PostScript files, Ventura converts all other line-art file formats when they're loaded. Among these other graphics formats, two of the most robust are CGM and VideoShow. The CGM format, developed by Graphic Software Systems, is a standard encoding scheme for storing graphic data used by many software packages, including several that generate statistical and analytical graphics from mainframe databases. The VideoShow format, developed by General Parametrics, uses yet another method for storing graphic data. Although Ventura converts color CGM files, it cannot convert color VideoShow files (color is turned into shades of gray). If the graphics program you're using can produce files in either the CGM or VideoShow formats, load the same file in both formats to see if Ventura does a better job of converting one format or the other.

Another excellent line-art format that Ventura supports is Apple Macintosh PICT, a graphics standard used by such draw programs as MacDraw and MacDraft. Before you can load Macintosh graphics into Ventura, however, you must transfer them into a PC-compatible format by using a network or communications program that supports both environments. After the PICT file has been transferred, you can load it into Ventura by using the Macinstosh PICT format.

The HPGL format is an encoding scheme used to send graphic data to a plotter or other vector-graphics device. The number of graphics packages that support the HPGL standard is vast, but not all of these programs can save HPGL pictures on disk rather than sending them directly to a printer. Three well-known programs that do offer the option of saving HPGL disk files that can be loaded into Ventura are AutoCAD, Microsoft Chart, and VersaCAD (as shown below).

`VideoShow`

`CGM`

`MAC PICT`

`HPGL`

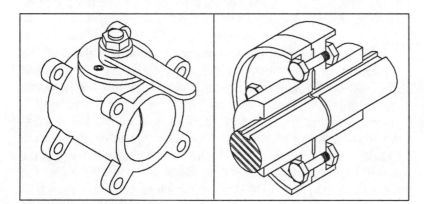

Shown here are two examples of line-art produced with VersaCAD, a well-known CAD program, and loaded as HPGL files.

AutoCad .SLD

Lotus .PIC

Mentor Gr

MS Windows

Most of the remaining line-art formats are program-specific. The AutoCAD (.SLD) option is used to import slide files created with AutoCAD, a leading CAD program. However, you can often obtain better resolution by instead converting AutoCAD files to the HPGL format. The Lotus (.PIC) format is used to load graphs created with 1-2-3, Symphony, and other programs that use the same format. The Mentor Graphics format is used to import files from Mentor Graphics CAD, manufacturing, and engineering software used on dedicated workstations, such as Apollo Computer machines. Before Ventura can load Mentor Graphics files into the program, however, they must also be transferred into a PC-compatible format.

MS Windows is the final line-art format supported by the Load Text/Picture menu option. Using the MS Windows format, you can load files created with any Microsoft Windows program that can save files in the Windows Metafile (WMF) format. If a Windows program cannot create WMF files, Ventura provides a special conversion utility that will save any metafile cut or copied to the Windows clipboard in the WMF format, which can then be loaded into Ventura. To use this program, first copy the CLIP2VP.EXE file on the Ventura Publisher Utilities Disk to the WINDOWS directory. Then start Windows and run the CLIP2VP program from inside the Windows Executive screen — CLIP2VP will occupy a small pop-up window at the right top of the screen — and proceed to start the Windows application, such as Windows Draw, from which you want the line-art drawing. Once the drawing is on the screen, select it and cut or copy it to the clipboard. Finally, select the Save As command in the CLIP2VP window and name the file under which you want to save the clipboard drawing (the .WMF extension is added automatically). You can now exit Windows, start Ventura, and use the Load Text/Picture option to import the WMF file you created.

Another line-art format that can be used in Ventura is the Drawing Interchange Format, usually identified by the .DXF file extension and supported by AutoCAD and similar programs. You cannot, however, load a .DXF file directly by using the Load Text/Picture option; instead you must first convert the .DXF file into a GEM file by using the "DXFTOGEM.EXE" conversion utility, supplied on the Ventura Utilities Disk. Copy your .DXF file to the same directory where the utility is located, type "DXFTOGEM FILENAME" (using the name of your DXF file in place of "FILENAME"), and press the Enter key. The utility will create a converted copy of your file, but with the .GEM extension. You can then use the line-art file format for GEM to load the converted .DXF file into Ventura. Because Ventura cannot convert a number of .DXF attributes — such as three-dimensional rendering, curve fitting, shape entity, ellipses that are not X-Y aligned, tapering widths in polygons, text mirroring, and text expansion factors — you'll need to check the converted drawing carefully to determine if it can be used or not.

Image Files

The other type of graphics file available in the Load Text/Picture dialog box is the "Type of File: Image" option, which supports the following graphics formats or programs:

- GEM/Halo DPE
- PC Paintbrush
- MAC Paint
- TIFF

The GEM/Halo Desktop Publishing Edition (DPE) format is used when you want to load files from GEM Paint and other graphics programs or from scanning software that creates GEM-formatted (.IMG) image files. Halo DPE, which is also distributed under the name Desktop Publisher's (DP) Graphics, is another paint program that can generate GEM-formatted image files by using a built-in conversion capability. The advantage of using these or other programs that produce GEM-formatted image files is that Ventura can load the files directly without converting them and taking up extra disk storage space.

The PC Paintbrush format (developed by ZSoft) is one of the most popular bit-mapped graphics standards supported by IBM PC publishing programs. This format, which is identified by the .PCX file extension, is used by PC Paintbrush Plus and Publisher's Paintbrush. Publisher's Paintbrush is particularly useful because it provides multiple zoom modes that make it easy to edit a full-page image at a resolution of 300 dpi (on a system with EMS memory). You can also load 1-2-3 graph (.PIC) files into these and other paint programs to enhance your business graphics before loading them into Ventura.

The Apple Macintosh Paint format is used to load files that conform to a bit-mapped graphics standard used by Macintosh paint programs, such as MacPaint and FullPaint, and other applications like

Image

GEM / HALO DPE

PC-Paintbrush

MAC Paint

Microsoft Chart and Excel. As with Macintosh PICT files, however, you must first transfer these files into a PC-compatible format before proceeding to import them into Ventura.

Thus far, the emphasis on using pictures in your documents has been to add business graphics or original illustrations. But with Ventura,

The images used in this document were produced with a scanner and Publisher's Paintbrush. A scanned image was flipped horizontally to produce both ends of the letterhead, and a 1-2-3 pie chart was enhanced by adding the scanned image of a coin behind the slices. All of the text, including the labels, was created with Ventura's Text Editing tools.

Crown Mining & Manufacturing

100 Zaveri Industrial Park
Crown City, Idaho 83703
208/345-6789

Dear Potential Investor:

The materials enclosed in this Private Placement Memorandum provide the corporate business plan and current business projections for Crown Mining & Manufacturing, herein referred to as the "Company." These materials are confidential and are to be released only to those who have a current or potential investment in the Company.

Executive Summary

In 1859, silver fever struck a group of prospectors in a gulch on the western side of Nevada when they discovered the Comstock Lode—the first and richest silver-mining camp in the United States. Today, silver is used so widely and rapidly that silver mines have not been able to meet world demand for decades. The expanding consumption of silver in industrial use accounts for much of this demand.

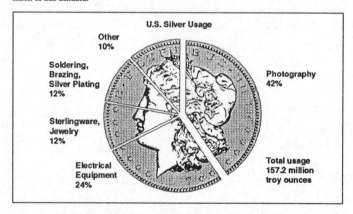

U.S. Silver Usage

Other 10%

Soldering, Brazing, Silver Plating 12%

Sterlingware, Jewelry 12%

Electrical Equipment 24%

Photography 42%

Total usage 157.2 million troy ounces

While the prospect of discovering another Comstock Lode in the United States may seem unlikely to some, the board of directors at Crown Mining & Manufacturing believe just the opposite. The problem is that it takes years of hard work to sink a shaft, bore tunnels, and develop deposits of silver — and that requires millions of dollars. But to paraphrase Mark Twain, once you are "smitten with the silver fever," it may be the road to fortune.

you can also add pictures of photographs and existing artwork that have been converted into graphics files by using an image scanner. In order to load image files created with a scanner, you must use a compatible image file format. Fortunately, most popular scanners save files in the TIFF or PC Paintbrush (.PCX) formats, which makes it easy to load them into Ventura. A few scanner programs, such as GEM Scan and MegaScan, will also save scanned images as GEM-formatted (.IMG) files. If you use gray-scale images, however, you must use the TIFF or PostScript (with shades of gray) formats, which are the only gray-scale formats that Ventura supports at this time.

TIFF

To operate most scanners, you can either use the scanner software or an image editing program that provides its own driver for operating the scanner, such as GEM Scan, Halo DPE, and Publisher's Paintbrush. However, the amount of control you have over the scanning process will vary, depending on the scanner and software used. With most scanning software, you should be able to control the image's brightness and contrast, as well as choose a line-art or dithering (often called "halftone") scanning mode. If you're scanning photographs, you'll need to use a scanner that provides a gray-scale scanning mode for the best and most flexible results.

Most scanner software also gives you a choice of resolution settings to use when scanning an image, typically ranging from 75 to 300 dpi. The resolution you should use depends on a number of factors, including the type of printer you expect to use, the amount of available memory and storage space, the type of image you're scanning, and how you plan to use the image in a document. As a general rule for scanning line art, you should set the scanner resolution to match your printer's resolution, whenever possible. If you plan to output an enlarged version of a scanned image, using the highest resolution ensures that more detail will be retained. If you expect to reduce the image, however, scanning it at a lower resolution won't hurt the quality as much because reducing it has the effect of actually increasing its resolution. With gray-scale images, however, you don't need to scan at 300 dpi to obtain good results. Normally, you can scan the image at a resolution that matches the screen frequency you intend to use when actually producing the digital halftone. In this book, for example, any gray-scale images that were output at 300-dpi were usually scanned at less than 100 dpi, since the screen frequencies used only ranged from 50 to 60 lpi.

If you use gray-scale TIFF images in a document that will be printed on a 300-dpi laser printer, you can scan the images at less than 300 dpi and still obtain excellent results. The image on the left, which is 86K in size, is scanned at 78 dpi, and the image on the right, which is 240K, is scanned at 133 dpi, yet the printed results (using the Image Settings menu option's defaults) don't show that much difference.

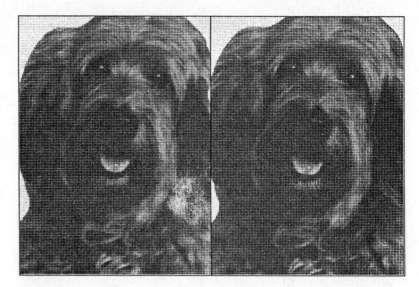

Those who haven't used scanners before are often surprised to discover how much disk storage space can be required to use a scanner on an ongoing basis. For example, a full-page graphic scanned at 300 dpi can easily require 1MB of disk storage. And because 300-dpi image scanning and printing can involve plenty of processing time, a high performance PC (a fast 286 or 386 system) is generally recommended. If you intend to use 300-dpi scanned images in your Ventura documents, remember that your disk must have enough space to store the converted copies that Ventura makes when it loads non-GEM image files. For example, if you load a scanned image using the PC Paintbrush (.PCX) format and the file is 75K in size, you'll need about 75K additional disk space for Ventura to store the converted GEM-formatted (.IMG) file.

Another feature offered by several graphics programs is a memory-resident utility that can capture the image on a PC screen when using other software. With Publisher's Paintbrush, this utility is called Frieze; with GEM Paint, it is called Snapshot. Since these screen shots are bit-mapped images, they can also be loaded into Ventura. For example, all of the Ventura screen shots in this book were prepared using Frieze. The Ventura Utilities Disk also contains a separate conversion utility (TXTTOPCX) that enables you to convert a screen shot captured with Sidekick into the .PCX format. HotShot is yet another RAM-resident utility that captures screen shots that can be converted into the .PCX format and imported into Ventura.

Part IV

The
Professional
Extension

Chapter 8

Adding Power to Ventura

*A*ny business that uses Ventura as an integral part of a regular publishing operation should consider using *Ventura Publisher: Professional Extension,* a powerful add-on program that brings higher-end capabilities to the base product. The Professional Extension (Extension) includes such enhanced features as an automatic table creation function, scientific and mathematical equation formatting, extensive cross referencing, sophisticated vertical justification, optional hyphenation dictionary, and EMS memory support, which lets you create voluminous documents, up to a practical limit of 32MB.

While anyone that requires advanced publishing capabilities will certainly benefit from using the Extension, the most likely candidates are technical, scientific, engineering, academic, commercial, and specialized (such as legal and medical) publishing operations, as well as those involved in database publishing. However, to take full advantage of the Extension's publishing prowess, you may need to procure a more advanced computer. Unlike the base product, which runs acceptably fast even on a PC-XT, the Extension performs best on a 286- or 386-based system, and with EMS memory highly recommended. Although you can run the Extension on a system without EMS memory, the more memory your computer has, the more voluminous and complex your Ventura documents can be and the faster you can access them.

While the Professional Extension provides useful features for virtually any publishing activity, two applications that should profit most are commercial publishing (e.g., books, magazines, and newspapers) and scientific and technical publishing.

Ventura Publisher: Professional Extension — Most Useful Features for Major Business Applications	Enhanced Features					
	EMS Support	English Dictionary	Table Editing	Cross Referencing	Vertical Justification	Equation Editing
General Business	✔		✔	✔	✔	
Education and Research	✔	✔	✔	✔		✔
Commercial Publishing	✔	✔	✔	✔	✔	✔
Scientific and Technical	✔	✔	✔	✔	✔	✔
Financial and Insurance	✔		✔	✔		✔
Government and Legal	✔	✔	✔	✔		

The Extension also requires at least 1.2MB of EMS memory in order to use the 130,000-word English hyphenation dictionary (licensed from Edco Services) provided with the program as an additional option. If your system has insufficient EMS memory, you can still use the Extension without installing the dictionary (the program will instead use the base product's hyphenation algorithms and smaller dictionaries), but you'll miss out on the improved hyphenation and added controls it provides. For example, you can designate the length of words and the minimum number of characters before or after the hyphen, and with about 2.5MB of EMS memory you can also use a utility provided to update the dictionary.

Enhanced Features

Installing the Extension is a simple matter of re-installing the base product along with the additional Extension disks provided. The incremental hard disk space required for the Extension is approximately 600K, plus another 1.2MB if the English hyphenation dictionary is installed. To run the Extension, you merely type "VPPROF" (instead of "VP") at the DOS system prompt. After the Extension is loaded, you'll see the same interface on the screen as you did with the base product, with one important difference: a new operating mode, Table Edit, appears in a box directly under the four function selectors in the side-bar.

After you select the Table Edit mode, the add button reads "Ins New Table," and you can easily create tables anywhere in a document. You just click on the add button or select the new Table command provided in the Edit menu's Insert Special Item option, and proceed to specify the table's width, number of rows and columns, and other settings in the dialog box provided. When finished, Ventura immediately inserts your customized table into the page at the exact spot you have designated. As you fill in the empty table using the keyboard, the program enlarges each cell vertically, as necessary, to contain the entries. Better yet, you can import a .PRN (printed to disk) spreadsheet file created with 1-2-3 (or compatible program) directly into Ventura, and the program automatically creates a table with the proper number of rows and columns. Editing a table's format is also easy: Simply click on one or more cells to insert rows or columns, join and split cells, set background tints for cells, change ruling line widths, and assign one cell's attributes to another. Each cell is a separate paragraph, so you can format the contents by defining styles, as with any other paragraph.

With the Extension's equation formatting feature, you can insert complex formulas and equations anywhere in a document. Based on a standard mathematical and scientific language called EQN, Ventura's equation formatter recognizes over 100 special words and commands (Greek characters, math operators, diacritical marks, and more) commonly required in physics, engineering, and other technical publications. Whenever you select the Equation command (which replaces the base product's Fraction command in the Insert Special Item menu option), Ventura provides the Equation Editing screen. As with the base product's Fraction Editing screen, you can type keyboard commands on top and see the formatted result below. After you finish and leave this screen, the typeset equation is inserted where the cursor is in the text. For example, typing the equation "y~=~sqrt {x sup 2 plus y sup 2}" produces the following example of a square root:

$$y = \sqrt{x^2 + y^2}$$

The cross-references feature provided in the base product is greatly enhanced in the Extension. At any location in a document, you can insert the current figure, table, or section number as well as the current page or chapter number. Move text and graphics around and

Ventura automatically updates all references at your command, including those that extend across chapters. You can also insert special markers throughout a text file and interpose a variable definition (substitute text of up to 54 characters) at each marker location, for example, to add the name of a specific client in the appropriate places in a standard contract.

Automatic vertical justification helps fit your text more evenly into a given vertical space, such as a frame or column. Ventura offers two types of vertical justification: Carding adds space in multiples of the line spacing, so you maintain baseline alignment across

With the Extension's automatic table function, you can compose technical charts, such as the one shown in this sample, much faster than you can with the base product.

Camera Lenses

Table 5- 7: Extreme Close-Up Focusing Chart for 2-, 3-, 4-, and 6-Inch Lenses with 16mm or 35mm Cameras

Distances from lens diaphragm to object and lens diaphragm to film are in inches.
Magnification Ratio is the number of times an object is enlarged on film.

No. of F/stops Increase Required	Exposure Factor Required	Magnification Ratio	2-INCH LENS		3-INCH LENS		4-INCH LENS		6-INCH LENS	
			Diaphragm to Object	Diaphragm to Film	Diaphragm to Object	Diaphragm to Film	Diaphragm to Object	Diaphragm to Film	Diaphragm to Object	Diaphragm to Film
2	4	1:1	4	4	6	6	8	8	12	12
3 1/8	9	2:1	3	6	4 1/2	9	6	12	9	18
4	16	3:1	2 5/8	8	4	12	5	16	8	24
4 1/2	25	4:1	2 1/2	10	3 3/4	15	5	20	7 1/2	30
5 1/8	36	5:1	2 7/16	12	3 5/8	18	4 3/4	24	7 3/8	36
5 1/4	49	6:1	2 3/8	14	3 1/2	21	4 5/8	28	7	42
6	64	7:1	2 5/16	16	3 7/16	24	4 9/16	32	6 7/8	48
6 1/4	81	8:1	2 1/4	18	3 3/8	27	4 1/2	36	6 3/4	54
6 1/2	100	9:1	2 3/16	20	3 5/16	30	4 7/16	40	6 5/8	60
7	121	10:1	2 1/8	22	3 1/4	33	4 3/8	44	6 1/2	66

Note: These values are approximate since lens focal length will vary slightly. Some lenses will deliver a better image if reversed in their mounts at high magnifications.

range of acceptably sharp focus in front and behind a subject. In summary, the three factors that affect depth of field are:

- F/stop setting — stop down to increase depth
- Distance of subject — rapid decrease in depth as lens is focused close
- Focal length — more depth for short focal length, less depth for long focal length

Close-Up Lenses

When a camera that does not have a macrofocusing capability is required to focus on objects closer than the normal focusing range of its own lens, a supplementary close-up lens can be used. If you use more than one supplementary lens at a time, you can calculate the combined power of the lenses by adding their individual diopter values.

The focus of the camera's own lens must be adjusted to vary the focusing distance. One way to determine the proper working distance from the supplementary lens to the subject

Figure 5-10: With a macrofocusing lens, a camera can focus at extremely close distances without requiring the use of a supplemental lens.

5-16

columns and facing pages; feathering adds the exact space required to make text reach the bottom of the column or frame, dividing the added space uniformly among all the lines.

There's no doubt that Ventura Publisher: Professional Extension places more powerful tools in the hands of virtually anyone using the base product. However, it also takes time and practice to learn how to harness the Extension's power most effectively. Chapter 9 provides more detailed information on applying the Extension's advanced features, to help you determine if you need the Extension's features for your publishing operation, or to help you learn more about using the Extension if you already have it.

Ventura on a Network

If you plan to use Ventura or the Extension in an environment where several contributors are involved in the document creation process (such as an in-house publishing division), you should consider using *Ventura Publisher: Network Server*. The Network Server (which comes with the base product) can be installed to run across multiple workstations connected on a 3Com, PC Net, Novell, or other local area network (LAN) system.

There are two different ways in which a publishing group can use the Network Server on a LAN: in an office where only one person uses Ventura at a time, or in an operation where multiple users need to access the program concurrently. In the first scenario, different members of a group must take turns using Ventura or the Extension, and the program can be customized to recognize each person's unique hardware setup and default preferences. You can also connect up to six printers to the PC running the Network Server and choose one easily from each workstation.

In the second case, each person on the LAN can still access the same copy of the Network Server, however, you'll also need to purchase an additional copy of the base program or the Extension for each concurrent workstation (the installation process makes a record of each additional copy's serial number). Although the investment required to run Ventura in this second scenario is higher, the advantage is that writers, editors, designers, illustrators, proofreaders, managers, and others can all be working on different parts of the same publication at the same time.

The Network Server version of Ventura, which can be used with either the base product or the Extension, includes special features for group publishing, such as a Browse command that lets you load and view a chapter but not make any changes.

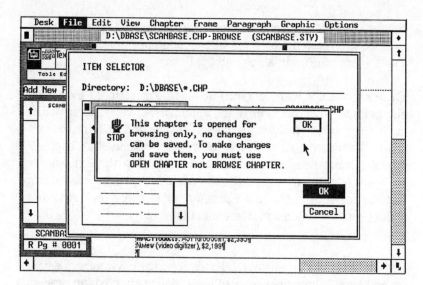

When the Network Server is used in this second type of networked publishing environment, some of its most useful features include:

- Chapter locking: Chapter files that are being worked on are locked to keep others from changing the same document.

- Conflict management: If you're editing a Ventura chapter that contains a text (or graphics) file and someone else is concurrently editing the original file, the Network Server informs you when you try to save the chapter and asks whether you want to overwrite the text (or graphics) file or save the edited chapter under a new name.

- Browse mode: With this feature (shown above), other group members can read the last saved version of a chapter but can't change it. You can also create read-only style sheets to avoid the potential conflict caused by group members accessing the same style sheets. This feature helps to ensure consistency of formatting across all company documents.

- Printer sharing: As in the first scenario, you can choose to print on any of the six different printers connected to the LAN. The upgraded printer drivers that are supplied with the Network Server will automatically issue end-of-job commands to the program's print spooler.

Chapter 9

Using the Professional Extension

*O*ne way to explain the difference between Ventura and the Extension is to describe the basic product as a general-purpose publishing program and the Extension as an industrial-strength version of the same tool. When you use the Extension, you work with the same interface, menus, and menu options as those found in the base product. However, several key features, including cross referencing, fraction editing, and hyphenation and justification, have been enhanced or altered to encompass more advanced capabilities. Finally, the new Table Edit function has been added to create tables and forms.

With the Extension's advanced capabilities, Ventura can provide features that professional, scientific, and technical publishers have come to expect from high-end composition and pagination systems. Unless you're a full-time publisher, however, you may be wondering whether or not you really need the Extension to facilitate your own publishing operation. Therefore, the purpose of this chapter is twofold: to provide those who already have the Extension (or plan to use it) with basic information on how the program's features work; and to help others determine if the Extension would make a worthwhile addition to their repertoire of publishing tools. Bear in mind, however, that it would take another book to fully examine the many ways in which you can apply all of the Extension's powerful features.

In the Publisher Info dialog box, the amount shown after "SYS" is the EMS memory taken by the Extension and other applications (such as a disk cache), and the amount shown after "APP" is the total EMS memory available for all text files in a Ventura document. As with the base product, you can access the program's Diagnostics screen by clicking on the word "Ventura" in the lower-left box.

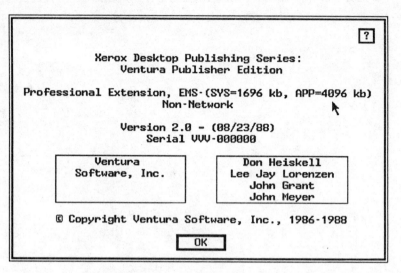

If you use EMS memory with the Extension, there are three main advantages. First, the program will be able to access larger documents much faster by eliminating much of the time spent spooling information to and from the hard disk as you move from page to page. Second, depending on how much EMS memory your system contains, the Extension can increase the paragraph size limit by over 10 times, compared to the base product. Third, with at least 1.2MB of EMS memory, you can also make use of the 130,000-word English hyphenation dictionary, included with the Extension as an option for users with the highest typographic standards.

In the Diagnostics screen, the program displays the current EMS memory in use (out of the maximum amount available), and it shows that the number of line elements per frame has increased from the base product's limit of 725 to 1,022 (this limit increases even more if additional EMS memory is available).

```
VENTURA PUBLISHER DIAGNOSTICS

Internal Memory in Use:      2850 /     25000 bytes
External Memory in Use:     18960 /     64024
    EMS Memory in Use:      49152 /   4194304
   Text Memory in Use:          0 /      4096
   Paragraphs in Use:          4 /      1024 paras
 Line Elements in Use:          0 /      1022 elements

  Ext. Mem. Swapped Out:        0
  Text Mem. Swapped Out:        0

       Width Table Size:     9786 bytes
    Graphics Buffer Size:    48000
      Screen Fonts Size:    52000
       Hyphenation Size:     9732
     Perm. Strings Size:    10007
   FARCODE Overlay Size:    61776
                                              OK
```

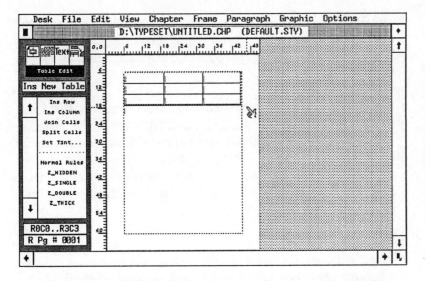

The interface used by the Extension is identical to that used by the base product except for the addition of the Table Edit mode, located under the original four functions in the side-bar. When the Table Edit mode is active (as shown here), the add button and assignment list display this feature's special tools, which are used to insert tables in a document, such as the default table shown in this screen shot.

Anyone who has ever used Ventura to publish tabular material knows what a tedious and time-consuming task it can be. With the base product, you normally create tables by inserting tabs and construct forms by applying the box text tool or adding frames. In each case, you may also rely heavily on using the various ruling line options (Ruling Line Above, Ruling Line Below, and Ruling Box Around) in the Paragraph and Frame menus in order to create a matrix of rows and columns. With the Extension, however, you only need to select a few commands and Ventura automatically places a table matrix on the page at the exact spot you selected. This feat is made possible by the addition of a new function, called Table Edit, which joins Frame Setting, Paragraph Tagging, Text Editing, and Graphic Drawing as the program's fifth operating mode.

As with the other program modes, Ventura provides several different methods for enabling the Table Edit function:

- Choose the Table Edit function selector in the side-bar
- Choose the Table Edit menu option in the View menu
- Choose the Edit menu's Insert Special Item option (Ctrl-C) and select the Table command (F9)

After you change to the Table Edit function, the contents of the side-bar's add button and assignment list change to reflect the different controls and commands available (as shown on the right).

Working with Tables

The Table Edit cursor is represented by a smaller version of the crossbar icon used by the Frame Setting mode, the add button reads "Ins New Table," and the assignment list is used to display various table-editing commands.

Before you can insert a table into a document, you must first insert the Text Editing cursor in a text file, just before any paragraph return or end of file symbol. Although inserting a table in a text file placed on the base page usually works best, you can also put tables in added frames and in box text, as long as the typing cursor is inserted there first. You cannot, however, insert a table in text that is part of a header, footer, footnote, or other table.

Inserting a Table

When you select the Insert New Table add button, Ventura provides a pop-up dialog box just as it does when you select the Add New Tag and Set Font add buttons (using the Paragraph Tagging and Text Editing modes, respectively). In this case, it is the Insert/Edit Table dialog box (shown below) and it can also be accessed by selecting the Insert Special Item option and the Table command (as shown on the left). If you accept the default values, a simple table consisting of three columns and three rows will be inserted at the typing cursor's location. The size of the table depends on whether you place it in a box text, an added frame, or the page frame itself. If placed in a frame, the table's size is governed by the frame's margins and

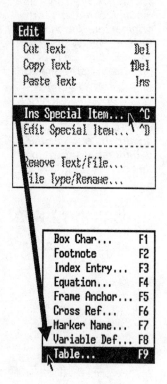

The parameters shown in this Insert/Edit Table dialog box are the default settings the Extension uses to produce a basic three-row, three-column table. After you click "OK," the Extension automatically inserts the table at the spot where the Text Editing cursor was prior to selecting the Insert Table add button or Table command from the Insert Special Item option (Edit menu).

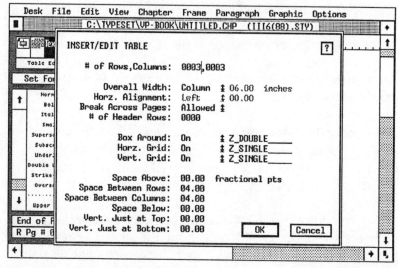

An empty table created by using the settings in the dialog box shown on the previous page.

columns settings as well. Each of the default table's cells (the enclosed areas in which a row and column intersect) is the same width and height, as shown in the example above.

Although you can always start with a default table and then change it into the form you want after it's inserted on the page, it's faster to change the default settings in the Insert/Edit Table dialog box at the outset. Use the keyboard to enter the number of rows you want for the first number in the "# of Rows, Columns" setting, and enter the number of columns you want for the second number. If you change the "Overall Width" setting from "Column" to "Custom," you can use the "Horz. Alignment" setting to make the table align horizontally against the left or right margin, centered, or indented by the amount you define. If you want a long table to automatically continue from one page frame to the next, use the "# of Header Rows" setting to specify how many header rows you want repeated on each additional page. If you don't want the header rows repeated, select the "Break Across Pages: No" setting.

The "Box Around," "Horz. Grid," and "Vert. Grid" settings tell Ventura which ruling lines to use when it creates the table matrix. For its default table, Ventura uses two program-generated tags, "Z_DOUBLE" (two thin lines) and "Z_SINGLE" (one thin line), however, you can type in other tag names that contain the ruling line specifications you want to use. For example, you might use a third program-generated tag, "Z_THICK" (one thick line), in place of "Z_DOUBLE" for the ruling box around the entire table, or you might want to create and use a tag called "RED BOX" for printing the ruling box in color. You can also choose the "Off" setting for all three ruling line options if you don't want the table to contain any lines at all.

The "Space Above" and "Space Below" settings add vertical space above and below the table itself. "Space Between Rows" adds vertical space between each row, while "Space Between Columns" adds horizontal space to the left of each column. "Vert. Just. at Top" and "Vert. Just. at Bottom" allow you to control the vertical justification at the top and bottom of the table. (Vertical justification is explained in the "Expanded Features" section later in this chapter).

Entering Table Text

After a table is inserted, the typing cursor is automatically located in the first cell (in front of a paragraph return symbol if the Show Tabs & Returns option is active) and you can immediately begin entering text into the table by using the keyboard. As you add text, the cursor will automatically move down and create new lines, as necessary, increasing the height of the row in order to accommodate each new line. Although only one paragraph return is allowed per cell, you can force additional lines of text inside a cell by using line breaks (hold down the Control key and press the Enter key).

Using the keyboard cursor keys, you can move the typing cursor through the text within a cell, and also move the cursor to the next cell. The Delete, Backspace, Shift, Tab, and other keys function as they normally do in the Text Editing mode. You can also use the mouse and keyboard to cut, copy, and paste text within a cell, however, you cannot select text in more than one cell at a time.

Finally, by using a special feature that recognizes columnar data from other programs, you can load a spreadsheet or database file and the Extension will automatically place it into a table for you. However, the columnar data file must be formatted with at least *two space characters* between each column in order for it to be loaded into the Extension successfully. With 1-2-3, for example, you can use that program's global column settings feature to ensure that the column widths are large enough before producing a print (.PRN) file that can be imported into the Extension. With dBASE, you can apply

The Extension provides new tools that make it easy to turn an ordinary spreadsheet file, such as the 1-2-3 worksheet file shown here, into an appropriately formatted and typeset table.

Golden Antiques Annual Expense Report		
Expenses:	1989	1988
Salaries	$253,450	$195,320
Rent	$50,950	$40,940
Warehouse	$20,920	$8,950
Travel	$7,500	$5,020
Telephone	$6,220	$4,020
Total	$339,040	$254,250

```
LOAD TEXT/PICTURE                                    [?]

    Type of File:  [Text]  [Line-Art]  [Image]

    Text Format:  [Generated]  [ASCII]  [WordStar 3]  [WS 4.0/5.0]

                  [MS-Word]  [WordPerfect]  [XyWrite]  [8-Bit ASCII]

                  [Writer]  [MultiMate]  [DCA]  [WordPerfect 5]

                  [PRN-to-Table]

    # of Files:  [One]  [Several]

    Destination:  [List of Files]  [Text Clipboard]  [Text Cursor]

                                        [OK ]  [Cancel]
```

With the Extension, the Load Text/Picture dialog box includes a special "PRN-to-Table" option that lets you import a spreadsheet, database, or other columnar data file and automatically place it into a program-generated table that is large enough to accommodate every row and column in the source file.

that program's Copy command to create a text (.TXT) file using the System Data Format option, or use its Report to File command to produce an ASCII text file with two spaces between each field.

To load a properly formatted spreadsheet or database file into the Extension, the typing cursor must first be inserted in a text file on a page. Next select the Load Text/Picture option (File menu) and choose "Type of File: Text," "Format: PRN-to-Table" (an option available only in the Extension), "# of Files: One," "Destination: Text Cursor," and click "OK." The Extension converts the .PRN file into a table (.TBL) file, leaving the original .PRN file intact, and automatically places the columnar information into a default table.

```
Desk  File  Edit  View  Chapter  Frame  Paragraph  Graphic  Options
      C:\TYPESET\UNTITLED.CHP  (DEFAULT.STY)

              | Golden Antique Annual Expense Report
Expenses:     | 1989       | 1988
Salaries      | $253,450   | $195,320
Rent          | $50,950    | $40,940
Warehouse     | $20,920    | $8,950
Travel        | $7,500     | $5,020
Telephone     | $6,220     | $4,020
Total         | $339,040   | $254,250
```

This screen shot shows the table automatically generated by the Extension to accommodate the sample spreadsheet file shown on the previous page. Although this table is only a "draft" version, you can usually turn it into a final table (as shown on the next page) with only a modicum of additional formatting.

Using the Table Edit function's tools, the three columns in the first row are joined together for the header. The Paragraph Tagging function can be used as usual to apply various typographic attributes to the text in each cell.

Golden Antiques Annual Expense Report		
Expenses:	1989	1988
Salaries	$253,450	$195,320
Rent	$50,950	$40,940
Warehouse	$20,920	$8,950
Travel	$7,500	$5,020
Telephone	$6,220	$4,020
Total	$339,040	$254,250

Editing Tables

After a table is inserted in a document, the Extension provides a host of editing features that makes it easy to modify the entire table or only selected portions, such as a group of cells, columns, or rows. To select the entire table, place the Table Edit cursor at the upper-left corner of the first cell, click and drag the mouse to the lower-right corner of the table, and release the mouse button. The Extension highlights the entire table with a gray-textured outline and indicates the range of cells in the selection box. For example, if you select the entire default table (Row 0, Column 0 through Row 3, Column 3), "R0C0..R3C3" is displayed in the selection box. Using this method, you can also select part of a table, and enlarge or reduce the selected part by applying the same mouse–keyboard technique (hold down the Shift key and click) used to select text in the Text Editing mode.

```
Edit
Cut Row/Column...    Del
Copy Row/Column...   ↑Del
Paste Row/Column...  Ins
- - - - - - - - - - - - - -
Set Column Width...  ^C
Edit Table Settings  ^D
- - - - - - - - - - - - - -
Remove Text/File...
File Type/Rename...
```

There are several ways to modify a table or part of a table once it is selected. Using the Edit menu, you can apply the Cut Row/Column, Copy Row/Column, Paste Row/Column, Edit Table Settings, and Set Column Width options. If the entire table is selected, for instance, you can use the cut, copy, and paste commands to move it from one page to another. In each case, the Extension will also prompt you with a pop-up dialog box asking you to confirm the operation before it is executed.

Choose the Edit Table Setting option and the Extension provides the same Insert/Edit Table dialog box you used to create the table, which allows you to change any of the values you originally specified. Choose the Set Column Width command and the program furnishes a highly useful dialog box that lets you scroll through the columns

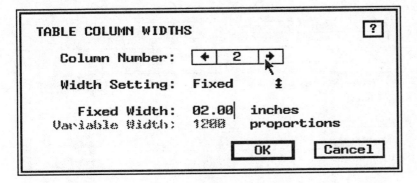

Using the Table Column Widths dialog box, you can select a fixed or variable width for each column in a table created with the Table Edit mode.

one by one (using the "Column Number" control), and select column widths that are "Fixed" (you specify the exact width) or "Variable" (relative to other columns) for each column in the selected table. To create variable widths, the Extension uses the proportions (percentages or integer multiples) you define for each selected column. Or, instead of using this dialog box (shown above), you can change column widths interactively by holding down the Alt key and using the mouse to drag the right column guide to the location you want. With a little practice, you can easily use the mouse in this manner to create a table form you desire.

Another way to edit a table is to apply any of the attributes provided in the Table Edit assignment list. Pick "Ins Row" or "Ins Column" and a pop-up screen tells you how many rows or columns you can insert at the selected part of the table before executing the command.

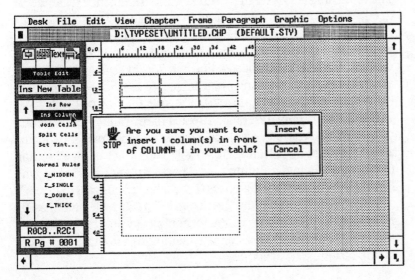

When the Table Edit mode is active, you can use any of the commands listed in the side-bar assignment list to edit an existing table. For the "Ins Row," "Ins Column," and "Set Tint" commands, the Extension provides additional dialog boxes, as shown in this screen shot.

With the Table Cell Tint dialog box, you can add a background color and fill pattern to one or more cells in any table created with the Table Edit mode. For example, you can place a solid background color, such as black, behind a table header and use the Paragraph menu's Font option (or the Text Editing mode's Set Font add button) to change the color of the header text to white.

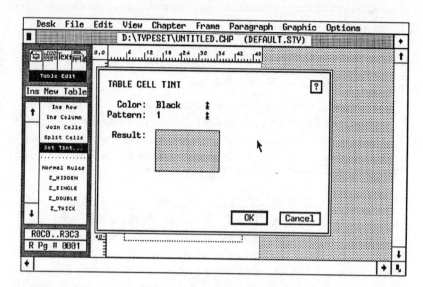

With the "Join Cells" and "Split Cells" commands, you can combine several cells into larger (wider or taller) cells or split them back into their original size. Larger cells are useful for headings that extend beyond a single column or row. The "Set Tint" command produces the Table Cell Tint dialog box (shown above), which lets you assign a background color and fill pattern to selected cells. As with all other program features that offer color, you can use the Define Colors option in the Paragraph menu to control the colors available.

The remaining attributes in the Table Edit assignment list allow you to edit any of the ruling lines used in the table. To do so, you must first click the mouse at the beginning of the ruling line or box you want to change, drag the cursor to the end of the line, and release the mouse button. The selected line will appear as a thick, gray line and you can now select any of the table rule tags in the assignment list ("Normal Rules," "Z_HIDDEN," "Z_SINGLE," "Z_DOUBLE," and "Z_THICK") to apply different attributes to the ruling line(s) or box you selected. You can also add your own table rule tags to the assignment list by selecting the "Table Rule List: Shown" setting (which appears in the Ruling Line Above, Ruling Line Below, and Ruling Box Around dialog boxes) for each tag you want to use. It's also possible to change the Extension's default table rule tags by following the standard procedure for editing any program-generated tag (the "Generated Tags: Shown" setting in the Set Preferences dialog box must be active).

Formatting Table Text

Because the Extension treats each cell in a table as a separate paragraph, the contents are formatted by using paragraph tags. Although the program automatically labels each cell with a default tag, called "Table Text" (which initially has the same attributes as the "Body Text" tag), you can change the default tag's attributes or assign different tags to various cells. Thus, you can use the Font, Alignment, Spacing, and other Paragraph menu options as you would with any paragraph. In most cases, however, you'll only need to apply a few tags to produce different types of alignment.

For example, you can create a variety of tables by using just five variations on the "Table Text" tag with these pivotal settings:

- Table Left: "Horz. Alignment: Left" (Alignment option)
- Table Center: "Horz. Alignment: Center" (Alignment option)
- Table Decimal: "Horz. Alignment: Decimal" and "In From Right to Decimal: 00,02 picas and points" (Alignment option)
- Table Leaders: "Auto-Leader: On" and "Leader Char: ..." for adding periods (or other leader characters) from the end of a paragraph to the next column guide (Tab Settings option)
- Table Rotate: "Horz. Alignment: Left," "Text Rotation: 90," and "Maximum Rotated Height: 03,00 picas and points" (Alignment option) primarily for rotating column headings

Finally, as with any text in a document, you can also use the Text Editing mode to change the attributes of table text by applying features from the assignment list (i.e., bold, italic, and so on), and by using the Set Font add button to change the typeface, type size, style, and color of any selected text.

NAME: Anderthal	FIRST: Nathaniel	EMPL OYEE: A5403
DOB: 07/08/55	SSN: 754-44-8077	
ADD: 7787 Woodcrest	DEPT: Operations	
CITY: Elmhurst Heights	JOB: Security Officer	
STATE: NY ZIP: 10878	HIRE: 08/07/87	
PHONE: 212 878-8877	GRADE: E12	

The Extension's Table Edit mode can also be used to create forms that incorporate graphics. The scanned image in this sample is placed in a separate frame added on top of a blank cell in the table.

Expanded Features

The philosophy behind the Extension is that many of the existing features in the base product could be broadened to include more of the enhancements and capabilities that many commercial and corporate publishers want most. Three of these expanded features are dictionary hyphenation, cross references, and vertical justification. This section takes a closer look at how each of these features work.

Dictionary Hyphenation

Among the stringent requirements that professional publishers demand from an electronic publishing system are the hyphenation and justification capabilities of the software program. While the base product provides sufficient hyphenation features for most common business purposes, the Extension offers superior hyphenation tools in the form of an optional, 130,000-word English hyphenation dictionary, prefix and suffix dictionaries, and related utilities.

During the installation process, the Extension automatically copies all of the optional hyphenation dictionary files onto your hard disk in a subdirectory named DICT, within the VENTURA directory. In order to use this dictionary, however, your PC must have at least 1.2MB of EMS memory. If your system has insufficient EMS memory, the Extension will instead use the base product's hyphenation algorithms and smaller dictionaries, and you can delete the files in the DICT subdirectory and regain about 1.2MB of disk space. If you've chosen to use the optional hyphenation dictionary by responding "Yes" during the installation process, the VPPROF.BAT file used to run the Extension will include the following lines:

```
DLOAD ENGLISH
DRTLCFG -M6 -B2 E3 -AA -PC:\VENTURA\DICT\
```

The first line tells the Extension to load the English hyphenation dictionary from the hard disk into EMS memory. The second line contains several parameters that allow you to control how words will be hyphenated. "-M6" indicates the minimum number of characters in a word that can be hyphenated. The default is six characters, which means that words containing five characters or less will not be hyphenated. "-B2" designates the minimum number of characters before the hyphen (the default is two characters); "E3" indicates the minimum number of characters after the hyphen (the default is three characters). The next setting tells the Extension how to treat an apostrophe: "-AA" sets the default for the language currently in use; "-AE" treats the apostrophe as the end of the word; and "-AC" treats it as a normal letter. The final setting ("-PC:\VENTURA\DICT") indicates the directory path where the dictionary files are located. If you change any of these default parameters, use an ASCII text editor (such as EDLIN, the MS-DOS utility) and make certain you use the same spacing as in the original file (i.e., one space between options).

After using the Extension, the dictionary remains in EMS memory unless you unload it by typing "DLOAD -U" from the DICT directory, or by adding the following lines at the end of the VPPROF.BAT file:

```
CD \VENTURA\DICT
DLOAD -U
```

Also located in the DICT subdirectory are two utilities: CHKWORD and DUPD. If you type "CHKWORD," the utility first displays the name of the currently loaded dictionary and the status of the prefix/suffix files in use, and then prompts you for a word that you want to check. After you type the word, the utility displays the word with all possible hyphenation points. The DUPD utility is a more powerful tool that you can use to update the hypenation dictionary, that is, you can insert and delete words, and change the hyphenation points of existing words. However, in order to use this utility, your PC must have about 2.5MB of EMS memory to hold both the original and the updated dictionaries.

To apply the DUPD utility, first use an ASCII text editor to create an update file that contains a list of up to 200 hyphenated words. Type one word on each line, in upper or lower case, and add hyphens where you want. Although the list does not have to be in alphabetical order, each word must be preceded by an update command character, as follows: Use a plus sign to add the word to the dictionary (e.g., +spread-sheet); an equal sign to change the word's hyphenation points (e.g., =Post-Script); and an exclamation mark to delete the word from the dictionary (e.g., !PostScript). After the update file is completed and copied to the same directory where the DUPD utility is located, you simply type the command "DUPD FILENAME" (using the name of your update file in place of "FILENAME") and the program goes to work and updates the hypenation dictionary, displaying a status report for each word as it is processed.

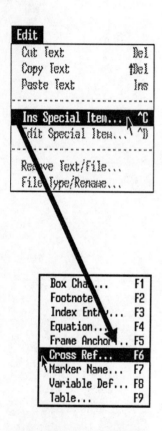

Cross References

Of all the expanded features the Extension has appended to the base product, the cross-references capability provides tools that virtually any publisher can put to good use. With this feature you can "flag" a location in a text file or frame caption, anywhere in a document, and instruct the program to generate one of several types of cross references (i.e., insert text) at that exact spot. These references include chapter, page, figure, table, and section numbers, as well as caption labels and variable text. Most of these references are related to other flags, called *markers,* which are hidden in other locations in the same document or chapter (.CHP) file, or that extend across different chapters belonging to the same publication (.PUB) file.

In creating a newsletter or magazine, for instance, you can insert cross references for "Continued on page *xxx*" and "Continued from page *xxx*" and the Extension will substitute *xxx* with the actual page numbers that link the continuation of an article. Or, you can just as easily cross reference a figure or table number. Even if a document is repaginated and the text and graphics move to new locations, the Extension will automatically update all cross references.

To insert the current page or chapter number anywhere on a page, follow the same procedure you used with the base product. Place the typing cursor wherever you want the reference located, select the Edit menu's Insert Special Item option (Ctrl-C), and pick the Cross Reference command (F6) from the pop-up menu to display the Insert/Edit Reference dialog box (shown below). Use the "Refer To" setting to pick page ("P#") or chapter ("C#") number for the reference type, leave the "At The Name" line blank, and change the

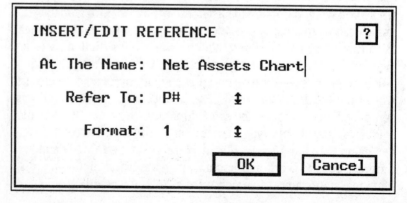

"Format" setting to a different numbering style if you don't want to use the default (arabic numerals). Click "OK" and the Extension inserts the page or chapter number on the page. If the Show Tabs & Returns command is active, a degree symbol (°) is shown where the cross reference is located and the word "Reference" is displayed in the current selection box. With the typing cursor in this location, you can also choose the Edit Special Item option (Ctrl-D) to recall the dialog box, or use the Delete key to remove the cross reference.

To insert a cross reference other than the current page or chapter number, you perform three separate actions: (1) insert a marker, (2) insert a reference to the marker, and (3) generate the cross-reference text. Before proceeding, however, you should know which text and graphics elements you want to cross reference in a document. To prepare for this, create a reference log that lists the names of various charts, tables, chapters, books, products, companies, individuals, and so forth. This log can be simple or extensive, depending on the complexity of the project, and it can serve as a guide for using cross references in future publications. Best of all, you can use this log when you create markers, labels, and other text that you must enter *verbatim* in various dialog boxes.

To proceed, the first step is to insert a marker where the item you want to refer to is located. If the location is in a text file, place the typing cursor in a convenient spot (e.g., directly in front of a key word or at the beginning of the paragraph), select the Insert Special Item option, and pick Marker Name (F7). This action produces the Insert/Edit Marker Name dialog box (shown below) and you can enter the label you want to use to identify the item (up to 16

Box Char...	F1
Footnote	F2
Index Entry...	F3
Equation...	F4
Frame Anchor...	F5
Cross Ref...	F6
Marker Name...	F7
Variable Def...	F8
Table...	F9

INSERT/EDIT MARKER NAME   ?

Marker Name: Net Assets Chart|

OK   Cancel

This Insert/Edit Marker Name dialog box is being used to place a hidden reference to the name "Net Assets Chart" in the title of a chart. This maker name can be linked to any number of additional cross refererences in the same document or in other chapter files in the same publication file.

characters) in the "Marker Name" line. If the location is a frame (e.g., a figure or table), select the frame, pick the Anchors & Captions menu, and enter the label (up to 16 characters) on the "Anchor Name" line. Because the marker name is hidden, be sure to record it on your reference log for easy referral. However, if you forget the name you used or just want to change it, place the cursor directly in front of the marker ("Marker Name" is shown in the current selection box) and select the Edit Special Item option to recall the dialog box for that particular entry.

The next step is to insert the same name in the text wherever you want a cross reference to the marker to appear. Insert the typing cursor in the proper location, select the Insert Special Item option, and pick Cross Reference to display the Insert/Edit Reference dialog box. Enter the marker or anchor name on the "At The Name" line, use the "Refer To" setting to select the reference type, and change the numbering format if necessary. In addition to page or chapter numbers, the other choices for reference type are figure number ("F#"), table number ("T#"), section number ("S*"), caption label ("C*"), or variable text ("V*").

Variable text lets you customize documents by inserting a substitute word or block of text (up to 54 characters) wherever the variable text is cross referenced, which is similar to applying the search-and-replace function offered by word processing programs. With the Extension, however, a single command can be used to insert substitute text in several different files all at once, and you can use substitute text on a selective rather than global basis. Each time you instruct the program to generate cross references, the latest entries for variable text are inserted throughout a publication. A practical application of this feature is the ability to instantly update any document with new dates, revision numbers, product names, part numbers, pricing information, and customer names.

To create variable text, place the typing cursor at the start of a text file so you can easily find it whenever you want to change it. Next, select the Insert Special Item option, and pick Variable Definition (F8) to display the Insert/Edit Variable Definition dialog box (shown on the following page). Enter the identifying name you want to use on the "Variable Name" line, and enter the actual text you want inserted on the "Substitute Text" line. For example, use "Net Assets"

```
┌─────────────────────────────────────────────────────┬───┐
│ INSERT/EDIT VARIABLE DEFINITION                      │ ? │
│                                                      └───┤
│   Variable Name:  Net Assets_____                        │
│                                                          │
│ Substitute Text: $12,650,000|_____     │
│                                                          │
│                                                          │
│                          ┌────────┐  ┌──────────┐        │
│                          │   OK   │  │  Cancel  │        │
│                          └────────┘  └──────────┘        │
└──────────────────────────────────────────────────────────┘
```

The information entered in this Insert/Edit Variable Definition dialog box will instruct the Extension to insert the specified substitute text, "$12,650,000," wherever it finds the hidden variable name "Net Assets."

as a variable name in a financial report and enter the current dollar amount for the substitute text. Whenever you want to change the substitute text, simply insert the cursor directly in front of the entry ("Variable Def." is displayed in the selection box) and select the Edit Special Item option to recall the appropriate dialog box.

After inserting all of the markers, variable text, and cross references, the last step is to generate the actual referenced text that will be inserted in the document. For this job, use the Multi-Chapter option (Options menu) to create a publication (.PUB) file that contains all of the chapters in your document, and then select the Renumber command. The Extension goes to work, loads each chapter in the publication, and generates and inserts the cross references in each designated location. If the program fails to match all of the cross references with markers (often due to a typing error), it produces an error message and generates a .GEN file that lists any incomplete references (as shown below). You can then load the file, read its contents, correct all errors, and reuse the Renumber command.

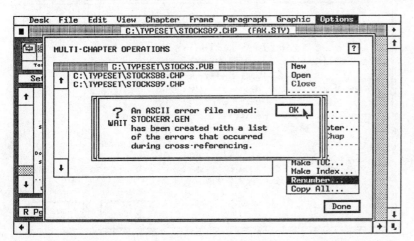

As shown in the pop-up message in this screen shot, the Extension automatically generated an error file (STOCKERR.GEN) when renumbering a publication (STOCKS.PUB) file. In this instance, the error file contained the following: "STOCKS88.CHP, page 1: Unresolved reference label (STOCK REPORT)."

Vertical Justification

Inconsistent spacing above or below the text and graphics elements in a publication is the nemesis of good design. It also tends to separate professional-looking documents from those that appear amateurish or hastily produced. Unfortunately, there are several reasons why unequal vertical spacing can occur in a Ventura document, not the least of which is the need to meet a deadline. Although the base product provides assorted tools to help you control spacing discrepancies caused by such culprits as mixed fonts (e.g., headlines, subheads, body text, captions), ruling lines, illustrations, and variable headers and footers, it often takes considerable skill and patience to produce harmonious results.

With the Extension, however, it's easier to attain consistent vertical spacing throughout a document without being overly assiduous. All you need to do is activate the automatic vertical justification controls that have been added to the Chapter Typography, Frame Typography, Paragraph Typography, and Insert/Edit Table menu options, as necessary, and the program will do most of the analyzing and adjusting for you. Provided in the dialog boxes for each of these options is a selection of tools that allows you to apply vertical justification in several different ways. In general, you instruct the program to align the text and graphics in an allotted space by adding as much vertical space as necessary to make the elements fit more evenly from the top to the bottom of a page or column, and without moving any of the elements across page or column boundaries.

With the Chapter (Default) Typography Settings dialog box, you can turn vertical justification on or off for an entire chapter by selecting "Feathering" or "Carding."

Vertical justification controls

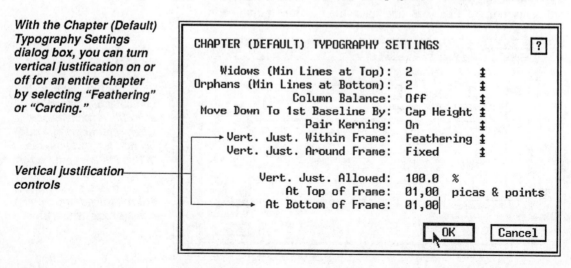

```
CHAPTER (DEFAULT) TYPOGRAPHY SETTINGS                    [?]

        Widows (Min Lines at Top):  2              ‡
    Orphans (Min Lines at Bottom):  2              ‡
                 Column Balance:    Off            ‡
       Move Down To 1st Baseline By: Cap Height    ‡
                   Pair Kerning:    On             ‡
           Vert. Just. Within Frame: Feathering    ‡
           Vert. Just. Around Frame: Fixed         ‡

             Vert. Just. Allowed:   100.0  %
                At Top of Frame:    01,00  picas & points
             At Bottom of Frame:    01,00

                                    [  OK  ]   [ Cancel ]
```

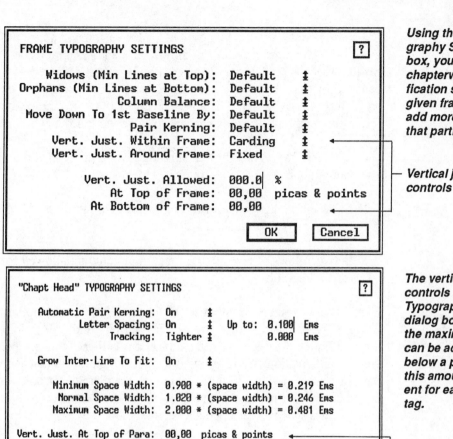

```
FRAME TYPOGRAPHY SETTINGS                          ?

       Widows (Min Lines at Top):   Default      ↕
Orphans (Min Lines at Bottom):      Default      ↕
              Column Balance:       Default      ↕
Move Down To 1st Baseline By:       Default      ↕
              Pair Kerning:         Default      ↕
       Vert. Just. Within Frame:    Carding      ↕  ←
       Vert. Just. Around Frame:    Fixed        ↕

       Vert. Just. Allowed:    000.0   %
          At Top of Frame:     00,00   picas & points
       At Bottom of Frame:     00,00

                          [ OK ]   [ Cancel ]
```

Using the Frame Typography Settings dialog box, you can override the chapterwide vertical justification settings for any given frame on a page or add more space around that particular frame.

Vertical justification controls

```
"Chapt Head" TYPOGRAPHY SETTINGS                   ?

  Automatic Pair Kerning:  On      ↕
       Letter Spacing:     On      ↕   Up to:  0.100  Ems
          Tracking:        Tighter ↕          0.000  Ems

  Grow Inter-Line To Fit:  On      ↕

     Minimum Space Width:  0.900 * (space width) = 0.219 Ems
      Normal Space Width:  1.020 * (space width) = 0.246 Ems
     Maximum Space Width:  2.000 * (space width) = 0.481 Ems

Vert. Just. At Top of Para:   00,00  picas & points
        At Bottom of Para:    01,01
   Between Lines of Para:     00,00
                          [ OK ]   [ Cancel ]
```

The vertical justification controls in the Paragraph Typography Settings dialog box let you specify the maximum amount that can be added above or below a paragraph, and this amount can be different for each paragraph tag.

Vertical justification controls

```
INSERT/EDIT TABLE                                  ?

   # of Rows,Columns:    0003,0003

          Overall Width:  Column  ↕ 06.00  inches
        Horz. Alignment:  Left    ↕ 00.00
   Break Across Pages:    Allowed ↕
       # of Header Rows:  0000

            Box Around:   On      ↕ Z_DOUBLE____
            Horz. Grid:   On      ↕ Z_SINGLE____
            Vert. Grid:   On      ↕ Z_SINGLE____

          Space Above:    00.00   fractional pts
   Space Between Rows:    04.00
Space Between Columns:    04.00
          Space Below:    00.00
     Vert. Just at Top:   00.00
  Vert. Just at Bottom:   00.00       [ OK ]   [ Cancel ]
```

The vertical justification controls in the Insert/Edit Table dialog box let you define the maximum amount of space that can be added above and below a table.

Vertical justification controls

Depending on the settings you define, the Extension will adjust the vertical space before and after frames, tables, and paragraphs until the text reaches the bottom of the column or page. If desired, you can also instruct the program to use vertical justification between each line of text. After it analyzes a given page or frame, the Extension methodically adds vertical space in the following order:

1. Between frames and the surrounding text, until the maximum amount allowed for each frame is added

2. Between paragraphs until the maximum amount allowed for each paragraph or table is added

3. Between lines of text until the maximum amount allowed for each paragraph is added

In most cases you can simply use the Chapter Typography option. Choose "Vert. Just. Within Frame: Feathering" and "Vert. Just. Around Frame: Moveable," and the program will apply the proper vertical justification. "Feathering" is a typesetting process that adds the exact space required to make text reach the bottom of a column or frame, dividing the space equally among all the elements. "Moveable" allows space to be added above and below frames.

The alternate choices for these two central options are "Carding" and "Fixed." "Carding" adds space only in exact multiples of the inter-line spacing in order to maintain baseline alignment across columns and facing pages. "Fixed" adds space only below the frame. As a general rule, feathering works best for books, brochures, and other documents where exact alignment across contiguous columns is not critical, while carding is well-suited for newsletters, newspapers, magazines, and other documents where precise alignment across contiguous columns is desired.

The "Vert. Just. Allowed" control, which is usually set at 100 percent, allows you to increase or decrease the maximum amount of vertical justification for each page. If a page still contains too much blank space, for example, you might try setting this control at 150 percent. The "At Top of Frame" and "At Bottom of Frame" controls let you set a limit on the maximum amount of vertical spacing for all of the frames in a chapter.

The Frame Typography option provides all of the same vertical justification controls offered by the Chapter Typography option and is applied by using the same techniques. With these controls, however, you can override the chapterwide vertical justification settings for any given frame, including any pages you may have added manually by using the Chapter menu's Insert/Remove Page option.

In order to control vertical justification for individual lines and paragraphs, you can use the Paragraph Typography option, which includes three settings — "Vert. Just. At Top of Para," "At Bottom of Para," and "Between Lines of Paragraph" — for specifying the maximum line spacing that can be added above and below the selected paragraph, as well as between each line.

Finally, the Insert/Edit Table option provides two vertical justification controls — "Vert. Just. at Top" and "Vert. Just. at Bottom" — which enables you to specify the maximum amount of vertical justification spacing above and below each table, in the same way you specified similar settings for individual paragraphs.

Working with Equations

At first glance, the Extension's equation editing feature doesn't look any different than the base product's fraction editing feature. However, once you begin working with this feature, you'll quickly discover that the equivalent of a scientific word processor has been added to the program. This powerful capability is designed to simplify the task of integrating text and complex technical material, such as mathematical and scientific formulas, and to produce attractive, readable results on paper. Virtually anyone who prepares technical publications, particularly those in the chemistry, physics, and engineering fields, should find that the Extension's equation editing tools are well-suited for typesetting the most sophisticated mathematical and scientific expressions.

Inserting and Editing Equations

To access the Extension's equation editing tools, select the Insert Special Item option (Edit menu) and choose the Equation command (F4) from the pop-up menu provided (as shown on the right). The Extension replaces the work area and side-bar with the same blank screen used by the base product for fraction editing, except that "Equation Editing" (instead of "Fraction Editing") is displayed in

Box Char...	F1
Footnote	F2
Index Entry...	F3
Equation...	F4
Frame Anchor...	F5
Cross Ref...	F6
Marker Name...	F7
Variable Def...	F8
Table...	F9

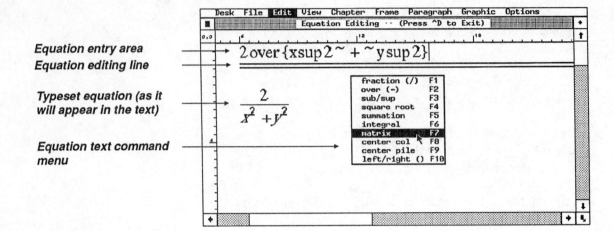

Equation entry area

Equation editing line

Typeset equation (as it will appear in the text)

Equation text command menu

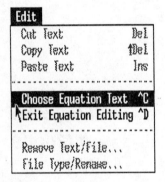

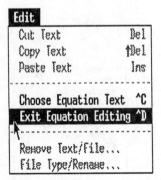

the title bar. Using the keyboard, you can now create equations by entering various commands and codes in the equation entry area, which is the part of the screen above the equation editing line, and within seconds the typeset result appears in the area below the line.

If you select the Choose Equation Text option in the Edit menu or use the Ctrl-C (^C) keyboard shortcut, the Extension provides an additional pop-up menu (shown above) that lists some of the most commonly used equation commands. As you can click on the various commands listed, or use the assigned function keys, the Extension will insert an example of that command at the text cursor's location in the equation entry area. For instance, if you select the square root command (F4), the Extension inserts "sqrt x" in the entry area and displays the following typeset result: $\sqrt{x}$

To edit an equation, simply use the Backspace key and retype it; the typeset result changes accordingly. You can also use the mouse to cut, copy, and paste any part of the equation material just like regular text. To return to the normal work area and insert the typeset equation at the typing cursor's location in the text, pick the Exit Equation Editing option (Edit menu) or use the Ctrl-D (^D) keyboard shortcut. To edit an equation after it is inserted into the text, place the typing cursor directly in front of the equation (the side-bar selection box will display the word "Equation") and select the Edit Special Item option (or press ^D) to return to the equation editing screen. As with the base product, this screen can also be displayed in any page view (i.e., enlarged, normal, etc.).

The Equation Commands

The Extension's equation editing feature is based on EQN, a standard mathematical and scientific language. As implemented in the Extension, there are five types of commands or special words that you can use to create equations, including symbol words, Roman words, diacritical marks, font commands, and equation commands.

Symbol words include Greek characters and certain mathematical symbols that are translated into symbol character equivalents (e.g., pi produces π). Roman words include math operators (e.g., cos, log, and sin) which are translated into normal (rather than italic) type. Diacritical marks include any character, symbol, or accent marks that appear above one or more letters (e.g., $\overleftrightarrow{xyz}$). Font commands change the font of the expression that follows (e.g., "a~+~b~=~bold x~+~y" produces "a + b = **x** + **y**"). Equation commands create math symbols or modify the position of an expression. A complete listing of the equation commands and special words or characters recognized by the Extension can be found in the *Ventura Publisher Professional Extension Reference Guide*.

A mathematical or scientific expression can be a word, a character, a group of characters not separated by a space, or anything placed inside of braces (i.e., the { } characters). However, in order to create a math/science expression using the Extension's equation editing feature, you must adhere to the following rules:

1. A space must be entered *before* and *after* all commands and special words (otherwise they are displayed as part of the expression). You can also put braces around an expression to ensure that it is formatted as a single unit.

2. To insert spaces within an equation, use the ~ (tilde) to add a regular space and use the ^ (caret) to add a thin space.

3. All commands must be entered *before* the expression they modify, except for diacritical mark commands, which are entered *after* the expression they affect.

Formatting Equations

Although the Extension doesn't generate special equations tags, there are several Paragraph menu options you can use to help format

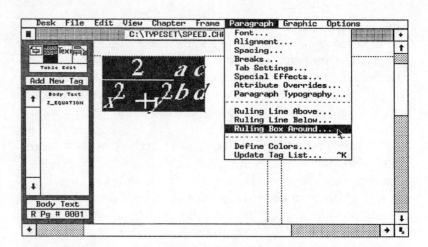

After you've inserted an equation into the text of a document, you can use the Paragraph Tagging mode to perform additional formatting. As shown in this screen shot, for example, you can apply a ruling box around an equation.

an equation. For example, with the Font dialog box, you can change the equation's typeface, type size, and color (but not type style); with the Attribute Overrides option, you can change the size and position for the subscripts and superscripts used in the equation; and with the Paragraph Typography option, you can turn on the "Grown Inter-Line to Fit" control to prevent the text from overlapping when equations are inserted. You can also use the various Ruling Line options in the Paragraph menu to add rules above, below, or around an equation, such as the following example:

$$\sum_{n=0}^{\infty}\left[\left(\frac{n+k}{n}\right)\right]^{-1}$$

If you want to change the type style used for part of an equation, you won't be able to use the Text Editing mode to highlight the text and then select the Set Font add button, or use the side-bar assignment list, to apply bold, italic, or other type styles to the equation. Instead, you must use return to the equation editing screen and use the equation font commands, mentioned earlier, to change the type style. However, you can apply the "Small," "Superscript," "Subscript," and "Normal" text attributes in the side-bar assignment list to a selected equation, if desired.

Index

A

Abandon option, 103
add button, 34 - 35, 45
Add New Tag button, 60 - 61
Add/Remove Fonts option, 143, 145 - 146, 232
added frames, 46
Adobe Illustrator, 21
Alignment option, 130, 177, 181, 191, 194, 201 - 202, 205, 216 - 217, 235
anchors, 131, 154, 164 - 165, 176
   defined, 164
   text codes, 240
Anchors & Captions option, 130 - 131, 176, 272
Apple Macintosh
   paint programs, 245
   PICT graphics format, 243
archiving chapters and publications, 148 - 149, 166
ASCII files, 4, 74, 108 - 109
aspect ratio, 172
Assign Function Keys command, 59, 224 - 225
assignment list, 34 - 35, 45, 57
Attribute Overrides option, 209 - 211, 280
attributes, text, 76
Auto-Numbering option, 121, 127, 129 - 130, 132, 150
AutoCAD, 243 - 244
automatic counting, 124, 126
automatic inter-line spacing, 141
automatic pagination, 18, 231

B

backup files feature, 140
base page frame, 46, 48, 124, 135, 139, 146, 154, 159, 166, 169 - 171, 179 - 180, 183, 194, 206
bit-mapped graphics, 21, 245
   bit-mapped image editing, 22
Bitstream Fontware, 23 - 24
Body Text tag, 57, 59, 112, 129, 135, 177, 223, 234
box characters, 63, 76
box text, 74, 91, 93
Breaks option, 130, 195, 200, 204, 217
Bring to Front option, 226
Browse command (Network Server), 256
bullets, 209, 216
button controls, 39

C

camera registration mark, 221
caption (.CAP) files, 100
change bar, 215
chapter files, 82, 100 - 105, 113, 147 - 148, 166, 169
chapter file locking (Network Server), 256
Chapter menu, 35, 57, 116, 119, 121, 125, 127, 130
Chapter Typography option, 121 - 123, 194, 212, 277
character sets, 77, 82
character shift, 83
Choose Equation Text option (Extension), 278
clip art software, 22
clipboard, 65, 154 - 158, 160, 184
color features
   CMYK process colors, 218
   four-color process printing, 218 - 219
   printing spot-color overlays, 6, 15, 218 - 219
   color separations, 219
   See also Define Colors option
column balance, 124
column guides, 146
Column Snap On/Off command, 174
conventional halftones, 185
Copy Text option, 65
Corel Draw, 21
crop marks, 114, 220 - 221, 225, 235
cropping pictures, 52
cross references (base product), 63, 76
cross references (Extension), 254, 270 - 272
custom column guides, 225
Cut Text option, 65
Cut, Copy, and Paste Options, 155

D

dBASE, 109, 262 - 263
decimal codes, 77, 82, 129
Define Colors option, 69, 218 - 221, 266
   creating PMS colors, 220
   mixing the CMYK process colors, 218 - 220
   printing color overlays, 220
   replacing the default colors, 219
   sample spot-color overlay pages, 221
   using with color displays, 220
   using with monochrome displays, 220